A new naval history

Manchester University Press

Cultural History of Modern War

Series editors Ana Carden-Coyne, Peter Gatrell, Max Jones,
Penny Summerfield and Bertrand Taithe

Centre for the
Cultural History
of War

https://www.alc.manchester.ac.uk/history/research/centres/cultural-history-of-war/

A new naval history

~

Edited by
QUINTIN COLVILLE AND JAMES DAVEY

Published in association with the National Maritime Museum

NATIONAL
MARITIME MUSEUM
GREENWICH

Manchester University Press

Published by Manchester University Press
Oxford Road, Manchester M13 9PL

www.manchesteruniversitypress.co.uk

British Library Cataloguing-in-Publication Data
A catalogue record for this book is available from the British Library

ISBN   978 1 5261 1380 1   hardback
ISBN   978 1 5261 1381 8   paperback

First published 2019
Paperback published 2022

Typeset in Minion by
Servis Filmsetting Ltd, Stockport, Cheshire

Published in association with the National Maritime Museum

NATIONAL
MARITIME MUSEUM
GREENWICH

Contents

Contents

List of figures and tables

Figures

List of figures and tables

Tables

Notes on contributors

Elaine Chalus (FRHS) is Professor of British History at the University of Liverpool. An expert on gender and political culture, Elaine's numerous publications – especially *Elite Women in English Political Life c. 1754–1790* (Oxford University Press, 2005) – have helped to reconfigure historians' understanding of women and eighteenth-century political culture. She is currently preparing a monograph for Oxford University Press, based on the forty surviving volumes of Elizabeth Wynne Fremantle's journals. She serves on editorial boards for *Women's History Review, Parliamentary History Journal* and the History of Parliament Trust, where she is Section Editor for the House of Lords, 1660–1832.

Quintin Colville is Senior Curator for Research at Royal Museums Greenwich. He was lead curator for its *Nelson, Navy, Nation* and *Forgotten Fighters: The First World War at Sea* galleries, and its special exhibition on Emma Hamilton. His work focuses on gender, material culture and the sociocultural history of the Royal Navy. His publications include (as editor) *Emma Hamilton: Seduction and Celebrity* (Thames & Hudson, 2016) and *Nelson, Navy & Nation: The Royal Navy and the British People, 1688–1815* (Conway Press, 2013, edited with James Davey). He is Visiting Professor at the University of Portsmouth, and Research Fellow at the University of York.

Mary Conley is Associate Professor of History at the College of the Holy Cross in Worcester, Massachusetts, where she directs the Scholarship in Action programme. She is the author of *From Jack Tar to Union Jack: Representing Naval Manhood in the British Empire* (Manchester University

Press, 2009). Her chapter forms part of a larger project about policing homosexuality below decks in the twentieth-century Royal Navy. In addition, she is currently working on a comparative colonialism history project about practices and policies that governed children's lives within and across the British Empire since the late eighteenth century.

James Davey is Lecturer in Naval and Maritime History at the University of Exeter. His research focuses on the history of the Royal Navy in a variety of political, economic and cultural contexts. His most recent book is *In Nelson's Wake: The Navy and the Napoleonic Wars* (Yale University Press, 2015) and his other publications include *The Transformation of British Naval Strategy: Seapower and Supply in Northern Europe 1808–1812* (Boydell Press, 2012) and *Nelson, Navy & Nation: The Royal Navy and the British People, 1688–1815* (Conway Press, 2013, edited with Quintin Colville).

Emma Hanna is a Senior Research Fellow in the School of History at the University of Kent. She is a Co-Investigator on two Arts and Humanities Research Council (AHRC) -funded projects: Gateways to the First World War, an AHRC-funded centre for public engagement with the centenary of the First World War (2014–19) and Reflections on the Centenary: Learning and Legacies for the Future (2017–20). Emma published her first monograph, *The Great War on the Small Screen* (Edinburgh University Press) in 2009, and she continues to publish widely on the themes of contemporary memory and memorialisation, the media, music and cinema, 1914–18.

Barbara Korte is Professor of English Literature at the University of Freiburg (Germany), where she is also a member of the collaborative research centre dedicated to heroes, heroisations and heroisms. She has worked on aspects of the heroic in Victorian periodicals and contemporary British television series, and has co-edited a collection of critical articles, *Heroes and Heroism in British Fiction since 1800* (Palgrave, 2017).

Cindy McCreery is Senior Lecturer in the Department of History at the University of Sydney and teaches eighteenth and nineteenth-century British and European history, including Britain's engagement with the wider world *c.* 1837–1914. Recent naval history publications include 'Neighbourly relations: Nineteenth-century Western navies' interactions in the Asia Pacific region' in Robert Aldrich and Kirsten McKenzie (eds.),

The Routledge History of Western Empires (Routledge, 2014) and 'Naval gazes: HMS Challenger, Swan River, and the Indian Ocean world c. 1832', *Studies in Western Australian History* (2014). She is currently writing a book on the first global British royal tour: Prince Alfred's world voyages in HMS *Galatea* (1867–71).

Katherine Parker specialises in the history of Pacific exploration and the cultural history of the Royal Navy. She received her training in history at the University of Pittsburgh, where she completed a dissertation on the production of geographic knowledge about the Pacific in Britain from 1669 to 1768. She is the Research Officer for Barry Lawrence Ruderman Antique Maps and is Administrative Editor of the Hakluyt Society.

Jonathan Rayner is Reader in Film Studies at the University of Sheffield, School of English. His research interests include Australasian cinema, genre cinema, naval history in film and popular culture and landscapes and moving images. With Julia Dobson he is co-director of SCRIF, the Sheffield Centre for Research in Film. He is author of *The Naval War Film* (Manchester University Press, 2007), *The Cinema of Michael Mann* (Wallflower, 2013), *The Films of Peter Weir* (Continuum, 1998/2003) and *Contemporary Australian Cinema* (Manchester University Press, 2000). He is co-editor of *Filmurbia* (Palgrave, 2017), *Mapping Cinematic Norths* (Peter Lang, 2016) and *Cinema and Landscape* (Intellect, 2010).

Cicely Robinson completed an AHRC-funded collaborative PhD in History of Art with the University of York and the National Maritime Museum. Titled *Edward Hawke Locker and the Foundation of the National Gallery of Naval Art (1795–1845)*, her thesis investigates the display and reception of naval art within one of Britain's first 'national' galleries. Subsequently Cicely curated the opening exhibition of British sporting art at Palace House, Newmarket. Specialising in nineteenth-century British art, she the Brice Curator at Watts Gallery – Artists' Village.

Jan Rüger is Professor of History at Birkbeck, University of London. He is the author of *The Great Naval Game: Britain and Germany in the Age of Empire* (Cambridge University Press, 2007) and *Heligoland: Britain, Germany and the Struggle for the North Sea* (Oxford University Press, 2017).

Daniel Owen Spence has been a historian of Empire, the navy and decolonisation, Research Fellow in the University of the Free State's

International Studies Group, Research Affiliate with the University of Sydney and Fellow of Leiden University's African Studies Centre. He became the first historian to be awarded a 'P' (Prestigious) rating by the National Research Foundation of South Africa, having published two monographs – *Colonial Naval Culture and British Imperialism, 1922–67* (Manchester University Press, 2015) and *A History of the Royal Navy: Empire and Imperialism* (I.B.Tauris, 2015) – as well as several international peer-reviewed journal articles and book chapters.

Evan Wilson is Assistant Professor in the John B. Hattendorf Center for Maritime Historical Research at the U.S. Naval War College. His first book, *A Social History of British Naval Officers, 1775–1815*, appeared with the Boydell Press in 2017. A recent recipient of the Sir Julian Corbett Prize in Modern Naval History, he has published articles in *The English Historical Review* and the *Journal for Maritime Research*. He contributed to and helped edit *Strategy and the Sea* (Boydell, 2016) as well as a new volume forthcoming with Palgrave, *Eighteenth-Century Naval Officers: A Transnational Perspective*. He holds degrees from Yale, Cambridge and Oxford.

Acknowledgements

The editors would like to thank Emma Brennan, Paul Clarke and Elizabeth Stone for their work on this volume, as well as the editors of the Cultural History of Modern War series. We are indebted to Robert Blyth for his careful reading of the manuscript and to Elizabeth Bowers, Kate Mason, Kirsty Schaper and Tina Warner at the National Maritime Museum. With gratitude also to Hannah, Douglas and Clara.

Introduction

Quintin Colville and James Davey

The last few decades have witnessed a transformation in the way that naval history is researched and conceived. A generation ago, this was largely – though by no means entirely – a self-contained world. Its priorities and themes were understood and accepted, revolving broadly around issues of warfare, command and leadership, strategy and tactics, technology and weaponry. While these crucial subjects remain, historians working within the discipline, and others from outside it who have identified the navy as fertile ground for analysis, have between them opened up new perspectives on the subject. The range and variety of research concerning the navy is now remarkable and continues to develop apace. Recent scholarship has examined issues of national identity and imperialism through naval affairs; the celebrity and legacy of Admiral Nelson; the social and cultural realities of life on board ship; the place of the navy within wider constructions of gender and class; and the myriad ways in which the relationship between the navy and British society has been mediated through art, music and popular culture. As a result, some of the assumptions of naval history have altered, and a variety of approaches now have a stake in defining it. Above all, there has been a distinct shift from a concern with the Royal Navy as a separate and separable institution, to an examination of the complex relationships between ship and shore, Britain and its empire, navy and nation.

Naturally, any discussion about the current state of naval history begs many questions about its earlier incarnations. As a discipline, it has not always had a strong sense of its past, for while there have been countless naval histories, there have been few works on the academic origins of the subject that have sought to explain how it has been conceived and understood. This unfamiliarity is beginning to change with the production of a number of 'state of the field' publications devoting attention to naval historiography, but for the most part, this historiography remains overlooked and frequently disregarded.[1] Few would disagree that it is a subject of long standing, with most historians tracing its origins to the flood of publications produced in the late nineteenth century.[2] It is worth remembering, though, that the roots of naval history go back much further than that. Navies, admirals and sailors had been the subject of chronicles and historical narratives from the earliest recordings of civilisations in the Western world. Thucydides devoted vast portions of his history on the Peloponnesian War to the naval aspects of the conflict, as did Polybius's account of the Punic Wars, and countless other works were produced in the subsequent centuries that referred, if only in part, to the actions of navies and their commanders. Nonetheless, these remained partial naval histories, with events at sea but one part of a broader narrative.[3]

It was not until the early eighteenth century that naval history emerged as a clearly defined, coherent and separate subject. The early decades of the eighteenth century saw the publication of the first general naval histories in the English language: Josiah Burchett's *A Complete History of the most Remarkable Transactions at Sea*, published in 1720; Samuel Colliber's *Columna Rostrata: Or, A Critical History of the English Sea-Affairs*; and finally Thomas Lediard's *The Naval History of England*, fifteen years later.[4] They were conscious that they were contributing something entirely novel, as Burchett made clear in his preface:

> I began to reflect that, among the numerous Subjects which have been treated in the *English* Tongue ... no one hath hitherto undertaken to collect somewhat of a *Naval History*, or general Account of the Wars on the Sea; whereof both ancient and modern Times have been so productive, that I know of no subject which affords more ample Circumstance.[5]

These works did not just appear out of the blue, but instead emanated from a society increasingly wedded to ideas of naval power, and with a growing need to record and debate Britain's naval past. While newspapers, prints, pamphlets and parliament continuously stressed the importance of the navy, it was not at all surprising that literate Britons would seek to find out more about the institution's history. From the outset, then, naval history was written by individuals who had identified it as a marketable subject, and who produced works aimed at a broad popular audience.

If naval history was primarily a subject aimed at a burgeoning reading public, it was also strident in its patriotism, deliberately reflecting broader mentalities about national naval prowess. Burchett's work was remarkably international in its focus, giving considerable attention to other nations that had 'flourished at sea' (including the Egyptians, Phoenicians, Greeks, Romans, Venetians, Swedes and Danes), but the historians who followed focused only on the English, and later British, Navy. Colliber saw the roots of British naval power in the maritime efforts of the Saxons, while Lediard began his *Naval History of England* on the only date that mattered – 1066 – ridiculing the idea that studying foreign navies would offer any useful lessons whatsoever.[6] Subsequent efforts wore their jingoism proudly: Charles Jenkins's *England's Triumph: or Spanish Cowardice Expos'd* can barely be described a history book, so blatant was its xenophobia, while John Campbell's 1759 work, *Lives of the Admirals and other Eminent British Seamen*, devoted its pages to highlighting fundamental characteristics intrinsic to the British naval admirals, including skilful navigation, virtue, heroism and success.[7] Even William James's superlative histories of the wars of 1793–1815, which remain the most comprehensive operational accounts of the conflict, were prompted by a moment of nationalistic pride.[8] Naval history would continue to be defined by its patriotic character into the modern era.

Most importantly, it had secured a robust and enduring popular audience. In the aftermath of the French Revolutionary and Napoleonic Wars, countless narratives and biographies of leading naval figures were produced, alongside autobiographical accounts written by both officers and seamen, which continued to be published into the second half of the century. What naval history had gained in popular audience, though, it missed in scholarly rigour, which grew increasingly evident as the study of history became more entrenched into British universities in the second half of the nineteenth century. From the 1890s, historians such as Alfred Thayer Mahan, Julian Corbett, Herbert Richmond and John Knox Laughton, began to refocus the discipline towards a more meticulous approach based on close analyses of surviving documentary sources, and in the process brought coherence to a subject that had previously lacked definition.[9] Institutions were set up that sought to further the reach of naval history: the Navy Records Society was established in 1893 to print original documents relating to the history of the Royal Navy, and it was followed in 1912 by *The Naval Review*, which published historical scholarship alongside papers on current professional concerns. Moreover, naval history was ensconced within the British university system for the first time: Laughton was a Professor of Modern History at King's College London throughout the 1890s and 1900s, while in 1919 the Vere

Harmsworth Chair in Naval History was endowed at the University of Cambridge.[10]

What was truly distinctive about the naval history produced in the 1890–1914 period was how attuned it was to contemporary political and professional issues. Most writers were naval officers or civilians closely tied to the navy, whose work promised to offer critical insights for the present.[11] For some, naval history provided a means of uncovering principles of naval strategy and tactics that could educate serving naval personnel. Laughton used academic methodologies to deliver texts and courses for the purposes of naval education, while Julian Corbett taught naval history on the Naval War Course from 1904; his *Official History of the War: Naval Operations* became the standard teaching resource of the interwar navy.[12] For others, naval history offered an obvious opportunity to argue for the importance of naval power against a backdrop of increasing imperial tensions and an escalating naval arms race. Herbert Richmond's operational histories demonstrated clear contemporary concerns – not least in *The Navy as an Instrument of Policy* – while in the United States, both Theodore Roosevelt and Alfred Thayer Mahan wrote to argue for a larger American navy. It seems likely that the Navy Records Society was also created with some degree of political intent: it was established at a time when Gladstone was attempting to reduce the naval budget.[13]

Naval history's reputation as a tool for naval education, and its obvious links to contemporary policy, gave it both resonance and relevance in the early years of the twentieth century. However, in the aftermath of the First World War – even as its influence on policy began to recede – it struggled to shake off its reputation as a narrow, specialised subject in thrall to the contemporary Royal Navy, and was all but excluded from the academic mainstream.[14] It did not help that its leading proponents continued to prioritise public and political influence. Herbert Richmond wrote in 1939 that there were 'three classes of individuals to whom an acquaintance of naval history is needful: the general public, the statesman, and the sea officer', deliberately omitting academia.[15] Certainly, in the decades after the Second World War, naval history had never been so popular with the British public: the National Maritime Museum saw its annual visitor figures double from 300,000 to 619,000 between 1954 and 1966, as visitors flocked to see its predominantly naval displays.[16] But within academia, naval history's focus on great men, tactics and technical detail seemed decidedly unfashionable to scholarly historians suddenly struck by the possibilities of social and economic history. By the 1960s, naval history had become almost invisible in British universities: King's College London failed to find a replacement for Laughton, while the Vere Harmsworth Chair in Naval History was converted to one in 'Imperial and Naval History' in 1932; since then it has been held only once by a naval historian.[17]

The second half of the twentieth century therefore saw naval history operating on the peripheries of academic discourse. It was in these shallows, however, that a 'new' naval history began to be forged that attempted to uncouple naval history from its patriotic, service-focused reputation. Inspired in part by broader historiographical trends, and encouraged by the remarkable body of source material available at the Public Record Office (now The National Archives) and the National Maritime Museum, scholars turned away from the strategic and operational histories favoured by Mahan and his peers (and which were still being taught in staff colleges). These historians looked anew at naval history, seeking to investigate the foundations of Britain's naval strength, rather than argue for its present utility, assessing navies in terms of politics, economics, administration, industry, material and manpower, finance and technological development, as well as taking account of non-institutional elements such as prize money and privateering.[18] John Ehrman's *The Navy in the War of William III*, published in 1953, was very influential, and he in turn supervised the thesis of Daniel Baugh, published as *British Naval Administration in the Age of Walpole* in 1965. These publications placed the navy at the heart of British history, and as Roger Knight and Hamish Scott have both noted, established a 'new agenda' that would in due course save naval history from its academic isolation.[19]

For the first time, naval history began to intervene in and enlighten wider historiographical debates. Paul Kennedy's *The Rise and Fall of British Naval Mastery*, published in 1976, was a landmark book, the first academic work dealing with naval history to make an impact on contemporary scholarship.[20] This publication focused not on battles or tactics, but instead examined all the elements that contributed to a nation's exercise of naval power, including geopolitics, economics, logistics and statecraft, all through the lens of Britain's national trajectory.[21] In the years that followed, countless other historians – including Patricia Crimmin, David Syrett, Roger Morriss, Jonathan Coad, Roger Knight, Brian Lavery, Michael Duffy, Andrew Lambert, Richard Harding, Patrick K. O'Brien and Jan Glete – produced analyses that uncovered how resources, economics and government have shaped naval power, and were in turn shaped by its activities.[22] By the 1990s, there was a corpus of work that

allowed naval history to intercede on debates that dominated the historical discipline: the history of military professionalism, the 'military revolution', and, by the 1990s, the discussion surrounding the 'fiscal-military
state'. This strain continued into the 2000s, with the study of navies at the
centre of discussions about the 'contactor state'.[23]

Furthermore, by the 1980s, naval history was being heavily influenced
by broader trends in historical study. Inspired by the 'new social history'
of the 1960s and 1970s, naval historians moved their focus away from
elites to a wider investigation of 'ordinary' people and the experience of
the individual.[24] Michael Lewis's *A Social History of the Navy* marked the
first attempt to build on this interdisciplinarity, with N. A. M. Rodger's
seminal *The Wooden World* replacing it as the definitive account of the
social worlds of the Royal Navy twenty-five years later.[25] J. David Davies's
Gentlemen and Tarpaulins did for the early modern era what Rodger's
work had done for the eighteenth-century navy, offering a sophisticated
and layered account of the Stuart navy's officer corps. Social histories
have since become a crucial part of naval history's bibliography, with
'histories from below' sitting alongside a wave of scholarship on shipboard hierarchies, naval officers and their interactions with wider British
society.[26] If naval history was quick to see the value of social history, it
was more resistant to the 'cultural turn' that grew in prominence during
the 1980s. However, in recent years a number of historians – Jan Rüger,
Kathleen Wilson and Timothy Jenks to name but three – have identified
the navy as an institution of significant cultural importance. It is unlikely
that any of these scholars would define themselves as 'naval historians',
but in turning to the Royal Navy, and outlining its remarkable sociocultural impact, they have shown just how interdisciplinary and historically
relevant the study of naval history can be.[27]

The engagement with wider historiographies has also seen naval history
benefit from the renaissance in maritime history. Numerous scholars,
such as Glen O'Hara, Karen Widen and David Cannadine, pointed to
the scholarly revival of this subject, highlighting its versatility and its
increased relevance in the globalised world of the twenty-first century.[28]
This popularity owes much to the prominence of Atlantic and global
history, which have used oceanic regional focuses to reveal transnational
networks and relationships, in the process challenging national and
imperial histories.[29] Navies are, by their very definition, tied to the idea
of the nation state and, at first glance, naval history's place in these avow-
edly transnational disciplines might seem limited. However, in recent
years a number of studies have shown any such doubts to be premature.

Scholars have revealed that navies were a crucial part of any oceanic system, creating networks of communication and cultural exchange, and acting as an instrument of globalisation.[30] Just as importantly, while a naval ship was for many a visible and even daunting manifestation of the state, it was frequently peopled by an ethnically and internationally diverse crew. Works such as W. Jeffrey Bolster's book, *Black Jacks*, have shown that Royal Navy ships were made up of a surprisingly high number of non-Britons, revealing a very different social make-up than previously understood.[31] The navy, it is clear, must not be excluded from the broader study of humankind's relationships with the sea.

Discussions over sailors, not least their social backgrounds and shipboard agency, have also prompted a gathering – and increasingly heated – discussion about naval and maritime manpower. What is more, it is a debate that has attracted scholars from a range of backgrounds, each of them bringing different methodologies and historical outlooks. Jeremiah Dancy's rigorous quantitative study of naval impressment in the late eighteenth century has argued that the number of sailors who suffered at the hands of the press gang was far lower than previous calculations allowed, suggesting instead that volunteers made up the majority of seamen in the Royal Navy. Other scholars have offered markedly contrasting views of the same subject. Isaac Land – a historian of political culture and a pioneer of 'coastal history' – has critiqued Dancy's work, accusing him of neglecting published discourse and relying too heavily on state archives. Christopher Magra, a historian of revolutionary America, has also criticised any attempt to downplay the importance of impressment, arguing that anger over British impressment was at the heart of American discontent in the lead-up to the American War of Independence.[32] The debate will continue to rage, but what is perhaps most notable about it is the variety of scholars who have turned to what ostensibly might be seen as a 'traditional' naval subject. The navy's search for sources of manpower is but one aspect of the debate, for these studies of naval impressment reveal just as much about the power of the state, radical politics and, in Magra's case, the origins of American independence.

In the early twenty-first century, we therefore find naval historical scholarship connected to the historical mainstream more firmly than ever before. This does not mean that its other audiences have receded. On the contrary, the subject has never been more popular with the general public than it is now, with countless books, television programmes and museum displays highlighting the crucial role of the navy in British history, while navies remain major consumers of naval history. Their concern with education and training will continue to shape scholarship; in the United States, almost all naval history teaching is in government educational facilities, especially the naval academy and naval war college.[33] However, it now finds itself deeply entrenched in British academia, with a growing range of naval history courses being taught across the country's universities. A new generation of naval scholars will move the discipline in new directions, for as this discussion demonstrates, the parameters of naval history have been continuously shaped through a prolonged and intense process of definition and redefinition. There have been many 'new' naval histories over the past decades, and there will no doubt be more again. Nonetheless, the contributions to this volume reflect the current reality of a field occupied, incorporated or borrowed by numerous scholarly constituencies, and they serve as a useful route marker on a journey that promises to become more rather than less complex and unpredictable.

The book is arranged in two parts. The first five chapters are sociocultural analyses of naval communities from the later eighteenth to the mid-twentieth centuries. Evan Wilson's chapter begins this section by opening a window onto an important but under-researched group within the eighteenth-century Georgian navy: warrant officers. In this regard, he contributes to the much-needed social historical analysis of the Royal Navy from this period pioneered by Michael Lewis and N. A. M. Rodger, and extended by volumes such as John Cardwell's on naval surgeons, Samantha Cavell's on midshipmen, Ellen Gill's on naval families and Thomas Malcolmson's work on order.[34] Wilson flags the relative scholarly neglect of warrant officers in comparison with their commissioned officer peers whose role and identity within understandings of shipboard organisation and status have been more readily grasped. Using a database drawn from the years 1775 to 1815, he examines the patterns of warrant officer careers, and assesses the opportunities for advancement and higher pay that emerged in the context of the French Revolutionary and Napoleonic Wars. He challenges some assumptions by concluding that the social distance within the wardroom between warrant and commissioned officers was generally small, with a large proportion of both constituencies drawn from professional backgrounds.

In an oft-quoted remark from his 2005 volume, *The Command of the Ocean: A Naval History of Britain, 1649–1815*, N. A. M. Rodger noted that 'there has been virtually no research undertaken into what one might call the female half of the naval community … [this represents] an enormous void of ignorance, and our knowledge of the social history of the navy will never be complete until someone fills it'.[35] The intervening years have begun to address this imbalance, in the process building on approaches to women's history within the broader maritime setting by scholars such as Lisa Norling and Margaret Creighton.[36] The eighteenth- and early nineteenth-century context has been explored by Margarette Lincoln, Jennine Hurl-Eamon, Cindy McCreery, Louise Carter and Patricia Lin; while Melanie Holihead has provided important insights into female lives in nineteenth-century portside communities.[37] Elaine Chalus's chapter in this volume reveals the intricate web of activities through which one naval wife, Betsey Fremantle, promoted the interests of her family and husband, the latter absent on active service for long periods between 1800 and 1815. Chalus exposes the concentric rings of Fremantle's emotional, sociocultural and political involvement, from the immediate anxieties surrounding parenthood and wartime dangers to her energetic advancement of schemes for the education of their children, the cultivation of local notables and powerful patrons and the financial management of their estate. From this perspective, the boundary between ship and shore becomes less important than the joint determination of husband and wife to act in the best interests of their family – whether through naval service or the careful and strategic cultivation of opportunities at home.

Another area where recent scholarship has interrogated the conceptual and experiential commonalities between naval and civilian realms lies in the study of male homosexuality and homoeroticism. Seth Le Jacq's work on the eighteenth-century Royal Navy, for instance, has traced this exchange within literature, the periodical press and the law, contending that naval personnel were often active agents in constructing broader debates surrounding homoeroticism.[38] Mary Conley's chapter here extends this form of analysis into the Victorian and Edwardian period where, as she notes, the rich history of homosexuality has been less concerned with exploring same-sex relations within the navy itself. Through an examination of naval courts-martial boards between 1900 and 1913, Conley illuminates sharpened Admiralty concerns that homosexual practices not only undermined service discipline but threatened the normative heterosexual foundations of naval and imperial manhood. She traces a changing legal language of condemnation from earlier references to 'lewd' and 'nasty' acts to a more codified vision of 'sodomy', 'gross indecency' and 'indecent assault'. Beyond this, though, she demonstrates how the anxieties of naval authority were amplified with regard to boy ratings, through fears that 'vice' could be incubated within the process of training, and that boys were vulnerable to the 'corrupting' influence of older sailors. However, the policing of naval bodies prompted by these apprehensions obliged the Admiralty to look beyond the institution to the pubs and music halls of portside communities.

Cindy McCreery's chapter expands our understanding of Royal Naval communities in the modern era from a different direction: the production and consumption of photographic images. In so doing, her work is part of a small but significant cluster of research focused on the social history of the navy during the later nineteenth and twentieth centuries by, among others, Mary Conley, Laura Rowe, Christopher McKee and Anthony Carew.[39] McCreery's focus is on overseas naval stations, and principally Simon's Town in South Africa. Within this context, she traces the role of photographs in defining and consolidating the sociocultural groupings that coalesced in these locations. Photographs were distributed and collected in order to cement links among networks of officers who effectively formed substitute families on foreign postings. Collected in albums, these assemblages were more enduring that the 'families' themselves, which naval life usually served to disperse and re-form. McCreery explores the functions of particular types of photograph, from the visual calling card of the carte-de-visite to group photographs taken on board ship or against landmarks ashore. She also identifies in these land-based images a rich resource for assessing both the leisure pursuits of naval personnel and their engagement with understandings of empire and race.

The latter categories of empire and race are also the subject for the final chapter in the first section of this book. Analyses of non-white experiences within naval and maritime life have also proliferated in recent years through the work of scholars such as Marcus Rediker, Peter Linebaugh, Charles Foy, Philip Morgan, Joshua Newton, Aaron Jaffer and Ray Costello.[40] Daniel Spence's chapter uses case studies considering India, the Cayman Islands and the Straits Settlement of Singapore to reveal how British imperial notions of racial hierarchy shaped the configuration of colonial naval forces. In each case, the British presented particular ethnic groups as 'naturally' predisposed to naval service. These judgements responded not only to ethnographic preconceptions but to local, geopolitical, imperial and strategic factors. They allowed the Royal Navy both to exclude communities deemed problematic and to legitimise the position of white naval personnel at the pinnacle of an organisational (and imperial) structure defined in their own interests. At the same time, Spence concludes that far from being simply the passive recipients of these authorised imperial messages, 'colonial peoples exerted agency to

Introduction

shape their own identities and take advantage of the opportunities that being perceived as martial races opened up to them.[41]

The five chapters that comprise the second part of the book address the public presentation of naval subject matter through a variety of representational forms. Ranging from the 1760s to the 1930s, these contributions demonstrate the diversity and complexity of the material involved. They move from the crisp iconography of commemorative medals to the curatorial ambitions of a naval gallery, and from the pages of popular periodicals to transient yet spectacular moments of public performance. The simple fact that these undertakings were planned and realised across such a broad chronology tells its own, albeit unsurprising story: that the roots of British culture are deeply set in naval narratives. However, the contributions here demonstrate, singly and collectively, the active and purposeful ways in which the navy has been fashioned for wider consumption. Though ostensibly 'naval', these cultural engagements typically had – and were meant to have – a resonance far beyond the navy itself, delineating for instance cherished national mythologies or idealised visions of male heroism. These agendas were also, of course, extremely mobile. They frequently promoted notions of national triumphalism but were equally the means, intentionally or otherwise, for exposing deep-seated national anxieties and evaluating troubling processes of historical change.[42] Disseminated through British society, these cultural beliefs about and expectations of the navy also became yardsticks against which the service might be judged in the present.

In her chapter, Katherine Parker uses both the eloquence and the muteness of a single object to explore the nature of eighteenth-century naval commemoration. In 1768, Thomas Anson commissioned the striking of a medal to celebrate the achievements of his late brother, Admiral Lord George Anson. Such medals had a long pedigree as acknowledgements of martial achievement. Parker shows, however, that both this commemorative tradition and the wider understanding of naval service to which it was attached lacked the flexibility to foreground the full scope of Admiral Anson's contributions. These lay at least as much in exploration and administration as they did in the master category of contemporary medal making: victorious battle. Through this object, she points to a fissure between the increasingly bureaucratic and professionalised realities of everyday naval life – which owed significantly to Anson's own work – and a parallel structure prioritising social honour and leadership in the heat of action. The latter was the currency of commemoration, buoyed by the enthusiastic public association of national prosperity with naval victory.[43]

The former, upon which success often depended, did not translate so readily into the existing visual and cultural vocabularies.

Cicely Robinson extends this analysis of the nature and uses of naval heroism into the nineteenth century, through the prism of the naval gallery opened at the Royal Hospital, Greenwich, in 1824.[44] The purpose of its displays was straightforwardly celebratory, asserting the centrality of naval power within an evolving story of national greatness boundaried by the Spanish Armada at one end and the conclusion of the Napoleonic Wars at the other.[45] Here, too, the focus was rigidly fixed on climacterics and moments of glory, with the dual aim of securing public admiration and incentivising new generations of naval recruits. One supreme hero stood out, and Robinson plots Admiral Lord Nelson's representation within the gallery through statuary, paintings and relics (including the undress coat that he was wearing when mortally wounded at the Battle of Trafalgar). As she points out, choosing the very location where Nelson's body lay in state in January 1806 supercharged the gallery's propagandist purposes, and placed Nelson still more firmly centre stage as the personification of an apparent national destiny.

General interest magazines from the period 1850 to 1880 provide Barbara Korte with material to demonstrate how this 'construction and reconstruction of heroic [naval] images' was both maintained and undermined in Victorian Britain. Her analysis involves titles such as *Chambers's Journal* and *The Leisure Hour* – sources considerably further removed from direct naval control than the Royal Hospital or the Anson legacy. While she notes the same teleological approach to naval and national history that informed the paintings hanging in Greenwich, cross-currents are also made evident. Above all, the readerships of these publications were presented with a picture of dramatic technological change in the navy that could be interpreted as both empowering and disempowering. The conjunction of oak and valour that had supposedly won command of the seas was moving towards a new synthesis, and one whose physical and scientific properties seemed so awesome that they threatened to render human heroism redundant. In the absence of large-scale conflict to repopulate the pool of naval exemplars – and with a Victorian queasiness surrounding the personal motivations of distant but important figures such as Drake and Benbow – Korte presents an image of increasing public uncertainty. Not least, defining the navy though its battle honours, and the qualities of its commanders and crews through proximity to conflict, had drawbacks in an era dominated by the institution's deployment on policing and peacekeeping duties.

The indications of cultural nervousness that Korte reveals within constructions of naval heroism become urgent and profoundly desta-bilising in Jonathan Rayner's examination of *War Illustrated* magazine's coverage of events at sea between 1914 and 1916. The British public had come to view naval confrontation with Germany as a performance rehearsed through Nelsonian precedent, with inevitable and decisive victory as its final act.[46] Rayner shows how *War Illustrated* interpreted the naval conflict for its readers when reality failed to conform to a charismatic cultural script. Positive naval stories were glossed with Nelsonian allusion, and British involvement with the new technologies of submarine warfare was presented as consistent with traditional heroic ideals. Nonetheless, and as Rayner demonstrates, the central problem-atic remained untreatable. The victory that the Royal Navy ultimately won through 'sea control' was not the annihilating fleet action that the nation had been promised, and which the public had savoured in advance. The sense, communicated by Anson's medal, that unglamor-ous administration and efficiency were undeserving of memorialisation was paralleled and writ large for the twentieth-century consumers of *War Illustrated*. They struggled to locate the grinding, incremental work of naval blockade, power projection and trade protection within the narrow parameters of a fetishised heroism.

The Royal Navy's failure to deliver a new Trafalgar during the First World War cut deeply into the place it occupied within navalist, nation-alist and imperialist opinion. During the interwar years, these prem-ises of conservative Britishness were also perceived as menaced from other quarters, most notably by socialism, industrialisation and their assumed challenge to the established order. Emma Hanna's chapter shows how – galvanised by these fresh anxieties and threats – the naval account of Britain's inexorable rise was relaunched, once again in Greenwich, in 1933.[47] Hanna explores the genesis of the great night pageant that was held there that June, with its familiar and mytholo-gised retelling of British history weighted towards a rosily conceived Elizabethan and Georgian past (and drawing a veil over Cromwell and the Protectorate).[48] The pageant represented society as a changeless community processing harmoniously through time, and defined by consensus, tradition, hierarchy and monarchical authority. With the 'cult of the navy' as its organising framework, the event was an enor-mous popular success. The naval and heroic narrative of British great-ness was always most powerful as an imagined and idealised reality. The anticlimactic disappointment of Jutland, and the myriad interwar signs of Britain's declining global status, created a desire within some constituencies for a return to 'normality', and a void that cultural performance readily exploited.

Notwithstanding the richness and variety of these ten studies, it is necessary to conclude with a brief consideration of what this volume cannot achieve. Perhaps this should begin with an acknowledgement that the evolution of naval history – and the agency of academic fashion – have worked to obscure as well as to reveal.[49] In spite of the title selected for this book, its editors are keenly aware that new approaches to naval history bring their own problems. Not least, revisionism and novelty are always eager to have their freshness highlighted by the supposed staleness of what went before. In recent years and in broad terms, the 'new' has become synonymous with studies that connect ship with shore, and the institution of the navy with much wider historical realities.[50] Earlier specialisms dealing with the idiosyncratic, internal workings of naval life have often suffered as a result, easily marginalised as works of enthusiastic but parochial traditionalism.[51] However, any resulting loss of fluency in the vocabularies of ship handling, command skills, weapons technologies, naval architecture or navigation comes at a cost. The significance of these subjects, and the ability of new research questions to reinvigorate apparently recondite material, are easily obscured.

Much vital work has been completed – though more needs to be done – to reveal the extent to which the Royal Navy is the expression of social, cultural, national and imperial agendas. At the same time, these essential insights need to be counterbalanced by a continuing curiosity regarding the specific human and professional alchemy of naval life from the port town to the deep sea.[52] More traditional naval history was vulnerable to the criticism that it ghettoised its subject, and artificially promoted its uniqueness. Newer approaches, and particularly from within cultural history, are vulnerable to the charge that they systematically erase naval exceptionalism, representing the institution through the media of popular culture rather than through fine-grained analyses of naval lived experience. The inherent hazard of this process is that naval history, however defined, forms a series of discrete strata deposited loosely one on top of the other, rather than fusing into something more solid and synthesised. The fact that a multitude of disciplinary approaches now interrogate naval material accelerates the accumulation of strata but does not necessarily provide the edifice itself with any greater stability or accumulated analytical power.

In a recent article, Isaac Land has considered what a more 'holistic' and 'integrated' naval history might look like.[53] He refers to Victor Davis Hanson's work *Carnage and Culture: Landmark Battles in the Rise of Western Power*, and quotes the author's contention that: 'Students of war must never be content to learn merely how men fight a battle, but must always ask why soldiers fight as they do, and what ultimately their battle is for.'[54] The value of this comment for naval history surely lies in its insistence that a complex field of study will become problematically compartmentalised or thought-provokingly interconnected in direct relation to the nature and quality of the questions historians ask.[55] As we have seen, the welcome status quo is that the questions being asked of the naval world are diverse and challenging; the issue lies in determining how, why and whether they intersect, and what their conjunction might permit us to reveal.

This, in turn, begs the fundamental question of what navies are actually for. The answer has most consistently and enduringly been identified in their development as instruments of conflict, a view closely connected to the nature of much naval history as an analysis of and preparation for war fighting.[56] There is, of course, an unarguable degree of common sense within this premise, and yet the instinct of historians to mistrust monocausal explanations is also well applied here. Without necessarily challenging the centrality of this battle-focused definition, the branches growing outwards from this 'trunk' have become so broad and luxuriant that they have long required other visible means of support. As we have seen, navies have, for instance, been assessed in terms of their active role within diplomacy, the functioning of the state, the operation of trade and commerce and the realm of industry and technology.[57] They have been illuminated as locations within which understandings of class, hierarchy, expertise, age, gender and sexuality have been communicated, entrenched and contested.[58] Their influence upon and involvement within a host of local, regional, national, imperial and global cultural forms and political agendas has been convincingly demonstrated.[59] Moreover, it has become clear that at any point of the early modern and modern periods addressed in this volume, every element in this amalgam of form and function invariably links to a dozen others.

Rather than a single tree, therefore, the naval world now appears more of a thicket, with a complex and often concealed labyrinth of roots and entanglements. War and the anticipation of war certainly prompted it to grow and change. Unlike a career in farming, the law or the priesthood, naval life *always* had a relationship to war, whether active or passive.

However, this connection to conflict also associated the navy's personnel with a charismatic and culturally validated masculinity, and the institution with the most straightforward route to promoting its usefulness and significance and defending its costliness. Under these circumstances, it is surely inevitable that the navy's myriad activities have been viewed and presented rather too consistently through the prism of combat readiness and warlike purpose. Few naval memoirs are written about desk-bound careers in the supply and secretariat branch. And yet, many of the levels on which the navy functioned owed as much or more to the undramatic realities of peacetime – from patronage networks to the patterns of sociability and recreation that defined and attracted particular groups within the institution.[60] War was an ever-present *raison d'être*, but its arrival could be experienced as an aberration, menacing settled routines of ceremony, training, professional hierarchy and family life.

To put it crudely, the fact that the bulk of naval historical scholarship has been focused on periods of conflict can thus create a circularity when it comes to plotting the underlying priorities of the organisation and its people. As has been noted for the nineteenth century, the failure of that era to deliver long periods of high-intensity sea warfare has, at times, even threatened to leave it without a naval history at all.[61] The aim of this book is not to replace one partiality with another, but instead to unsettle the notion that any single master category should enjoy necessary pre-eminence. The potential exists for the plurality of current approaches to naval history – defined as broadly as possible – to meet on a more level playing field, where their interaction will provide new answers and new questions for all participants. This book can only provide a step in that direction. It does not ask to be viewed as the expression of a newly resolved and internally coherent approach to naval history itself, even if that was either desirable or achievable.[62] It does, however, hope to promote the interdisciplinary exchange and communication that holds out so much promise for future scholarly insight and public engagement.

It is fitting, too, that this volume developed from papers presented at the National Maritime Museum, Greenwich, in 2013. Greenwich, of course, has been implicated for centuries in the making and – as several chapters in this collection explore – the representing of naval history. These connections began with the Tudors and the royal dockyards at Deptford and Woolwich, and then flourished from the commissioning of the Royal Hospital for Seamen in the 1690s through to the operation of the Royal Naval College from 1873 to 1997. The National Maritime Museum itself occupies buildings once used for naval training by the

Introduction

Royal Hospital School and is thus physically and conceptually the product of this legacy. The agendas that led to its opening in 1937 were the socio-culturally conservative, navalist, nationalist and imperialist motivations that had energised the Navy League in the late nineteenth century.[63] By the 1930s, the writing was clearly on the wall for such triumphalist visions of naval mastery and British pre-eminence. However, amid imperial destabilisation and international competition, 'the supporters of the National Maritime Museum project could still believe that such an institution would help to turn the tide'.[64] Those founding aspirations are now only a ghostly presence within a site that – like naval history itself – has long charted a determinedly different course through British and global history.

Notes

1 For an assertion about the weakness of naval historiography see Andrew Lambert, 'The Construction of Naval History, 1815–1914', *The Mariner's Mirror*, 97:1 (February 2011), 217, 223. For recent examples of 'naval gazing' see: John B. Hattendorf (ed.), *Ubi Sumus? The State of Naval and Maritime History* (Newport, RI: Naval War College Press, 1994); Hattendorf (ed.), *Doing Naval History: Essays Toward Improvement* (Newport, RI: Naval War College Press, 1995); Richard Harding, *Modern Naval History: Debates and Prospects* (London: Bloomsbury, 2016). A few works have attempted to analyse naval historiography in focused periods: see Andrew Lambert, *The Foundations of Naval History: Sir John Knox Laughton, the Navy and the Historical Profession* (London: Chatham Publishing, 1998); Don Schurman, *The Education of a Navy: The Development of British Naval Strategic Thought, 1867–1914* (London: Cassell, 1965). The centenary issue of the *Mariner's Mirror* included a number of articles about the history of naval history: see *The Mariner's Mirror*, 97:1 (February 2011).
2 See, for instance, N. A. M. Rodger, 'Britain' in Hattendorf, *Ubi Sumus?*, pp. 42–3; Lambert, *Foundations of Naval History*.
3 Harding, *Modern Naval History*, p. 4.
4 Josiah Burchett, *A Complete History of the most Remarkable Transactions at Sea, from the Earliest Accounts of Time to the Conclusion of the Last War with France. Wherein Is Given An Account of the most considerable Naval-Expeditions, Sea Fights, Stratagems, Discoveries And Other Maritime Occurrences that have happen'd among all Nations which have flourished at sea: And in more particular manner of Great Britain, from the time of the Revolution, in the years 1688, to the aforesaid Period. In Five books* (London, 1720); Samuel Colliber, *Columna Rostrata: Or, A Critical History of the English Sea-Affairs: Wherein all the Remarkable Actions of the English Nation at Sea*

are described, and the most considerable Events (especially in the Account of the three Dutch Wars) are proved, either from Original Pieces, or from the Testimonies of the Best Foreign Historians (London: R. Robinson, 1727); Thomas Lediard, *The Naval History of England, In all its Branches; from the Norman Conquest in the Year 1066 to the Conclusion of 1734. Collected from the most Approved Historians, English and Foreign, Authentik Records and Manuscripts, Scarce Tracts, Original Journals, &c. With Manny Facts and Observations, never before made public*. (London: John Wilcox, 1735). See also James Davey, 'The Birth of Naval History: Audience and Objectivity in Eighteenth-Century Historical Writing' (forthcoming).

5 Burchett, *A Complete History*.

6 Burchett, *Complete History*, pp. 1–34; Lediard, *Naval History*, preface.

7 Capt. Charles Jenkins, *England's Triumph: Or Spanish Cowardice expos'd. Being a Compleat History of the Many Signal Victories Gained by the Royal Navy and Merchants Ships of Great Britain, for the Term of Four Hundred Years past, over the insulting and haughty Spaniards. Wherein is related a true and genuine Account of all the Expeditions, Voyages, Adventures &c. of all the British [English-British interchangeable] Admirals from Time above mentiond, whose Successes have already filled all Europe with Amazement*. (London, 1739); John Campbell, *Lives of the Admirals and other Eminent British Seamen* (London, 1742).

8 Dismayed to discover that American accounts of recent naval victories had failed to take into account the British inferiority in size and gunnery, William James wrote a book that sought to overturn any misconceptions, so beginning a debate about frigate sizes that continues to this day. For an excellent overview of James's career see Andrew Lambert's introduction to William James, *Naval Occurrences of the War of 1812: A Full and Correct Account of the Naval War Between Great Britain and the United States of Americas, 1812–15* (London: Conway Maritime Press, 2004), pp. i–vii. See also William James, *The Naval History of Great Britain during the French Revolutionary and Napoleonic Wars*, 6 vols. (Mechanicsburg, PA: Stackpole Books, 2002).

9 Harding, *Modern Naval History*, p. 5. For each historian's defining works, see Alfred Thayer Mahan, *The Influence of Sea Power Upon History, 1660–1784* (Boston, MA: Little, Brown and Company, 1890); Mahan, *The Influence of Sea Power Upon the French Revolution and Empire, 1789–1812* (Boston, MA: Little, Brown and Company, 1892); Mahan, *Sea Power in its Relation to the War of 1812*, 2 vols. (Boston, MA: Little, Brown and Company, 1905); Julian Corbett, *England in the Seven Years' War* (London: Longmans, Green and Company, 1907); Corbett, *The Campaign of Trafalgar* (London: Longmans, Green and Company, 1910); Corbett, *Some Principles of Maritime Strategy* (London: Longmans, Green and Company, 1911); Herbert Richmond, *The Navy in the War of 1739–48* (Cambridge: Cambridge University Press, 1920); Herbert Richmond, *National Policy and Naval Strength and Other Essays*

(New York: Longman, Green and Company, 1928, 1934, 1993); Herbert Richmond, *The Navy as an Instrument of Policy, 1558–1727* (Cambridge: Cambridge University Press, 1953).

10 Rodger, 'Britain', pp. 42–3, 45.

11 Rodger, 'Britain', pp. 42–3; Harding, *Modern Naval History*, p. 5.

12 Lambert, 'The Construction of Naval History'; Harding, *Modern Naval History*, p. 5.

13 Rodger, 'Britain', pp. 42–3.

14 Lambert, 'The Construction of Naval History', 217; Harding, *Modern Naval History*, p. 6.

15 H. W. Richmond, 'The Importance of the Study of Naval History', *The Naval Review*, 27 (May 1939), 201–18, quote from p. 201.

16 Kevin Littlewood and Beverley Butler, *Of Ships and Stars: Maritime Heritage and the Founding of the National Maritime Museum, Greenwich* (London: National Maritime Museum, 1998). Visitors in the 1950s would have seen galleries focusing on Anson, Vernon, Cook, Nelson, Trafalgar, the transition from sail to steam and the First and Second World Wars.

17 Rodger, 'Britain', p. 45.

18 Roger Knight, 'Changing the Agenda: the "New" Naval History of the British Sailing Navy', *The Mariner's Mirror*, 97:1 (February 2011), 225, 227–9.

19 H. M. Scott, 'The Second Hundred Years War', *The Historical Journal*, 35:2 (June 1992), 453.

20 Lambert, 'The Construction of Naval History', 219.

21 See the new edition, Paul Kennedy, *The Rise and Fall of British Naval Mastery* (London: Allen Lane, 1976; published with new introduction, London: Penguin, 2017), p. xix.

22 There is not enough space to list the many works produced in this period so the most important will suffice (in order of publication): P. K. Crimmin, 'Admiralty Relations with the Treasury, 1783–1806: the Preparations of Navy Estimates and the Beginnings of Treasury Control', *Mariner's Mirror*, 53:1 (1969), 63–72; David Syrett, *Shipping and the American War, 1775–83: A Study of British Transport Organization* (London: Athlone Press, 1970); R. J. B. Knight, 'The Royal Dockyards in England at the Time of the American War of Independence' (PhD thesis, University of London, 1972); Roger Morriss, *The Royal Dockyards during the Revolutionary and Napoleonic Wars* (Leicester: Leicester University Press, 1983); Jonathan Coad, *The Royal Dockyards, 1690–1850: Architecture and Engineering Works of the Sailing Navy* (Aldershot: Scholar Press, 1989); Brian Lavery, *The Ship of the Line*, 2 vols. (London, 1983–4); Michael Duffy, *Soldiers, Sugar and Seapower: The British Expeditions to the West Indies and the War against Revolutionary France* (Oxford: Clarendon Press, 1987); Andrew Lambert, *The Last Sailing Battlefleet: Maintaining Naval Mastery, 1815–50* (London: Conway Maritime Press, 1991); Richard Harding, *Amphibious Warfare in the Eighteenth Century:*

The British Expedition to the West Indies, 1740–1742 (New York: Boydell and Brewer, 1991); Patrick Karl O'Brien, *Power with Profit: the State and the Economy, 1688–1815* (London: Institute of Historical Research, 1991); Jan Glete, *Navies and Nations: Warships, Navies and State Building in Europe and America, 1500–1860*, 2 vols. (Stockholm: Almqvist and Wiksell, 1993).

23 Roger Knight and Martin Wilcox, *Sustaining the Fleet, 1793–1815: War, the British Navy and the Contractor State* (Woodbridge: Boydell Press, 2010); H. V. Bowen and A. Gonzales Enciso (eds), *Mobilising Resources for War: Britain and Spain at Work during the Early Modern Period* (Pamplona: Eunsa, 2006); R. Torres Sanchez (ed.), *War, State and Development: Fiscal-Military States in the Eighteenth Century* (Pamplona: Eunsa, 2007); Gareth Cole, *Arming the Royal Navy, 1793–1815: The Office of Ordnance and the State* (London: Pickering and Chatto, 2012); James Davey, *The Transformation of British Naval Strategy: Seapower and Supply in Northern Europe, 1808–1812* (Woodbridge: Boydell and Brewer, 2012); Robert K. Sutcliffe, *British Expeditionary Warfare and the Defeat of Napoleon 1793–1815* (Woodbridge: Boydell Press, 2016).

24 Harding, *Modern Naval History*, pp. 6–7.

25 Michael Lewis, *A Social History of the Navy, 1793–1815* (London: Allen & Unwin, 1960); N. A. M. Rodger, *The Wooden World: An Anatomy of the Georgian Navy* (London: Harper Collins, 1986).

26 J. D. Davis, *Gentlemen and Tarpaulins: The Officers and Men of the Restoration Navy* (Oxford: Oxford University Press, 1991). For more recent examples of naval social history see Margarette Lincoln, *Naval Wives and Mistresses* (London: National Maritime Museum, 2007); S. A. Cavell, *Midshipmen and Quarterdeck Boys in the British Navy, 1771–1831* (Woodbridge: Boydell and Brewer, 2012); Evan Wilson, *A Social History of British Naval Officers 1775–1815* (Woodbridge: Boydell, 2016); Ellen Gill, *Naval Families, War and Duty in Britain 1740–1820* (Woodbridge: Boydell, 2016).

27 Jan Rüger, *The Great Naval Game: Britain and Germany in the Age of Empire* (Cambridge: Cambridge University Press, 2009); Kathleen Wilson, 'Empire, Trade and Popular Politics in mid-Hanoverian Britain: The Case of Admiral Vernon', *Past and Present*, 121 (November 1988), 74–109; Timothy Jenks, *Naval Engagements: Patriotism, Cultural Politics, and the Royal Navy, 1793–1815* (Oxford: Oxford University Press, 2006).

28 Karen Wigen, 'Oceans of History', *American Historical Review*, cxi (2006), 717–21; Glen O'Hara, '"The sea is swinging into view": Modern British Maritime History in a Globalised World', *English Historical Review*, cxxiv (2009), 1109–34; David Cannadine (ed.), *Empire, the Sea and Global History: Britain's Maritime World, c. 1763–c. 1840* (Basingstoke: Palgrave, 2007).

29 The literature on Atlantic history – and increasingly global history – is vast. For important 'state of the field' pieces see Bernard Bailyn, 'The Idea of Atlantic History', *Itinerario*, xx (1996), 19–41; Bernard Bailyn, *Atlantic History: Concepts and Contours* (Cambridge, MA: Harvard University Press,

2005); Richard Blakemore, 'The Changing Fortunes of Atlantic History', *English Historical Review*, cxxxi:551 (2016), 851–68; Cannadine, *The Sea and Global History*.

30 For a good example of this, see Christer Petley and John McAleer (eds), *The Royal Navy and the British Atlantic World, c. 1750–1820* (London: Palgrave Macmillan, 2016).

31 W. Jeffrey Bolster, *Black Jacks: African American Seamen in the Age of Sail* (Cambridge, MA: Harvard University Press, 1998); see also Charles R. Foy, 'The Royal Navy's Employment of Black Mariners and Maritime Workers, 1754–1783', *International Journal of Maritime History*, 28:1 (2016), 6–35.

32 J. Ross Dancy, *The Myth of the Press Gang: Volunteers, Impressment and the Naval Manpower Problem in the Late Eighteenth Century* (Woodbridge: Boydell and Brewer, 2015). For his critics, see Isaac Land, 'New Scholarship on the Press Gang', http://porttowns.port.ac.uk/press-gang-1/ and http://porttowns.port.ac.uk/press-gang2/ (accessed 18 December 2017); and Christopher P. Magra, *Poseidon's Curse: Naval Impressment and Atlantic Origins of the American Revolution* (Cambridge: Cambridge University Press, 2016).

33 Lambert, 'The Construction of Naval History', 217–18; Kenneth J. Hagen and Mar R. Shulman, 'Mahan Plus One Hundred: The Current State of American Naval History' in Hattendorf, *Ubi Sumus?*, pp. 379–80.

34 Lewis, *Social History*; Rodger, *Wooden World*; John Cardwell, 'Royal Navy Surgeons, 1793–1815: A Collective Biography' in David Boyd Haycock and Sally Archer (eds), *Health and Medicine at Sea, 1700–1900* (Woodbridge: Boydell & Brewer, 2009), 38–62; Gill, *Naval Families*; Cavell, *Midshipmen*; Thomas Malcolmson, *Order and Disorder in the British Navy, 1793–1815: Control, Resistance, Flogging and Hanging* (Woodbridge: Boydell Press, 2016). See also Isaac Land, *War, Nationalism, and the British Sailor, 1750–1850* (London: Palgrave Macmillan, 2009), for a particularly integrated social and cultural approach.

35 N. A. M. Rodger, *The Command of the Ocean: A Naval History of Britain, 1649–1815* (London: Penguin, 2005), p. 407.

36 M. S. Creighton and L. Norling (eds), *Iron Men, Wooden Women: Gender and Seafaring in the Atlantic world, 1700–1920* (Baltimore, MD: Johns Hopkins University Press, 1996); Lisa Norling, *Captain Ahab had a Wife: New England Women and the Whalefishery, 1720–1870* (Chapel Hill, NC: University of North Carolina Press, 2000); L. Abrams, *Myth and Materiality in a Woman's World: Shetland, 1800–2000* (Manchester: Manchester University Press, 2005); V. Burton, '"Whoring, drinking sailors": Reflections on Masculinity from the Labour History of Nineteenth-Century British Shipping' in M. Walsh (ed.), *Working Out Gender: Perspectives from Labour History* (Aldershot: Ashgate, 1999), pp. 84–101; M. S. Creighton, '"Women" and Men in American Whaling, 1830–1870', *International Journal of Maritime History*,

4:1 (1992), 195–218; T. Bergholm and K. Teräs, 'Female Dockers in Finland, *c.* 1900–1975: Gender and Change on the Finnish Waterfront', *International Journal of Maritime History*, 11:2 (1999), 107–20; Jo Stanley, 'With Cutlass and Compress: Women's Relations with the Sea', *Gender and History*, 12:1 (2000), 232–6; Hugh Murphy, '"From the Crinoline to the Boilersuit", Women Workers in British Shipbuilding during the Second World War', *Contemporary British History*, 13:4 (1999), 82–104.

37 Melanie Holihead, 'Cut Adrift or Towed Astern: Sailors' Wives in Mid-Nineteenth-Century Portsea Island Considered in Perspective', *Journal for Maritime Research*, 17:2 (2015), 155–68; Linda Colley, *The Ordeal of Elizabeth Marsh: How a Remarkable Woman Crossed Seas and Empires to Become Part of World History* (London: Harper Perennial, 2008); see also Quintin Colville, Elin Jones and Katherine Parker, 'Gendering the Maritime World', *Journal for Maritime Research*, 17:2 (2015), 97–101.

38 Seth Stein Le Jacq, 'Buggery's Travels: Royal Navy Sodomy on Ship and Shore in the Long Eighteenth Century', *Journal for Maritime Research*, 17:2 (2015), 103–16. For a twentieth-century exploration of homosexuality and the maritime world see Jo Stanley, '"They Thought They Were Normal – and Called Themselves Queens": Gay Seafarers on British Liners, 1945–85', in Duncan Redford (ed.), *Maritime History and Identity: the Sea and Culture in the Modern World* (London: I.B.Tauris, 2014), pp. 230–52. For an analysis that demonstrates the currency of naval homosexual identities within wider British culture see: Matt Houlbrook, *Queer London: Perils and Pleasures in the Sexual Metropolis, 1918–1957* (Chicago: Chicago University Press, 2005). See also B. R. Burg, *Boys at Sea: Sodomy, Indecency, and Courts Martial in Nelson's Navy* (Basingstoke: Palgrave, 2007).

39 Mary Conley, *From Jack Tar to Union Jack: Representing Naval Manhood in the British Empire, 1870–1918* (Manchester: Manchester University Press, 2009); Laura Rowe, *Morale and Discipline in the Royal Navy during the First World War* (Cambridge: Cambridge University Press, 2017); Rowe, 'Their Lordships Regret That … Admiralty Perceptions of and Responses to Allegations of Lower Deck Disquiet' in J. D. Keene and M. S. Neiberg (eds), *Finding Common Ground* (Boston, MA: Brill, 2010); Christopher McKee, *Sober Men and True: Sailor Lives in the Royal Navy, 1900–45* (Cambridge, MA, and London: Harvard University Press, 2002); Anthony Carew, *The Lower Deck of the Royal Navy, 1900–39: The Invergordon Mutiny in Perspective* (Manchester: Manchester University Press, 1981).

40 Marcus Rediker, *The Slave Ship: A Human History* (London: John Murray, 2007); E. J. Christopher, *Slave Ship Sailors and their Captive Cargoes* (Cambridge: Cambridge University Press, 2006); Peter Linebaugh and Marcus Rediker, *The Many-Headed Hydra: Sailors, Slaves, Commoners and the Hidden History of the Revolutionary Atlantic* (London: Verso, 2012); Charles R. Foy, 'The Royal Navy's Employment of Black Mariners and Maritime Workers,

1754–1783', *International Journal of Maritime History*, 28:1 (2016), 6–35; Philip Morgan, 'Black Experience in Britain's Maritime World, 1763–1833' in Cannadine, *The Sea and Global History*; Joshua Newton, 'Slavery, Sea Power and the State: the Royal Navy and the British West African Settlements, 1748– 1756', *Journal of Imperial and Commonwealth History*, 41:2 (2013), 171–93; Aaron Jaffer, *Lascars and Indian Ocean Seafaring, 1780–1860: Shipboard Life, Unrest and Mutiny* (Woodbridge: The Boydell Press, 2015); Ray Costello, *Black Salt: Seafarers of African Descent on British Ships* (Liverpool: Liverpool University Press, 2012).

41 Daniel Owen Spence, Chapter 5, this volume.

42 See Jan Rüger, *The Great Naval Game: Britain and Germany in the Age of Empire* (Cambridge: Cambridge University Press, 2007).

43 See James Davey, 'The Naval Hero and British National Identity, 1707–50' in Duncan Redford (ed.), *Maritime History and Identity: The Sea and Culture in the Modern World* (London: I.B.Tauris, 2014), pp. 13–37; Nicholas Rogers, 'From Vernon to Wolfe: Empire and Identity in the British Atlantic World of the Mid-Eighteenth Century' in Frans de Bruyn and Shaun Regan (eds), *The Culture of the Seven Years' War: Empire, Identity, and the Arts in the Eighteenth-Century Atlantic World* (Toronto: University of Toronto Press, 2014), pp. 25–52; Kathleen Wilson, 'Admiral Nelson and the People: Masculinity, Patriotism and Body Politics' in David Cannadine (ed.), *Re-Discovering Nelson* (London: Palgrave, 2005), pp. 49–66.

44 See also Geoffrey Quilley, 'The Battle of the Pictures: Painting the History of Trafalgar' in David Cannadine (ed.), *Trafalgar in History: A Battle and its Afterlife* (Basinstoke: Palgrave Macmillan, 2006), pp. 121–38.

45 See Rüger, *The Great Naval Game*: p. 3: 'the Royal Navy became one of the most important metaphors of Britishness in the nineteenth century'.

46 See *ibid.*, especially pp. 1–4.

47 For a useful counterpoint addressing an earlier moment of public naval display see: Huw W. G. Lewis-Jones, 'Displaying Nelson: Navalism and "The Exhibition" of 1891', *International Journal of Maritime History*, 17:1 (2005), 29–68.

48 See Rüger, *The Great Naval Game*, for example, pp. 173–4, 269.

49 See Knight, 'Changing the Agenda', 236.

50 See, for instance, Land, *War, Nationalism, and the British Sailor*, p. 166.

51 Lewis R. Fischer, 'Are We in Danger of Being Left with Our Journals and not Much Else: The Future of Maritime History?', *The Mariner's Mirror*, 97:1 (2011), 366–81: 'When I first entered the profession in the mid-1970s, maritime history was dismissed by many scholars in other sectors of the historical discipline as a haven for antiquarians who posed narrow questions of interest only to enthusiasts and no one else … the late Frank Broeze, in my view the best maritime historian of his generation, referred to this narrow approach as "nautical history"', p. 366.

52 From a naval perspective, see the following previously cited contributions: Lewis, *Social History*; Rodger, *The Wooden World*; Rowe, *Morale and Discipline*; Mckee, *Sober Men and True*; Carew, *The Lower Deck of the Royal Navy*.

53 Isaac Land, 'Gender History: Inclusion versus Integration', http://www.britishnavalhistory.com/gender-history-inclusion-versus-integration/, 2 March 2014 (accessed 18 December 2017).

54 Victor Davis Hanson, *Carnage and Culture: Landmark Battles in the Rise of Western Power* (New York: Doubleday, 2001), p. 131.

55 See Lambert, 'The Construction of Naval History', 224: 'The issue is not what we know, but what questions we ask, and how our work engages with other scholars, and other audiences'.

56 See Lambert, 'The Construction of Naval History', 208, 217.

57 For work approaching the latter category of 'technology' from cultural perspectives see, for instance: Don Leggett and Richard Dunn (eds), *Re-Inventing the Ship: Science, Technology and the Maritime World, 1800–1918* (London: Ashgate, 2012); Don Leggett, *Shaping the Royal Navy: Technology, Authority and Naval Architecture, c. 1830–1906* (Manchester: Manchester University Press, 2015); Crosbie Smith, '*Dreadnought* Science: The Cultural Construction of Efficiency and Effectiveness' in Robert Blyth, Andrew Lambert and Jan Rüger (eds), *The Dreadnought and the Edwardian Age* (Farnham: Ashgate, 2011), pp. 135–64.

58 See Quintin Colville, 'Corporate Domesticity and Idealised Masculinity: Royal Naval Officers and their Shipboard Homes, 1918–39', *Gender and History*, 21:3 (2009), 499–519; Quintin Colville, 'Jack Tar and the Gentleman Officer: The Role of Uniform in Shaping the Class- and Gender-Related Identities of British Naval Personnel, 1930–39', *Transactions of the Royal Historical Society*, 6:13 (2003), 105–29.

59 See Margarette Lincoln, *Representing the Royal Navy: British Sea Power, 1750–1815* (London: Ashgate, 2002); Cannadine, *Trafalgar in History*; David Cannadine (ed.), *Admiral Lord Nelson: Context and Legacy* (Basingstoke and New York: Palgrave Macmillan, 2005); Nicholas Rogers, *The Press Gang: Naval Impressment and its Opponents in Georgian Britain* (London: Continuum, 2007); Timothy Jenks, *Naval Engagements: Patriotism, Cultural Politics, and the Royal Navy* (Oxford: Oxford University Press, 2006).

60 See, for example, a recent thesis that explored the network and influence of naval patronage in the late eighteenth century: Catherine Beck, 'Patronage and the Royal Navy, 1775–1815' (unpublished PhD thesis, University College London, 2017).

61 See Lambert, 'The Construction of Naval History', 207: 'Edwardian naval history examined admirals and operations – ships and men, dismissing the nineteenth century as an unremarkable catalogue of gunboat diplomacy; tedious technology and dull books that separated Nelson from the next world

conflict … Never a headline area for research or teaching, the nineteenth century rarely achieved a critical mass of scholarship, and the main debates have been driven by twentieth century concerns'.

62 See Knight, 'Changing the Agenda', 242: 'Over-defined labels as to whether a historian is a "naval" or "maritime" historian are of little consequence and misleading to boot. The future is at least in part interdisciplinary. After all, economic, political, war studies and cultural histories of the navy are but dialects of a greater language'.

63 See, for instance, John C. Mitcham, 'Navalism and Greater Britain, 1897– 1914' in Duncan Redford (ed.), *Maritime History and Identity: The Sea and Culture in the Modern World* (London: I.B.Tauris, 2014), pp. 271–93; Neil C. Fleming, 'The Imperial Maritime League: British Navalism, Conflict, and the Radical Right, c. 1907–1920', *War in History*, 23:3 (2016), 296–322.

64 Kevin Littlewood and Beverley Butler, *Of Ships and Stars*, p. xv.

Part I
Sociocultural analyses of the Royal Navy

Particular skills: warrant officers in the Royal Navy, 1775–1815

Evan Wilson

Warrant officers are the forgotten men of the Georgian navy. Above them, commissioned officers have received substantial historical attention, beginning with, but not limited to, the ever-increasing biographies of Nelson.[1] Below them, the lower deck has come under growing scrutiny, much of it focused on the question of impressment.[2] Warrant officers of wardroom rank, on the other hand, have only been studied in fits and starts. These men – the master, the purser, the surgeon and the chaplain – lack the glamour of commissioned officers and the political salience of impressed men on the lower deck. But the failure of the historical profession to study warrant officers should not be seen as a reflection on their value to the navy and its operations. They were prominent members of every ship, and the master, purser, and surgeon had particular skills that were unique on board and essential for life at sea. They ate and in some cases berthed alongside commissioned officers in the wardroom, and saw themselves as socially and professionally comparable.

What has been written about warrant officers originates, as does so much of the social history of the navy in this period, with Michael Lewis. His pioneering work on commissioned officers relied on a large database; he was unable to compile a similar database for warrant officers because of a lack of available sources, but he did study warrant officers in the context of other members of the ship's company.[3] Few since have followed his lead. More recent studies have tended to focus on only one kind of warrant officer, such as Gordon Taylor and N. A. M. Rodger's work on naval chaplains, or Janet Macdonald's research on pursers.[4] The most common of these studies focus on surgeons.[5] Medical historians have contributed significantly to our understanding both of surgeons' roles in medical discoveries and their naval careers. While the work of John Cardwell, in particular, has significantly advanced our understanding of surgeons' lives, its scope is narrow.[6] It is long past time to revisit Lewis's work and include all warrant officers – not just surgeons – in the new social history of the navy.

The foundation for this chapter is a database of warrant officers selected at random from seniority lists compiled by naval administrators from 1775 to 1815. It includes all four warrant officers of wardroom rank, and it is designed to cover roughly 10 per cent of the men who served during the French Revolutionary (1792–1802) and Napoleonic Wars (1803–15). The database provides opportunities to compare warrant officers both to each other and to commissioned officers. Using online genealogical databases, we can suggest some preliminary conclusions about warrant officers' families and their geographic origins. By tracing the paths that warrant officers took into the navy, the pattern of their movements from ship to ship within the navy, and whether they decided to remain in the navy for their whole careers, we can reveal a more comprehensive picture of warrant officers' careers and lives than any previous study.[7] They were typical members of Georgian Britain's middle classes, and they aspired to the respect and status of professionals, including doctors, lawyers, and clergymen as well as commissioned army and navy officers. Some succeeded, using the navy as a platform for advancement in the civilian world, while others remained in naval service. Those who remained waged a successful campaign for higher pay and more elaborate uniforms to close the social gap with commissioned officers. Masters and chaplains, though, struggled with lingering uncertainty about their employment prospects and their place in the naval hierarchy.

Most warrant officers were English, and few were born outside the British Isles, as Table 1 shows. Within the British Isles, there are some interesting patterns. Note that there are no Scottish chaplains in the database, because chaplains not born in England tended to come from Church

Table 1 Geographic origins in the wardroom[8]

	England	Scotland	Ireland	Wales	Overseas
Commissioned	72%	13%	7%	3%	5%
Masters	61%	31%	4%	2%	2%
Pursers	82%	11%	2%	2%	2%
Surgeons	34%	36%	25%	4%	2%
Chaplains	81%	0%	8%	11%	0%

of England territory – namely Wales and Ireland. As naval historians have long suspected, and as Cardwell's work also shows, surgeons were disproportionately Scottish and Irish.[9] Educational opportunities were significantly greater for surgeons in Ireland and Scotland, as will be discussed later. Surprisingly, nearly one in three masters seems to have been Scottish but, unlike surgeons, the remaining majority was heavily English rather than split between England and Ireland. Masters' records were the most difficult to uncover and, as a result, the percentage of Scottish masters may be exaggerated. But Master Murdo Downie's career provides some hints as to why there may have been so many Scottish masters. Born in Aberdeen, Downie grew up working in the North Sea coastal fishing trade before joining the navy. He published a chart of the east coast of Scotland in 1792, and was later cited as an expert on the North Sea in a book entitled *The New Seaman's Guide, and Coaster's Companion*.[10] The maritime communities of Scotland were a fertile recruiting ground for the navy. English-born masters were also likely to come from maritime communities, where they would have been exposed at an early age to the seamanship and navigation skills necessary for survival at sea.

Warrant officers came from social backgrounds broadly similar to those of commissioned officers.[11] This conclusion goes against most of what has been written about members of the wardroom. Historians have assumed that since a commission was undoubtedly more prestigious than a warrant, commissioned officers would naturally have come from more socially elite backgrounds than warrant officers.[12] Instead, it is more accurate to say that the majority of commissioned and warrant officers shared similar professional and commercial backgrounds. A typical wardroom in a ship of the line might have five lieutenants, four warrant officers and three marine officers. On average, nine of these twelve men would have come from middling backgrounds, and only one or two from a landed family.[13] The social distance between wardroom members, and in particular between the commissioned and warrant officers, was small. Chaplain Edward Mangin provides corroborating evidence when he notes that there was only one 'independent man' in his wardroom on board the third-rate *Gloucester*; the rest came from backgrounds on the fringes of genteel society.[14]

We need not spend any time on the 'titled people' category here, since no warrant officers came from the elite. The professional category similarly requires little explanation: professionals were often the sons of other professionals. Two straightforward examples are surgeon James Thynne, whose father was an apothecary and surgeon in Scotland, and chaplain Edward Brice, whose father was also a clergyman.[16] Purser John Henry Bond crossed two categories: his father was a surgeon in the navy, and his grandfather was a purser.[17] There are dozens of other examples in the database, as roughly half of all members of the wardroom came from professional backgrounds. The 'business and commerce' category refers to the widest range of family incomes, from Surgeon Samuel Gage Britton, whose father was a tailor in Bristol, to Captain Christopher Bell, whose father was a merchant who owned one of the largest houses in Great Yarmouth.[18]

It is noteworthy that that the commissioned officer, Bell, came from a relatively wealthy commercial background, while the warrant officer, Britton, did not. There was a social gap between the backgrounds of commissioned and warrant officers, such that in each category commissioned officers tended to come from the higher end of the social spectrum. They were more likely to be the sons of prominent professionals – admirals, generals, physicians, bishops – than warrant officers. Nevertheless, the gap was not so large that warrant officers would have necessarily felt socially inferior to commissioned officers. Most men in the wardroom were members of the upper quartile of British society, but not members of the landed elite. As members of the middle classes, they could not rely on family wealth and so followed their fathers in pursuing a profession requiring training and education.

The most surprising result in Table 2 though is that, on a typical ship of the line, the surgeon was as likely to come from a landed background as one or two of the lieutenants. For a Scottish or Irish gentry family, sending their son into the medical profession was a relatively safe, if moderately expensive, choice. Surgeons incurred medical training expenses

Table 2 Social backgrounds in the wardroom[15]

Officer	Titled people	Landed gentry	Professionals	Business and commerce	Labourers and minor farmers
Commissioned	4%	17%	45%	26%	8%
Masters	0%	5%	53%	32%	10%
Pursers	0%	0%	48%	39%	13%
Surgeons	0%	19%	45%	34%	2%
Chaplains	0%	41%	53%	6%	0%

Source: Wilson, 'The Sea Officers', chapter three. The categories derive from Lewis' work on commissioned officers, and while they are imprecise and slightly old-fashioned, they are still helpful in distinguishing wardroom members' relative social prestige

of between £50 and £100, but the potential payoff for such an investment was a steady career as a medical service provider with the chance of further education leading to becoming a physician.[19] Service in the navy, as we will see, was a useful way to gain valuable experience and possibly a useful connection. The reputation of naval surgeons also increased steadily across the eighteenth century.[20] In his 1748 novel *Roderick Random*, Tobias Smollett famously portrayed naval surgeons as incompetent and untrained. At his exam, Random is asked, 'If during an engagement at sea, a man should be brought to you with his head shot off, how would you behave?'. Smollett was aiming more for black humour than truth, but other commentators were similarly sceptical of surgeons' abilities. A former surgeon lamented the 'absurdity' of employing 'raw apothecaries' boys … whose whole education had been acquired in the course of a year or two behind the counter.'[21] By the end of the century, though, training and expertise seem to have improved. Surgeon John McHugh had in fact been trained as an apothecary before he joined the navy, but he was more than just an apothecary's boy: he was a licensed apothecary in Dublin in his own right.[22]

Other surgeons attended teaching hospitals or attended classes at a Scottish university before joining the navy. Since the ancient English universities did not offer medical classes in the same way, we can see one reason why a disproportionate number of surgeons were Scottish. Even those without any kind of higher education would have been educated locally and learned at least the fundamentals of Latin, which was essential for medical practice. Peter Cullen, for example, attended a grammar school in Glasgow for four years before matriculating at the College of Glasgow; he began his apprenticeship with a local surgeon when he turned fourteen.[23] Most future naval surgeons joined the navy as young men in their late teens or early twenties as assistant surgeons. There was no qualifying exam, and naval service provided ample opportunities for hands-on learning. As the contemporary commentator John Atkins argued, 'I know of no better School to improve in, than the NAVY, especially in Time of War, Accidents are frequent, and the Industrious illustrate Practice by their Cures'.[24] When the candidate felt he was prepared, he would attend one of the twice-monthly meetings of the Surgeons' Company at its headquarters near Newgate Gaol. There, with other candidates for service as surgeons in the armed services and the East India Company, he would be interviewed by one of the examiners. The examination was entirely oral and tested his knowledge of anatomy, physiology and surgery. As with the lieutenants' exam, it is likely that some examiners were more rigorous than others. Successful candidates paid a guinea to the Surgeons' Company before heading to the Navy Board, certificate in hand, to solicit a warrant.[25]

Chaplains were also examined before they could enter naval service, though their exams were neither rigorous nor universally completed. In theory, the Archbishop of Canterbury or the Bishop of London interviewed candidates for naval chaplaincies. In practice, many chaplains seem to have either conducted the interview by letter or simply been in the right place at the right time. Mangin recalls having to produce 'the proper certificates' before joining the navy, but those seem to have been simply a few letters of recommendation.[26] When the Reverend Henry Duckworth found himself in debt, he joined the navy and used it to escape to Jamaica. It is unlikely he took the time, while running from his creditors, to attend an interview with the Bishop of London.[27] All chaplains, though, had attended a university, where they studied Greek, Latin and theology.[28] They were not trained for the unique challenges of ministry at sea.

While chaplains were barely vetted and surgeons sat an oral exam of uncertain rigour, masters' experiences were substantially different. They were examined thoroughly and repeatedly: not only did they have to sit an exam for their first warrant, but they also had to sit an exam each time they sought employment in a larger ship. The navy – via the examining body, Trinity House – invested so much time and resources in masters' qualifications because masters were expected to be the experts in seamanship and navigation on board.[29] The transcript of an exam survives in the archives, and it contains more than one hundred specific questions about navigation and seamanship. 'Suppose you're bound for the Downs in the night time and coming from the westward. How will you proceed, and [what are] your marks for anchoring there?' Follow-up questions often forced the master to think quickly about changing conditions: 'Suppose you're taken with a gale of wind in the night time, and want to go in to Portland Road. What are your marks?'[30]

To learn how to answer these questions, masters followed one of two paths into the navy: some spent years in merchant service first, while others were trained by the navy, much as commissioned officers were. Masters from the merchant service often had command experience in merchant ships operating in the coastal trade, and some had far more experience than that. Before he joined the navy, John Buyers was the chief mate of the merchant ship *Margaret*, which spent more than three years trading in the South Pacific before she was wrecked on a reef. Using considerable ingenuity and expertise, Buyers and his crew fashioned a raft from the wreck and managed to sail it back to Tahiti.[31] Masters trained in the navy were also likely to be experienced in a variety of roles and conditions. They often had early careers largely indistinguishable from commissioned officers. George Forbes joined the navy in 1787 and served for the next five years as a variety of ratings, which was common for future officers. He spent 1795 as a midshipman and 1796 as an acting lieutenant, suggesting that he was bound for a commission; instead, he received his first warrant as a master.[32] His authority in the wardroom derived in part from the similarities between his experience and that of a commissioned officer.

Among the members of the wardroom, only pursers and marine officers did not have to sit qualifying exams to earn their warrant or commission. From 1813, though, that changed as aspiring pursers now had to be examined by three experienced pursers, much as lieutenants were examined by three post-captains. The regulation came too late for the members of the present database. Instead, many of them learned their profession by first attending one of the growing network of mathematical schools that aimed to educate accountants, clerks and sometimes future commissioned officers.[33] The next step was to secure a position as a clerk in naval service, either ashore or with a captain. The database suggests that pursers received their first warrants, on average, when they were twenty-five years old. Surgeons, interestingly, received their first warrant at nearly the same age, suggesting that it took about as long for a clerk to learn how to manage a ship's accounts as it did for a surgeon to learn the basics of the medical profession. This pattern may reflect the rudimentary nature of the education expected of a naval surgeon, but it may equally suggest that pursery was challenging, requiring diligence and attentiveness. It was the purser's responsibility to track how much every man on board consumed. Shipboard life for a purser therefore meant spending a good deal of time shuttling between his books and the hold, and working closely with the cooper.[34]

After spending years in training to prepare for all the necessary exams, warrant officers were finally ready to assume their positions of authority. Though the database contains a purser who was seventeen at his first warrant and a chaplain who was sixty, they represent the extremes. Three-quarters of all pursers and surgeons earned their first warrants in their twenties, as did half of all masters. Those masters who joined in their thirties or later had spent the bulk of their careers prior to the navy in merchant service. An officer's first warrant was almost always in the navy's smallest ships. Some 90 per cent of pursers, masters, and surgeons first joined a fifth-rate frigate or smaller. This was a formal policy for masters, since they had to pass an exam to be qualified to serve in each larger rate. It was not an official written policy for surgeons and pursers, but there is ample evidence that naval administrators placed them in small ships deliberately. In 1782, at the end of his tenure as First Lord of the Admiralty, Lord Sandwich insisted that pursers begin their careers in sloops.[35] This practice ensured that no fresh-faced surgeon would be immediately responsible for the health of 800 sailors, no rookie master would be asked to make a crucial decision at the height of a fleet action and no teenage purser would be responsible for keeping track of a fleet's supplies.

A newly warranted officer could expect to stay with his first ship for a year or two before moving on to – he hoped – a larger ship with higher pay. A warrant tied an officer to a particular ship in a way that a commission did not, which has caused some historians to assume that warrant officers tended to stay with one ship for many years.[36] Precise numbers are difficult to uncover, since the only way is to track officers from ship to ship in the Admiralty's succession books.[37] It is a time-consuming process, liable to omissions, but doing so suggests that, in fact, turnover from ship to ship for both commissioned and warrant officers was high. Masters joined a new ship on average every twenty-one months, and other warrant officers have a similar pattern. A quick survey of a few commissioned officers' careers suggests they averaged slightly shorter tenures on each ship, perhaps about twelve to fifteen months.[38]

The previous two paragraphs require two minor qualifications. The first is that turnover was only high in wartime; in peacetime, most officers, both commissioned and warrant, were unemployed. The navy demobilised quickly when eighteenth-century wars ended, and most members of the wardroom, not to mention the lower deck, were rather unceremoniously turned ashore. Secondly, chaplains need to be discussed separately from other warrant officers. Every ship needed a master, a purser and a surgeon; chaplains were unnecessary. Throughout the eighteenth century, chaplains rarely sailed on frigates; early in the century, they seem to have seldom sailed at all. One warrant officer claimed in 1743 that he had heard prayers on board once in his life; another captain said he spent sixteen years in the mid-century navy without ever hearing prayers. Later in the century, divine services became more common, and more chaplains found a home on board ship, but they did so almost exclusively on ships of the line.[39] There was nothing comparable for chaplains to the practice of appointing inexperienced masters, pursers and surgeons to the navy's smallest ships. In the database, every chaplain's first appointment was to a ship of the line.

Unsurprisingly, chaplains had the shortest and most irregular careers of all members of the wardroom. Some 20 per cent of naval chaplains served on only one ship before leaving the navy. Some, perhaps, found it an unpleasant experience: the chaplain's role on board was ill defined and depended in large part on the captain's good graces. Mangin suggested that he was unwelcome in the sick-bay because '[t]he entrance of the clergyman is, to a poor seaman, often a fatal signal'. He complained about the impossibility of ministering to sailors, whose habits and lifestyles he found bizarre and barbaric.[40] Mangin was, as others have noted, temperamentally unsuited to naval life, but he does provide important insights into the difficulties that chaplains faced. Though there are examples of chaplains who spent long enough in naval service to suggest that they saw it as a rewarding and fruitful employment, no chaplain in the database had a career longer than fifteen years. More common were chaplains who spent two to five years at sea before securing a more desirable living ashore. Naval connections could sometimes be helpful for that transition. Joseph Charles Thomas may have met his powerful patron, Edmund Boyle, eighth Earl of Cork and Orrery, while serving as chaplain of *Vanguard*. After Thomas left the navy, his patron provided the connections that helped him marry an heiress and support the work of William Blake.[41]

Whether warrant officers' skills transferred easily to civilian life shaped the length of their careers. Chaplains sit at one extreme, non-essential outsiders in the maritime world but ubiquitous ashore. Masters sit at the other extreme. The navy was the largest maritime employer, and masters' skills were entirely maritime. Masters therefore had good incentives to remain in naval service for as long as possible, and their careers were on average the longest among warrant officers at more than a dozen years. Some served far longer than that. William Price was appointed master of *Isis* in the American War of Independence, and was still serving more than four decades later. Methuselah Wills and James Murray joined the navy at about the same time as Price, and though they were not quite as durable, they both served for more than twenty-five years.

In between masters' long and chaplains' short careers, pursers and surgeons tended to remain in naval service for, on average, about four or five warrants. Though pursers' skills were essential at sea, they were not particular to naval life: bookkeeping and accounting were in demand ashore as well. It is therefore surprising to find that some pursers' careers were as long as the masters' careers listed above. Thomas Jennings, for example, served from 1806 until the end of the Napoleonic Wars, and then again from 1832 to 1847. Richard Bromley joined the navy just after the Nootka Sound mobilisation in 1790, and remained afloat throughout the French Revolutionary and Napoleonic Wars. Men like Bromley and Jennings skew the mean length of a purser's career to more than eleven years, but the median length is much lower, about six years. Surgeons share the same median career length: their skills were central to civilian life and many seem to have used the navy as training for a career spent largely ashore.

While some warrant officers' careers ended because they pursued more attractive careers ashore, others left the navy because they could no longer find a ship. However, the latter scenario usually only applied during peacetime; in wartime, most warrant officers could choose whether to seek civilian or naval employment because naval demand was high. It has escaped the notice of historians that the navy suffered from frequent shortages of warrant officers, particularly masters and surgeons. The Navy Board informed the Admiralty in 1821 that, 'the difficulty of procuring suitable Masters for small Vessels, which was so much felt during the War, has not been removed since its termination'.[42] Once a master had passed for a ship of the line, he was unlikely to want an appointment in a sloop because larger ships paid more. Only in peacetime, when employment prospects plummeted for all members of the navy, were masters likely to concede ground. David Blackburn accepted a warrant as master of a brig sailing with the First Fleet to Australia in 1787. He complained to his sister, 'She is a brigg [*sic*] and I shall be paid only as a sixth rate viz. £5 per month, which of itself is a hardship as I have passed for a third rate which is £7 monthly'.[43] In wartime, though, there are examples of vacancies even in the navy's largest ships, suggesting that experienced masters enjoyed good employment prospects. In 1801, one officer reported to the Admiralty: 'Masters are much wanted; the *Orion* [a ship of the line] has none, and there will be difficulty in getting one'.[44]

Demand for surgeons was highest on the navy's unhealthiest stations. Charles Bunting, stationed in the West Indies, suffered from 'Attacks of Fever' and requested a transfer, 'but with this he could not succeed on account of the great want of Surgeons'.[45] Demand was not quite as high on home stations, but a qualified surgeon could still expect to be employed quickly. Peter Cullen noted in 1793 that '[m]edical officers were very scarce at this time', and was surprised when, in 1796, he applied for a ship and was told there were no vacancies. The next day, though, he met an old friend who was taking command of a ship and requested his services.[46] The Sick and Hurt Board complained in 1805 that the navy was '[suffering] materially in the present war from want of surgeons and surgeons' mates'.[47] As we will see, part of the problem identified by the Sick and Hurt Board and by surgeons themselves was the navy's comparatively low pay.

Since chaplains were not employed on all ships, or even on all ships of the line, their employment prospects are difficult to define. It is likely that a chaplain who hoped to serve in the navy could do so easily, so long as he found a captain interested in having a chaplain on board. Pursers, however, could struggle with unemployment. A survey of pursers' services from 1834 asked respondents to describe their naval employment history. Few had served in peacetime, as we would expect, but most listed extensive service in wartime. On average, the respondents had been employed for six out of every ten wartime years.[48] Further evidence for some minor unemployment problems for pursers comes from the navy's seniority lists in 1809 and 1810, which listed nearly 300 more pursers than masters. We know that there was a shortage of the latter, and that every ship sailed with one purser and one master. It is likely that there were slightly more pursers than could be employed by the navy, even at the height of the Napoleonic Wars.

To attract qualified masters and surgeons to naval service, the Admiralty increased warrant officers' pay. It was a long time coming, as surgeons had been calling for better pay since at least the American War of Independence. In 1779, a former assistant surgeon wrote to the navy's Comptroller, Charles Middleton, asking for half pay to be extended to every surgeon. Middleton admitted that the navy was not an attractive employer for surgeons, but he also seems to have been one of the administrators responsible for delaying action until the Napoleonic Wars.[49] In a series of reforms enacted between 1802 and 1807, the Admiralty finally responded to pressure from warrant officers and increased pay for all members of the wardroom except chaplains. The most junior surgeon of a sloop received a huge raise, more than double his old income, and surgeons' incomes were disconnected from the size of their ship or crew and linked instead to seniority. This was a deliberate ploy to encourage experienced surgeons to serve in small ships. Masters and pursers continued to be paid by the rate of their ship, but they now earned, on average across all rates, 37 and 25 per cent more, respectively.[50]

Though we cannot compare surgeons' pay increases directly to the others because they were no longer paid by rate, they were the largest beneficiaries of the reformed pay scale. Senior surgeons now earned similar wages to post captains, and junior surgeons were paid almost twice as much as lieutenants. The Admiralty was clearly concerned about the shortage of surgeons, and eager to make their pay more competitive with other employers of medical professionals. Even after the reforms, surgeons were still paid less and were of lower status than their medical colleagues in the army and the East India Company.[51] In part to address this persistent gap, the Admiralty belatedly moved to recognise the importance and prominence of warrant officers by issuing them with uniforms. The first uniforms were barely worthy of the name, no more than plain blue coats issued in 1787. A group of physicians led a campaign to revise the original pattern, writing to the Sick and Hurt Board and citing the rank they held 'in the Service and Society'. They were successful in 1805, and the revised pattern was deliberately designed to mimic commissioned officers' dress, with gold buttons on the front and gold lace on the collar.[52]

The new uniforms can be seen in the context of the shortage of masters and surgeons as deliberate attempts to make a career at sea more attractive. They were also an indication that warrant officers saw themselves as the social equals of commissioned officers. A useful way to test where warrant officers fitted on the social spectrum is to follow their careers after they left the navy. As we saw with chaplain Joseph Charles Thomas, connections made in the navy helped many former warrant officers set up high-status civilian careers. Chaplain Charles Inglis became the Bishop of Nova Scotia.[53] Surgeon Robert Crowe compiled a chemistry textbook and established a practice in Versailles, while Thomas Downey published a book of original poems.[54] Henry George Windsor, a former purser, was one of the founding members of the Barbados Chamber of Commerce, and James Lawson Drummond, a former surgeon, helped establish the Belfast Natural History Society.[55] Most famous were two former pursers who used their connections to powerful admirals to become Secretary of the Admiralty. Philip Stephens and Evan Nepean also both served as MPs, and were made baronets at the end of their careers.[56] Not all warrant officers were as successful as these men, and after 1815 many endured unemployment; but there are a number of examples of former warrant officers who moved easily among the upper quartile of British society thanks to their connections in the navy.

The navy's expansion to meet the demands of the Napoleonic Wars provided warrant officers with opportunities for social and professional advancement. They were highly skilled men from middling backgrounds similar to those of commissioned officers. As a result, they expected to enjoy the same social status as commissioned officers, even if the highest ranks and opportunities for national celebrity available to commissioned officers were closed to them. While there were far more commissioned officers than could be employed at sea, there was a shortage of warrant officers. Recognising their value to the navy during a war for national survival, warrant officers waged a successful campaign for higher pay and status. Those that left the navy boasted skills and sometimes connections and prize money that eased their transition to civilian life.

Running parallel to this story of advancement is a narrative of decline and obsolescence. Surgeons and pursers could be assured of their place in seagoing life; masters and chaplains could not. From a nadir at mid-century, chaplains' fortunes improved during the wars with revolutionary France, and particularly following the mutinies of 1797, as senior officers saw a role for chaplains in combatting discontent on the lower deck. The growing naval evangelical movement also ensured that some senior naval officers encouraged ministry at sea. But many did so without chaplains. James Hillyar was a leading captain and prominent evangelical, but when he took *Phoebe*, a thirty-six-gun frigate, on a multi-year voyage to the Pacific, he did so without the aid of a chaplain. Instead, he conducted services himself every Sunday.[57]

Masters also faced the threat of obsolescence. The master usually berthed in the second-largest cabin in the wardroom after the first lieutenant, and he was one of only three men, along with the first lieutenant and captain, who signed all the important ship's documents such as the muster and pay books. Masters were also the only warrant officers who normally stood watches. The lieutenants' exam, introduced in 1677, slowly eroded masters' dominance of sailing and navigation skills, as well as their positions in the naval hierarchy. By the end of the eighteenth century, many commissioned officers were expert sailors and navigators. Masters nevertheless remained the navy's on-board insurance against shipwreck into the nineteenth century. The likely explanation for the persistence of the position, other than bureaucratic momentum, is that newly commissioned officers were not always reliable sailors. Passing the lieutenants' exam was akin to a teenager passing a driving test: the passing certificate indicated that the bearer understood the basics of seamanship and navigation, but it did not mean he could be entirely trusted. Masters, examined more frequently and rigorously, still had a role to play. As the shortage of masters identified earlier suggests, though, many recognised that the position was becoming obsolete. After James Bowen performed heroic service at the Battle of the Glorious First of June in 1794, while serving as master of Lord Howe's flagship, Howe offered him his choice of reward. Bowen chose a commission as a lieutenant, even though he would be placed at the bottom of the lieutenants' seniority list.[58] Lieutenants had opportunities for promotion, and indeed Bowen died an admiral; masters did too – many aspired to be superintending masters of dockyards – but such positions were far less prestigious and well paid than being a senior commissioned officer. By the mid-nineteenth century, masters were clearly no longer needed, and the Admiralty eliminated the position.

What can this chapter tell us about the 'new' naval history? First, Michael Lewis deserves credit for marrying social history with naval history in the 1960s. In addition to his important work on the officer corps and the lower deck, he was also the first serious academic to notice the men in the middle. This chapter has revised and reinforced his work. Despite Lewis's efforts, we have an incomplete picture of the sailing navy's command structure. In particular, warrant officers have been comparatively under-researched and underappreciated, even though they provided unique and essential skills and they were recognised by their contemporaries and colleagues as full members of the ship's elite. Calling attention to these men highlights other gaps in our knowledge of the shipboard hierarchy. For example, petty officers and warrant officers not of wardroom rank (the gunner, boatswain and carpenter) await a future scholar.

This chapter has also applied new techniques, not available to Lewis, to the social history of the navy. It does not claim to be alone in these efforts: quantitative digital history – the application of computing power to large datasets – is flourishing. Other naval historians are doing similar work. John Cardwell has produced a prosopography of surgeons, mentioned earlier, and J. R. Dancy has approached the historiographical problem of the press gang by overwhelming it with data. Dan Benjamin has also applied new techniques to old problems – in his case, the techniques of economic history to the questions of motivations and prize money.[59] These scholars and those included in this volume demonstrate that naval history cannot survive in isolation from the rest of the academy. This is not to suggest that naval historians should blindly follow academic fashions; rather, it is essential that naval historians engage with other historical disciplines and methodologies, drawing from them the techniques appropriate for the study of men and women at sea.

Notes

1 The research for this chapter was conducted for my doctoral dissertation, 'The Sea Officers: Gentility and Professionalism in the Royal Navy, 1775–1815' (University of Oxford D.Phil. thesis, 2014), now published as *A Social History of British Naval Officers, 1775–1815* (Woodbridge: Boydell and Brewer, 2017). This chapter was written with the financial support of the National Maritime Museum's Caird Senior Research Fellowship, which I gratefully acknowledge.

2 The most recent work is J. R. Dancy, *The Myth of the Press Gang: Volunteers, Impressment and the Naval Manpower Problem in the Late Eighteenth Century* (Woodbridge: Boydell and Brewer, 2015).

3 M. Lewis, *A Social History of the Navy, 1793–1815* (London: Allen & Unwin, 1960), pp. 228–55.

4 G. Taylor, *The Sea Chaplains: A History of the Chaplains of the Royal Navy* (Oxford: Illustrated Press, 1978); N. A. M. Rodger, 'The Naval Chaplain in the Eighteenth Century', *British Journal for Eighteenth-Century Studies*, 18:1 (1995), 33–45; J. Macdonald, *Feeding Nelson's Navy: The True Story of Food at Sea in the Georgian Era* (London: Chatham Publishing, 2006). Rodger also describes the responsibilities and administrative origins of each warrant officer in *The Wooden World: An Anatomy of the Georgian Navy* (London, 1986) and *The Safeguard of the Sea: A Naval History of Britain, 660–1649* (London: Harper Collins, 1997).

5 Some examples include B. Vale and G. Edwards, *Physician to the Fleet: The Life and Times of Thomas Trotter, 1760–1832* (Woodbridge: Boydell and Brewer, 2011); G. L. Hudson (ed.), *British Military and Naval Medicine, 1600–1830* (Amsterdam: Brill, 2007).

6 J. Cardwell, 'Royal Navy Surgeons, 1793–1815: A Collective Biography' in D. B. Haycock, and S. Archer (eds), *Health and Medicine at Sea, 1700–1900* (Woodbridge: Boydell and Brewer, 2009), pp. 39–62.

7 For a full description of the database and how it was compiled, see Wilson, 'The Sea Officers', introduction and appendix.

8 Wilson, 'The Sea Officers', pp. 42, 107. Some parts of the table cannot add up to 100% because of rounding errors.

9 Cardwell, 'Royal Navy Surgeons', p. 40.

10 G. Chalmers, *Caledonia: or, An account, historical and topographic, of North Britain; from the most ancient to the present time* (London, 1810), p. 59; J. Chandler, *The New Seaman's Guide, and Coaster's Companion* (London, 1809), title page.

11 For a discussion of commissioned officers' social backgrounds, see E. Wilson, 'Social Backgrounds and Promotion Prospects in the Royal Navy, 1775–1815', *The English Historical Review*, cxxi (2016), 570–95.

12 The quotation cited most frequently in support of this argument comes from a letter written by midshipman Edward Barker to his uncle in 1800. In it,

he explained that he was desperate for help from a patron to secure a naval commission, which he said was equivalent to 'an independency and the rank of gentleman in every society and in every country'. J. B. Hattendorf et al. (eds), *British Naval Documents, 1204–1960* (London: Navy Records Society (hereafter NRS), 1993), p. 546.

13 Marine officers' backgrounds seem to have been broadly similar to warrant officers'. They were not included in the database; instead, see B. Zerbe, *The Birth of the Royal Marines, 1664–1802* (Woodbridge: Boydell and Brewer, 2013).

14 H. G. Thursfield (ed.), *Five Naval Journals, 1789–1817* (NRS, 1951), p. 33.

15 Wilson, 'The Sea Officers', chapter three. The categories derive from Lewis's work on commissioned officers, and while they are imprecise and slightly old-fashioned, they are still helpful in distinguishing wardroom members' relative social prestige.

16 J. Maxwell, *Paisely Dispensary: A Poem* (1786), dedication; *Alumni Oxonienses: The Members of the University of Oxford, 1715–1886*, J. Foster (ed.), 4 vols. (Oxford, 1888), s.v. 'Brice, Edward'.

17 TNA, ADM 6/353/66 (Admiralty: Service Records, Registers, Returns and Certificates: Certificates and other papers submitted by applicants to the Charity, 1814).

18 Bristol Record Office, Miscellaneous Bristol Deeds 5918/29/e; C. J. Palmer, *The Perlustration of Great Yarmouth, with Gorleston and Southtown*, 3 vols. (Great Yarmouth, 1875), vol. 3, p. 339.

19 Cardwell, 'Royal Navy Surgeons', p. 46.

20 G. L. Hudson, 'Introduction: British Military and Naval Medicine, 1600–1830' in Hudson (ed.), *British Military and Naval Medicine*, p. 10; M. Lincoln, *Representing the Royal Navy: British Sea Power, 1750–1815* (Aldershot: Ashgate, 2002), p. 167; G. Holmes, *Augustan England: Professions, State and Society, 1680–1730* (London: Allen & Unwin, 1982), p. 10.

21 Vale and Edwards, *Physician to the Fleet*, p. 22.

22 *Parliamentary Papers 1829*, xxii (235), 'Return of Persons examined and certified as Qualified by Apothecaries' Hall in Dublin, and Number of Prosecutions, 1791–1829'.

23 *Five Naval Journals*, pp. 44–5.

24 J. D. Alsop, 'Warfare and the Creation of British Imperial Medicine, 1600–1800' in Hudson (ed.), *British Military and Naval Medicine*, pp. 23–50.

25 Vale and Edwards, *Physician to the Fleet*, pp. 21–2.

26 *Five Naval Journals*, p. 5.

27 A Cambridge Alumni Database, *University of Cambridge* (hereafter ACAD), s.v. 'Duckworth, Henry Robert', available at http://venn.lib.cam.ac.uk/acad/2016/search-2016.html.

28 It was possible to find educational affiliations for 70 per cent of the chaplains in the database. In descending order, they attended Oxford, Cambridge or Trinity College, Dublin.

29 Henry VIII had granted Trinity House, located in Deptford, a royal charter to regulate pilotage on the Thames; by the seventeenth century, their responsibilities had expanded to include examining masters on behalf of the navy. A. Adams and R. Woodman, *Light Upon the Waters: The History of Trinity House, 1514–2014* (London: Corporation of Trinity House, 2014).

30 National Maritime Museum, DRY/10 (H.M.S. *Dryad*, 1780). I am grateful to Lena Moser for the reference. Her forthcoming dissertation will be the first scholarly study focused on masters: 'Eine sozial- und kulturwissenschaftliche Untersuchung der masters der Royal Navy als vormoderne Funktionselite' (University of Tübingen PhD thesis, forthcoming).

31 'Explorers of the Pacific: European and American Discoveries in Polynesia', *Victoria University of Wellington Library*, available at http://nzetc.victoria. ac.nz/tm/scholarly/tei-BucExpl.html (accessed 3 August 2018); J. Turnbull, *A Voyage round the World* (London, 1813).

32 The National Archives, Kew (hereafter TNA), ADM 29/1/60 (Admiralty: Royal Navy, Royal Marines, Coastguard and related services: Officers' and Ratings' Service Records (Series II), Navy Pay Office: Entry Books of Certificates of Service, 1802–14).

33 E. G. R. Taylor, *The Mathematical Practitioners of Hanoverian England, 1714–1840* (Cambridge: Cambridge University Press, 1966), p. 79.

34 Rodger, *Wooden World*, pp. 87–98.

35 Macdonald, *Feeding Nelson's Navy*, p. 92.

36 *Ibid.*; R. Morriss, *The Foundations of British Maritime Ascendancy: Resources, Logistics and the State, 1755–1815* (Cambridge: Cambridge University Press, 2011), p. 264.

37 TNA, ADM 6/192 (Admiralty: Service Records, Registers, Returns and Certificates. Succession book of standing officers, 1800–1812); TNA, ADM 11/66–7 (Admiralty: Officers' Service Records (Series I), Succession Books of Commissioned & Standing Officers, 1785–1803).

38 TNA, ADM 9/4/1152; TNA, ADM 9/6/1823; TNA, ADM 9/6/1955 (Admiralty: Survey Returns of Officers' Services, 1817–28).

39 R. Blake, *Evangelicals in the Royal Navy, 1775–1815: Blue Lights & Psalm-Singers* (Woodbridge: Boydell and Brewer, 2008); G. Atkins, 'Religion, Politics and Patronage in the late Hanoverian Navy, *c.* 1780–*c.* 1820', *Historical Research*, 88:240 (2015), 272–90.

40 *Five Naval Journals*, pp. 7–14.

41 'Biographical Note: Rev. Joseph Thomas (1765–1811): Connoisseur, Emblem Writer and Patron of William Blake', *Erfurt Electronic Studies in English*, available at http://webdoc.gwdg.de/edoc/ia/eese/artic22/hoeltgen/thomas.html (accessed 3 August 2018).

42 TNA, ADM 106/3571 (Navy Board: Records. Miscellaneous, 26 September 1821).

43 D. Neville, *Blackburn's Isle* (Lavenham: Terence Dalton Ltd., 1975), p. 116.

44 *Selections from the Correspondence of Admiral John Markham during the Years 1801–4 and 1806–7*, ed. C. Markham (NRS, 1904), p. 405.

45 TNA, ADM 6/323 (Admiralty: Service Records, Registers, Returns and Certificates. Register of officers' widows & orphans applying to the Compassionate Fund, 1809–27).

46 *Five Naval Journals*, pp. 75, 91–2.

47 M. Crumplin, 'Surgery in the Royal Navy during the Republican and Napoleonic Wars (1793–1815)' in Haycock and Archer (eds), *Health and Medicine at Sea*, pp. 72–3.

48 TNA, ADM 6/193–6 (Admiralty: Service Records, Registers, Returns and Certificates. Survey of age and services of Pursers, Nos.1–450, 1834).

49 *Letters and Papers of Charles, Lord Barham, Admiral of the Red Squadron, 1758–1813*, ed. J. K. Laughton, 3 vols. (NRS, 1907, 1910, and 1911), vol. 1, p. 48 and vol. 2, pp. 284 and 425–6.

50 Between 1797 and 1807, commissioned officers also received pay increases of 35 per cent on average across all rates. N. A. M. Rodger, *The Command of the Ocean: A Naval History of Britain, 1649–1815* (London: Allen Lane, 2004), pp. 622–7.

51 Members of the army's medical branch were commissioned officers, while East India Company surgeons could trade privately to augment their incomes. Vale and Edwards, *Physician to the Fleet*, pp. 16–18.

52 D. Jarrett, *British Naval Dress* (London: J.M. Dent and Sons, 1960), pp. 63–4.

53 ACAD, s.v. 'Bedford, Francis'; *Dictionary of Canadian Biography* (online edn.), s.v. 'Inglis, Charles'.

54 *The British Review, and London Critical Journal* (London, 1816), vol. 7, p. 297; T. Downey, *Naval Poems: Pleasures of the Naval Life, and the Battle of Trafalgar* (London, 1813).

55 'Our History', *Barbados Chamber of Commerce & Industry*, http://bcci.point-sourcenetworks.com/bcci/OurHistory (accessed January 2016); *Oxford Dictionary of National Biography* (hereafter ODNB), s.v. 'Drummond, James Lawson (1783–1853)'.

56 ODNB, s.v. 'Stephens, Sir Philip (1723–1809)', 'Nepean, Sir Evan (1752–1822)'.

57 TNA, ADM 51/2675 (Admiralty: Captains' Logs. *Phoebe*, 1813–15); ODNB, s.v. 'Hillyar, Sir James (1769–1843)'.

58 ODNB, s.v. 'Bowen, James (1751–1835)'.

59 Cardwell, 'Royal Navy Surgeons'; Dancy, *The Myth of the Press Gang*; D. K. Benjamin and C. F. Thornberg, 'Organization and Incentives in the Age of Sail', *Explorations in Economic History*, 67:4 (2007), 968–1000.

2

'My dearest Tussy': coping with separation during the Napoleonic Wars (the Fremantle papers, 1800–14)

Elaine Chalus

The French Revolutionary and Napoleonic Wars (1792–1802, 1803–15) saw thousands of naval and military families separated for extended periods of time.[1] While social scientists and medical practitioners have focused on modern military and naval wives' responses to their husbands' lengthy and/or repeated deployments, especially during wartime, we still know relatively little about how their counterparts coped with separation in earlier wars.[2] As now, they experienced the anxiety of parting, loneliness of separation, vicissitudes of communication and fearful uncertainty of outcomes for their loved ones. Moreover, their separations were longer (three-year deployments were not unusual), and communication was much slower and sporadic at best. Many women – particularly sailors' wives – also struggled with financial insecurity. The Royal Navy's remittance system, established during the Seven Years' War (1756–63), enabled sailors to allot a portion of their salaries to their wives or mothers, but it was little used until modified to allow monthly payments in the 1790s.[3]

N. A. M. Rodger, writing in 2004, deplored the lack of research into the experiences of women ashore and argued that until this 'enormous void of ignorance' was filled 'the social history of the Navy will never be complete'.[4] The gap is now beginning to be filled. Research by historians such as Margarette Lincoln, Cindy McCreery, Louise Carter, Jennine Hurl-Eamon, Patricia Lin, Helen Doe and Melanie Holihead, among others, has begun to recover the diverse histories of naval women ashore and presents a complicated and diverse picture of naval women's life experiences.[5] Taken together, their work suggests that eighteenth-century naval women responded to separation in broadly similar ways to their modern counterparts. Age, class, status, education and financial circumstances all shaped their experiences; so too did personal traits of intelligence, optimism, resilience and resourcefulness.[6] Those who coped most effectively, as with their modern counterparts, took problem-solving rather than emotional approaches to their husbands' absences.[7] Successful eighteenth-century naval officers' wives, such as Frances Boscawen and Henrietta (Henny) Rodney, for instance, accepted their situations, planned ways forward, took action to solve problems and kept themselves busy.[8]

Elizabeth (Betsey) (née Wynne) Fremantle (1778–1857) was one of these, and the Fremantle papers provide us with a case study that illuminates the multiple demands – emotional, practical and socio-political – that separation placed on women in ambitious naval families. A lifelong diarist, Betsey's journals and the Fremantles' letters to each other survive for 1800–14. They serve as a testimony to a working naval marriage carried out largely at one remove against the backdrop of the French Revolutionary and Napoleonic Wars. Thomas Francis Fremantle (1765–1819) returned to sea in 1800 after a prolonged recovery from injuries sustained in 1797. For approximately eleven of the next fourteen years, the Fremantles were separated, leaving Betsey responsible for the running of her house, estate and family, and for furthering her husband's career and the family's best interests. Their separation only ended in 1814, when Betsey and the children left Swanbourne in Buckinghamshire to join Thomas Francis on Jersey.

As a couple, the Fremantles were representative of many ambitious naval couples of the period: they were energetic, hard-working and committed – committed to each other, to his career and to their family's future advancement. Both shared a firm belief in the need to defeat Napoleon and the rightness of the British cause. Betsey, as the daughter of an Anglo-Italian country gentleman and his French wife who had actively supported the French Royalist cause, had spent her early adolescence with French royalist agents and *emigrés* in Switzerland. Fear of attacks from pro-revolutionary mobs had then prompted the family to move to safety in the imperial city of Ratisbon in the mid-1790s. Finally, in 1797, the Wynne family fled the advancing French armies, racing from Florence to Livorno, where they were evacuated by the British Navy. The Revolution and its subsequent wars had shaped Betsey's life and she had, from early adolescence, sided strongly with the British. For Thomas Francis, as a younger son of an English gentry family, who had been involved in the naval campaigns against the French since the outbreak of

Figure 1 Portrait of Betsey Fremantle

the wars, the struggle against the French was personal as well as national. It offered him unprecedented opportunities for advancement, glory and economic gain. Each of the Fremantles therefore accepted that s/he had a part to play in a joint enterprise that demanded duty, service and sacrifice.[9] They coped with separation imaginatively and practically. They sustained their relationship through a regular correspondence. Betsey

Figure 2 Print showing Vice-Admiral Sir Thomas Fremantle

wrote once or twice a week, sending her letters post-paid to Plymouth, or directly via naval connections. Thomas Francis responded in turn. Their letters are thus compendiums of personal and family news, gossip and discussions of shared concerns and plans. Whether consciously or unconsciously, they created a virtual family circle that bound ship to shore, ensuring that Thomas Francis continued to be included in the wider life of the family.

The remainder of this chapter examines the ways that the Fremantles – specifically, but not only, Betsey – coped with separation between 1800 and 1814. It considers the virtual family circle, explores their responses to loneliness and anxiety, and suggests that it was due to the Fremantles' commitment to each other, and especially to Betsey's positive practicality, her drive and social nous that the family was effectively embedded into the Buckinghamshire gentry community and retained its visibility in the naval and social circles, and that the Fremantle children were well prepared for their future roles. As such, it illustrates the multi-layered personal, emotional, practical and socio-political demands that separation placed upon naval officers' wives, and underlines the importance of personal character and social networking to family success.

Snapshots of separation

Two snapshots of separation, reconstructed from 1803 and 1812 respectively, set the scene and exemplify the multiplicity of threads that wove the Fremantles' separated lives together.

On a quiet evening in December 1803, with HMS *Ganges* finally riding comfortably at anchor, its thirty-eight-year-old captain, Thomas Francis Fremantle, sat down to answer his wife Betsey's last letter. He had been up for the best part of thirty-six hours, most of it on deck, striving to prevent his ship from being driven on to the rocks in the face of a fierce winter gale. Bridging the miles between them with imaginative tenderness, he addressed Betsey by her nickname, his 'dearest Tussy', and commiserated with her on her bad cold:[10] 'I … fancied I saw You suffering in Your bed, wrapped up with handkerchfs and Night Caps'.[11] He teased her light-heartedly, calling her 'Mrs Crimper', before complimenting her on the state of the household accounts, which she sent him monthly. He then turned to their shared projects of family and estate. A domestic man, he was much concerned with the upbringing of their children (especially their sons, aged five, three and two). He was a younger son of a gentry family with a fortune and a reputation to make, and he was realistic about his sons' financial prospects. Consequently he warned Betsey yet again not to mollycoddle them: 'as they have to seek their fortunes in the great world *bring them up hardy*, that their Constitutions may not suffer hereafter'. Moving on to estate affairs, she was right to get Hawkins's cottage rethatched and if the villagers persisted in robbing the new trees of their supports she should threaten to stop donating coals for the poor. Finally, he added a plea of his own: could she please charm their neighbour into getting the new path and bridge completed?

Only then did he turn to his own situation. Betsey had sailed with him into battle in 1797, so he felt secure in confiding in her: 'I was so much Alarmed for the ship that I carried an immense press of Sail the Whole Night and never left the Deck for one minute – All the head was fairly washed away, and I was for a time under great apprehensions for the safety of the Ship'. The letter ended warmly, however, reinforcing the bonds between them:

> pray Dearest Betsey do not torment Yourself about Money concerns, I am so satisfied of Your prudence that you many depend on my making up any deficiencies that may arise, and pray do not harass Yourself by thinking too much about it ... do You my Dear Betsey go on as You have always done, which will be the greatest possible comfort to me, – peeper my Girls for me [kiss them], whip Charles and Henry, & tell Tom I hope he continues a good boy, that he is Obedient to his Mama and shews a good example to his Brothers and Sisters.

Nearly a decade later, in February 1812, the Fremantle family was complete: of the eight surviving children (five boys and three girls) Tom, the eldest, was thirteen and a highly promising scholar at Eton; Charles, eleven, was back at home briefly from the sea to recover from a fever and improve his French. Thomas Francis had risen to rear-admiral. Based in Sicily, he was in charge of securing the Adriatic. Still fiercely ambitious for himself and his family, he had had a good war. While his naval and diplomatic successes had been lauded and his career was firmly established, he had been at home for little more than three years in the last ten. This had necessitated sharing and delegation on his part, resulting in increased autonomy and independence on Betsey's. Over the years, their relationship had become more complementary. He had grown to trust in and rely upon her unflappability and solid good sense, while she – always his friend and lover – had gained confidence in her own judgement and become his full working partner.

Thus it was on the night of 4 February 1812 that Betsey wrote to her 'Dearest Husband'.[12] The fire in their small country house in Swanbourne, had been lit and six of the children were already in bed. She numbered her letter in case any were lost in transit. This was no. 49.[13] It had been a long time since August 1810, when Thomas Francis left for sea. She longed for his return and let him know that she missed him, but never whined or complained about his absence. Instead, she used her prose to bring the home and the children that he had not seen for years to life before his eyes. 'Emma & Charles' (then aged eleven and ten), she began, 'are making so intolerable a noise in *conversation* with their Cousin Fanny that I scarcely know what I am writing at this moment, luckily it has struck ten & I shall send them to Bed, when I hope to have a moment's peace'. Emma then interjected, taking the pen from her mother to plead her own case: 'Dear Papa, Indeed we are very agreeable company and I only wish you were here to make more noise but I must go to bed or else Mama will be in a pet'. Betsey then continued, crafting a vivid image of the children's lively antics, calling to mind familiar domestic objects and reminding him of his comfortable, well-worn family home and all who were awaiting him:

I often think that when you first return among us, you will be quite made *nervous* by the children after having been so long unaccustomed to their noise, & am surprised the doors still hold on their hinges & that the old *Green* carpet, which was almost threadbare when you went away still holds together it has many a patch, but I am determined to make it do until you come home. I wish you could have witnessed my agony yesterday when Charles led in the Shetland Poney into the library I would not allow him to go through, for fear of *my carpet*, & insisted on the poor beast going out the way it came in through your dressing room, Emma almost in tears as she was certain the poney would break his legs, going down the steps, it certainly was a *dangerous leap*, but he went safe out of the House ... You will scarcely believe that with all these riots & my eight rude children, I still contrive to keep the *rooms* in high order, but indeed it is the case ... Indeed I think you will find everything as you left it, a little the worse for *Age*, neither you or I will look younger after three years absence, but our children improve daily in appearance & looking at them I quite forget that I myself am growing an old woman, I dance & play with them & you would be amused to see me become so active.

Betsey was thirty-three at the time.

After a discussion of local news and national politics, she returned to familial themes, addressing her husband's repeated concerns about his daughters' *tournure*. Thomas Francis feared that his girls, growing up in the country, might not acquire the easy ladylike carriage and elegance of movement that he deemed absolutely necessary for their future social success (and good marriages). Betsey had been brought up in courtly society on the Continent, where she had benefited from Italian and

French dancing masters, and was more than capable of inculcating these social skills; however, she was adamant that her girls should be children as long as possible. She was particularly concerned that Emma, who was rapidly approaching menarche, had plenty of outdoor exercise: '[I am] so delighted to see her amuse herself like a perfect child that I let her fly her kite, & brush down her poney, provided she holds herself up like a *Gentlewoman* in the drawing room, & plays upon the Piano Forte, *à ma façon*, if you were here, you would do the same'. And, as with other decisions about the children, Betsey had the last word.

Loneliness and anxiety

The Fremantles felt their separations deeply. When Thomas Francis left Swanbourne to take up command of HMS *Ganges* on 24 August 1800, Betsey was only twenty and had three children under the age of three. Born in Venice, and brought up largely in Italy and Switzerland, she had only returned to England as a young wife in 1798. She knew more about courts than counties and, although a skilled household manager, had little experience of farms and estates. Nor did she have extensive support networks: her parents died in 1799; her three sisters were still teenagers and living with guardians in London; and her female networks, especially among the local gentry women in Buckinghamshire, were commensurately recent.

It would have been surprising had Betsey not felt anxious and alone under such circumstances. She characteristically refrained from complaining in her letters, however, and had no patience with officers' wives like Mrs Blackwood who bewailed her husband's absence: 'had I begun to lament in the same way we must have sung a dismal *ditty* together'.[14] The emotional wrench of parting was very real, though. Naval officers were often summoned to sea at short notice, and Thomas Francis's departures were no exception. In 1800, he left for sea after only three days' warning, leaving Betsey feeling bereft: 'I need not say I never felt so unhappy during all my life as I did this evening'.[15] It was the first time since their marriage in 1797 that they had been separated. Her words at the end of her first day alone echo across the centuries: 'I feel quite at a loss & wretched alone – poor little Tom distressed me many a time in the course of the day enquiring when his Papa would come home again'.[16] Never one to mope, Betsey coped by keeping busy. By the end of her second day alone she was already more positive: 'I employed myself in different ways & spent the day better than I expected'.[17]

As with their modern counterparts, the Fremantles found repeated deployments difficult. Neither was happy when Fremantle left again for sea in 1803: 'He really goes to sea quite *à contre coeur* as he was now so comfortably settled here, and I feel not a little anxiety at being left alone with five such young children and so much to manage'.[18] Unsurprisingly, they took every possible opportunity to see each other. When Thomas Francis docked in Portsmouth but was unable to return to Swanbourne, Betsey would scoop up several children and post to join him.[19] These precious moments were inevitably followed by renewed separations. Thomas Francis captured the raw emotion of an unexpectedly abruptly ended visit in 1805 in a letter marked 'not to be opened until five or six Miles from Portsmouth':

> My feelings are too poignant to suffer me to come near You & those poor Children whose absence from me I shall deplore until we next meet, – think well and seriously how much I am annoyed in every way, and You I am sure will compassionate [*sic*] me, however submit I must, and I live only in the hopes that this accursed War cannot last long or keep me any great length of time from all & every thing I hold dear in this world keep up your spirits and be assured how faithfully and affectly I remain Your loving husband.[20]

From their earliest separations, Thomas Francis imagined himself into Betsey's activities at home – 'I suppose Swanbourne is quite gay now and that all your roses are nearly in blossom, I should like to peep in upon You whilst You are perambulating in Your parterre'.[21] In turn, he sent her details of naval actions and ship life, enlivened by the antics of his pets or servant, the state of his ship band or his ideas for redecorating his cabin. He was always at his most lonely when bored and cruising: 'I do nothing but take snuff and read Shakespeare when I am off the Deck'.[22]

The distance between them was the most difficult to bear when there was a family crisis, as there was at the beginning of their last and longest separation in 1810. When Thomas Francis was promoted to rear-admiral in early August, both he and Betsey knew that it was his duty to return to active service: 'there is no remedy, & we must get reconciled to an Event, which I trust will lead to future comfort & the welfare of our Family'.[23] By 20 August, he was gone. The timing, however, could hardly have been worse. Betsey was a week away from giving birth to her ninth and final child, and the doctors had ordered their seriously ill five-year-old daughter, Louisa, to Brighton. Not only did Betsey's pregnancy prevent her from accompanying Louisa (she had to send her with a trusted servant), but she also had the added stress of preparing ten-year-old Charles, mentally and materially, to leave home for the first time and join his father at sea. Unsurprisingly, the Fremantles' correspondence reflected these strains. Thomas Francis's relief was palpable when he learned of her safe confinement: 'I need not tell You how much my happiness in life depends on Your doing well, and the horror that appears at the contrary for my poor Children makes me shudder'.[24] Believing that Louisa was gradually improving, Betsey sought to reassure him: 'nothing is wanting but Yourself to make us completely happy'.[25] Only a week later, however, she sent him a brief, anguished – and tellingly unnumbered – note informing him that Louisa had suddenly sickened and died.[26] By this time, however, Thomas Francis had sailed. When the news reached him nearly three weeks later, he was stunned, even though the doctors had warned him (though pointedly not Betsey) of the gravity of Louisa's condition. His response, which he knew would take weeks to reach her, captured his impotence and pain; like his sister Marianne, who had recently lost one of her children, he felt dazed:

> My Dearest and best of Women, how am I to begin a letter to You in answer to the very melancholy one I received two days ago, naming the death of our poor Louisa? since the arrival of the Hibernia I have not had the courage to put my hand to paper, and the anxiety I feel about You, as well as the distress of mind for our severe loss, has made me at times feel like poor Marianne in a state of stupor.[27]

Betsey's own distress over Louisa's death was exacerbated by her concern that Thomas Francis would only have Charles with him to bear the news: 'had we been together at such a period, I think we might have better Supported this Severe blow'.[28] While she had returned to her estate business, her hobbies and to teaching her daughters French and piano by mid-November, her spirits only really began to revive after she received her first letters from him late that month. They reassured her that he was in good company on his new ship and so busy as to be fully occupied.[29]

Fortunately, both the adult and surviving young Fremantles were generally sturdily healthy, so serious concerns about health seldom arose. What is perhaps significantly more surprising, given that the Fremantles were separated by war, is how little anxiety either she or Thomas Francis expressed about his safety. Whether this was because she/they chose not to share her/their fears, or because Betsey had spent enough time with the fleet at war to understand his situation, or because her Catholic faith sustained her, is impossible to determine. This is not to say that she was unconcerned, or that he did not appreciate the danger he was in. His letters to her after the Battle of Copenhagen are a case in point. As a naval officer in the model of Lord Nelson, Thomas Francis knew just how important it was to be his own marketing man: it was far too easy for a naval officer to be forgotten while he was away at sea, especially if he could not count upon having his praises sung in his admiral's despatches. Thomas Francis consequently wrote Betsey two distinctly different letters for two very different audiences on 5 April 1801. The first was a professional officer's account containing a plan of the attack, the orders given by Nelson and the news that Nelson had made his ship his second in the action. It was manly, martial and matter-of-fact. It was also designed to be copied by Betsey and shared among 'your County acquaintance'.[30] Enclosed with this letter was another that was intensely personal, a post-battle outpouring of emotion:

> I went through the action without reflecting *much* on those who were so much interested in my wellfare[sic] but when every thing was over I could not suppress tears which at this time again flow from my eyes, – You know my regard & attachment to You, which Your very proper Conduct so justly entitles You to, I remain so perfectly satisfied with every thing You have done & am so assured of Your judgement in Whatever relates to Yourself and the Children that I shall not enter into any detail, Whatever I possess in this World is at Your devotion, make Yourself happy & easy, & do not become too parsimonious.[31]

The only time that Betsey appears to have been truly anxious for Thomas Francis's safety was with regard to the Battle of Trafalgar. She knew that the fleet was preparing for battle, as Thomas Francis had written on 1 October 1805 of his preparations and his pleasure that Nelson had promised him 'my old place in the line of battle, which is *his second*'.[32] News of the battle reached her after breakfast on the morning of 7 November, when her servant burst in to tell her that there had been a 'most dreadful action' off Cádiz with 'Nelson & several captains killed'. This left her in 'undescribable misery', but only until the arrival of the post later that morning, which brought a reassuring letter from Lord Garlies, an old naval friend at the Admiralty, 'who congratulated me on Fremantle's safety & the conspicuous share he had in the Victory'. The mail also brought congratulatory notes from Lord and Lady Buckingham. Buckingham, who was Thomas Francis's patron, also sent copies of the *London Gazette* so that Betsey could read the latest news of the action.[33]

A virtual family circle

Betsey used her accounts of the children and her colourful descriptions of their activities to entice her husband in to her world, making him part of a virtual family circle and letting him know that he was loved and missed: 'I must say something of my brats, the inexhaustible Subject & certainly the pleasantest to us'.[34] She was especially good at depicting intimate scenes in domestic spaces that he knew well, and in capturing the children as characters. Her letters from 1810–11 are illustrative. She was especially pleased with Tom, who was excelling at Eton: 'Really Tom is perfection if you could see how very attentive he is, to me, full of spirits & fun & still always tractable & obedient, you would be delighted with him, & he grows remarkably handsome'.[35] Harry was rather a rough diamond; time at home, away from his Brighton schoolmates, had done wonders for his manners though.[36] Talking about Billy, who was rather a handful, gave her the opportunity to remind him that he was needed. Billy was, she wrote, 'always out & runs away from us all; he wants you much to keep him in order'.[37] The baby, Stephen, whom Thomas Francis had never seen, had Billy's big dark eyes.[38] He was much like their other boys in character, too: 'the boys are all so grave, Stephen seldom laughs, & is Just such another serious looking little man as Billy'.[39]

Thomas Francis had a decidedly soft spot for his daughters, and Betsey's depictions of them – especially his favourite, Emma, and hers, Cecilia (Cicey) – were always particularly evocative: 'I wish you could see Your Daughter [Emma] at this moment, pasting some papers in the inside of her writing desk, where she unfortunately spilt some ink this morng[?]. She is *vrai fille de son père* & is working & slaving as you would yourself'.[40] Betsey was pleased with Emma's progress: both she and Augusta read French with as much ease as English and both, she told her husband, spoke French with good accents. They were also continuing with their Italian. Moreover, Thomas Francis's mother had been very taken with Emma at their last visit: 'She finds her improved in every thing, and the cunning puss, was so *complaisant* & attentive, that she has quite won her GrandMama's heart'.[41] Most importantly, Emma and Cecilia, who had only been a toddler when he left, were great fun:

I find Cecilia more like Emma in manners & drollery than any of the other Children … Emma is at this moment singing all your vulgar Songs, & regretting you did not leave her the words of the one beginning with, 'I that once was a ploughman, a sailor am now'. I can[not] [paper torn] say that I regret it much, but I wish you [were] [paper torn] here to sing it to her.[42]

Cecilia, too, proved to be a singer. Betsey's description of the toddler in bed with her, singing merrily, conjured up the warm intimacy of their bedroom:

Cecilia amused me singing all last night God save the King, Oh What can the Matter be! – & a multitude of Songs, She often keeps me awake for several hours in the night but She is Such a fussy little puss & dear little darling that I cannot Send her back to her own bed. My whole Fremantle tribe send their love to you.[43]

A year later, Cecilia, then aged three, gave Betsey another excuse to remind him, obliquely, of how much he was missed: 'She cannot understand why you are never at home, & says her Papa must come home *one day*, this day will certainly be a day of happiness to us all'.[44]

Both of the Fremantles were intensely interested in ensuring that their children had the best educations possible. For the girls, this meant schooling at home under Betsey's watchful eye and, c.1810–11, the direction of a French governess. From 1812 onwards, Betsey took on these duties herself, supplementing her own efforts with specialist dancing masters and trips to London for social polish during the Season. Once Thomas Francis was settled in Sicily, she lobbied him to allow her to join him, arguing that the girls were at a stage when they would benefit immensely from a Continental experience.[45] Thomas Francis was tempted in 1812, but decided against it, despite encouragement from his brother William. It would have been a major family upheaval for only one year's residence (as he expected to return to England in 1813), but it may also have been because the reputation of the Sicilian court was so bad that he did not wish to expose his daughters to it.[46]

Betsey and Thomas Francis regularly discussed their sons' educations and plans for their futures, but, as the person on the ground, much of the final decision-making was hers. She regularly sought male expertise, though, and over the years had developed strong working relationships with Thomas Francis's childless brother, William, and with the family's patron, Lord Buckingham. William, who was a courtier and politician, and lived near Windsor (thus close to Eton), acted effectively as a surrogate father to the two intellectual, non-naval Fremantle boys, Tom and William (Billy); whereas Lord Buckingham took an active interest in the naval Fremantle boys, especially Charles. When Charles was sent home from the Mediterranean after an illness in the summer of 1811, he arrived while Betsey was in Scotland visiting her married sisters. Lord Buckingham promptly wrote to tell Betsey not to interrupt her visit. He would have Charles brought directly to Stowe, where he and Lady Buckingham would care for him until her return.[47] Then, in 1812, when Betsey was preparing to send Charles back to sea, she considered sending him with Admiral Sir John Warren, who agreed to take him whenever he was posted, but in the end took Lord Buckingham's advice and sent Charles out with Sir Thomas Hardy. She knew and respected Hardy from her time at sea; moreover, Hardy had the reputation of taking good care of his midshipman. The fact that he was posted to the Halifax station was an added benefit, as Charles had been sent home from the Mediterranean after contracting a fever and the North American climate was deemed healthy.[48] Betsey was also reassured by Buckingham's promise to recommend Charles to the notice of Lady Warren. She was sailing with the *Ramillies* to join her husband, and Buckingham assured Betsey that he would arrange for Charles to be taken to their house '& attended to very particularly', should he get ill.[49]

Shared interests

While their children were the largest of the Fremantles shared projects, their correspondence reveals a number of other mutual interests. The family's finances were one of these. Betsey was a good financial manager whose meticulous household accounts survive from shortly after her marriage until only a few years before her death. Thomas Francis teased her repeatedly about her frugality and reluctance to spend money on herself, but he trusted her implicitly with his finances:

> You know my Dearest Woman, I donot[*sic*] want to save Money, that I am not extravagant myself either in my living or in my person, and that if I can maintain You and my Children in the Sphere of life I wish always to see You, I am most happy & Contented and that is only to be done by an unbounded Confidence which I so properly place in Your hands, and anxious at all time to give You the advice and assistance of so many more Years of experience ... I tell You in a few words that the Bankers receive annualy[*sic*] from me £1125 – all of which is perfectly at Your Disposal and

Command, and if You want more they have my directions to answer your
bills to any amount; are You content! *You hateful Creature!*[50]

His 'advice and assistance' in their earliest years apart tended to focus
upon the children, the estate and how to negotiate the socio-political
arena successfully, that is, to the best advantage of his career and their
family, and without damage to her/their reputation. This was fully understandable given that he was leaving a very young wife in a country that
was new to her, where she still knew few people, but it was also entirely
unnecessary. Betsey was scrupulous of her reputation; furthermore, her
cosmopolitan upbringing, particularly her adolescence which had been
spent with aristocratic French émigrés in Switzerland and at the imperial
court in Ratisbon, had exposed her early to all sorts of people and honed
her socio-political skills. After their second separation in 1803, he gave
progressively less advice and came instead to defer increasingly to her
judgment, especially when it came to the children, the management of
the farm or their dealings with neighbours.

The challenge of managing the estate and making it profitable appealed
to Betsey. She was a fast learner and quickly developed a strong working
relationship with her factotum, Henley. Her pride in the smooth, pros-
perous running of the estate was apparent in her letters:

> I have Settled this last week my account with the Does to Michaelmas, when
> they owed me five pounds of the rent, besides for Bullocks, hay, & every
> thing else they bought. Henley is a *treasure* & helped me to make out their
> Book, which he understood much better than I did. I have also deducted in
> the accounts the 10 Guineas of the poor's Coals for this year, so that I hope
> I shall manage with them very well, & I only take Seven pounds of[f] Butler
> Weekley [*sic*].[51]

Networks and social politics

As this chapter has already intimated, strong support networks played
an important part in helping Betsey cope with separation. They provided
her with emotional support and distraction and gave her opportunities
to raise the family's visibility in the social arena with people who mattered. For Betsey personally, the importance of strong female support
networks cannot not be underestimated. While she was close to her
three younger sisters, especially Eugenia who was next to her in age,
their contact was almost entirely limited to correspondence after they
all made Scottish marriages by 1810. Similarly, Betsey was fond of her

mother-in-law and sisters-in-law, but they lived near London and she usually only saw them for short periods every year. It was female society in Buckinghamshire which provided her with her greatest support while Thomas Francis was away. Her social world was very much that of Jane Austen's heroines: it was dominated by walks, visits, dinners, trips to the big house in the area (in this case, Stowe), and the occasional house party or ball in Buckingham. It is a testimony to Betsey's ability to make friends and to the way that women stepped in to assist each other that Thomas Francis's absences were swiftly followed by visits and invitations from female neighbours. Thus, the day after Thomas Francis left for sea in 1800, the Misses Hislops from nearby Adstock called to invite her and the children to stay for several days.[52] Betsey met them again at a large dinner party the next evening at another neighbour's, Mrs Howard's. Mrs Howard, 'very friendly & kind', asked Betsey to stay overnight, presumably to save her the return trip home alone in the dark. The following morning Betsey took her two boys to Adstock for five days, returning home with the promise that Miss Hislop would come to stay with her the next Friday.[53]

Betsey's female network was also particularly helpful during the stressful period surrounding Thomas Francis's departure in 1810. Her concerns about sending Louisa to Brighton were eased when one of her neighbours, then in Brighton with a sick husband, volunteered to house the little girl and her maid, and to keep Betsey regularly informed. Nor was Betsey allowed to be alone for long. The day after Thomas Francis's departure, her closest friends, the Poulett sisters, drove over to spend the evening with her. Varying combinations of these four unmarried sisters called another three times before Betsey gave birth the following week. They then rapidly resumed visiting as soon as she could see company.[54] Other female friends and acquaintances also called and/or sent invitations to teas, dinners and visits. Even Betsey's mother-in-law paid her a flying visit, going miles out of her way to stay overnight at Swanbourne.[55]

With her husband away, Betsey immediately became head of the household and her intangible duties in the socio-political arena took on added importance. A good naval wife publicised her husband's exploits and reminded the people who mattered of his existence; an accomplished naval wife advanced her husband's and the family's best interests in elite society, not least by constructing a public image of the family as polite, cultured and worthy of advancement. Betsey took her responsibilities seriously. Although she had been charitably involved in the lives of the villagers, especially the old and the poor, since moving to Swanbourne, she now stepped in to her husband's position as head of the household. Despite being a practicing Catholic, she frequently had the local vicar, the pitiable Mr Haddock, over for dinner. When it became known that Haddock was actually starving himself in order to support his two sons, she joined in the subscription that the local farmers raised to help him. Moreover, she made a point of underlining the family's status by giving more than the leading farmer: 'I was a little at a loss what to give but as I understood Mr. Biscoe would pay a Guinea, I gave *two*'.[56]

Betsey enjoyed society and immersed herself in the local gentry community, using regular visits and teas, and occasional dinners and assemblies, to build and maintain her networks. Usually these were small-scale affairs; the assembly that she gave in January 1812, to celebrate a visit from her in-laws and their children, was the largest she held:

> All the neighbourhood assembled by nine oClock & the dancing began early, & was kept up with great Spirit till six in the morning. We Supp'd at one, & sat down Sixty people, Woodward & four of the Band, played, the whole went off uncommonly well, John Poulett was one of the best Beaux, & *a supply* from Stowe.[57]

The fact that she had Woodward, who led the county's most sought-after band, and that the Grenvilles of Stowe had shown their support for the event by despatching some of their house-party guests to the event, was a mark of the Fremantles' standing and would not have been missed by her guests.

Maintaining the Fremantles' connexion with the Grenvilles of Stowe was of central importance, as George Nugent-Temple-Grenville, Marquess of Buckingham, had long been both William and Thomas Francis's patron and their political leader.[58] In this, Betsey shone. While her Catholicism gave her an immediate connexion with Lady Buckingham, who was herself a Catholic convert, Betsey genuinely liked the Buckinghams and her musical ability, cosmopolitan past and personal charm appealed to them. She became a frequent guest at Stowe, invited for such special events such as the grand visit of the Prince of Wales and his brothers in 1805, and for the elaborate entertainment given for Louis XVIII and his brothers in 1808. The fact that she had been given away in marriage by Prince Augustus, and that she had met and played for the French king when he was in exile in Italy, would only have added to her cachet. She also usually attended the extended Stowe Christmas party, which ended with Lady Buckingham's birthday celebrations in early January. Her comment from near the end of the 1801 house party could stand for her experience over many years: 'I am almost tired of accompanying *catches* & Glees of an eveng. but L^d. Temple [Buckingham's heir] is so civil to us, th^t I must do it, as he likes no other music, & is only fond of hearing himself sing'.[59] Much as she might have been tired of playing music she disliked, she knew that maintaining good relations with the next generation of the family would be of benefit to the family's future.

Whenever possible, Betsey travelled to London for the Season. While these sojourns gave her children the benefit of specialist masters and allowed her to catch up with music and plays, they also served distinctly socio-political familial ends. She represented her husband, and her visiting reflected Thomas Francis's connexions and obligations. Thomas Francis attached great importance to this sort of socialising, and sent her specific instructions prior to her first solo London Season in 1801. She was to avoid naval cliques and any open association with the leading Catholic families, make the most of her musical skills, and pay a careful round of visits to the womenfolk of influential naval families.[60] Music was Betsey's *entrée* into London society. An outstanding pianist who had been tutored as a child by musicians such as Dragonetti, who was very popular in London at the turn of the century, she used her musical abilities and contacts to advantage over the years. It is telling that by 1813, when both of the Fremantles were longing for their separation to end, Betsey summed up her London Season, which had included two private concerts, one of which was certainly in a naval household, by saying, 'I think that I have now done my duty'.[61]

Conclusion

In 1814, when the Fremantles were finally reunited, Betsey was thirty-six and Thomas Francis was forty-nine. That they emerged from these years of separation with their relationship intact, their estate well cared for and their family embedded in the local and national elite, was as much a testimony to Betsey's ability to cope effectively with separation as it was to Thomas Francis's skills as an admiral. Their letters over these years apart demonstrate the ways that they used intimacy and sharing to span distance and forward their shared interests and ambitions. They reflected Thomas Francis's growing trust in Betsey, and her own growing confidence and competence.

For the Fremantles, and for hundreds of other naval families during the Revolutionary and Napoleonic Wars, extended separations were a fact of life. They posed the women left ashore with a range of personal, emotional, economic and practical challenges. The need to cope with anxiety and loneliness affected women at all levels of the social scale; so too did the need to step into husbands' shoes and assume the mantle of heads of households, with whatever responsibilities that entailed at different levels of society. While elite women like Betsey Fremantle did not share the financial uncertainties and struggles that blighted the lives of some sailors' wives, they too often had to assume new financial duties and learn new skills, including responsibilities for estate management. Those women who coped most successfully appear to have approached separations in much the same way as their modern counterparts: they took problem-solving approaches to the situations in which they found themselves, worked hard to maintain their relationships with their husbands and sustain their family units, developed and/or drew upon pre-established male and female networks to provide emotional as well as practical support, and kept themselves busy. In this, in a time of war, they were not exceptional: the expectation that women could and would fill both their own traditional roles as wives and mothers, and those of their menfolk in time of need, was not new. What bears further study is how this elasticity of gender roles reacted to peace – and what implications the experience of extended wartime separations had on both the development of more equal, complementary, relationships among couples and, on a societal level, on how the experience of so many women over such a long period of time fed into changing assumptions about women's capabilities in the first half of the nineteenth century.

Notes

1 Special thanks to Betsy and Iain Duncan Smith, the late Lord Cottesloe and the Fremantle Trust for permission to consult Elizabeth Wynne Fremantle's journals. Extracts from the early journals were published as Anne Fremantle (ed.), *The Wynne Diaries*, 3 vols. (London, 1935–40). All references here are to the original letters and manuscript journals which are now in the Centre for Buckinghamshire Studies (hereafter CBS): Spellings in the quotations are as given in the sources. Unless otherwise specified, Betsey's letters are taken from D/FR38/11–12.

2 See, for instance, Evelyn Millis Duvall, 'Loneliness and the Serviceman's Wife', *Marriage and Family Living*, 7:4 (1945), 77–81; R. Hill, *Families under Stress: Adjustment to Crises of War Separation and Reunion* (New York: Harper & Brothers, 1949); Hamilton I. McCubbin et al., 'Coping Repertoires of Families Adapting to Prolonged War-Induced Separations', *Journal of*

Marriage and Family, 38:3 (1976), 461–71; Diane L. Padden, Rebecca A. Connors and Janice G. Agazio, 'Stress, Well-being and Coping in Military Spouses during Deployment Separation', *Western Journal of Nursing Research*, 33:2 (2011), 247–67; Brian Cafferky and Lin Shi, 'Military Wives Emotionally Coping during Deployment: Balancing Dependence and Independence', *The American Journal of Family Therapy*, 43:3 (2015), 283–95.

3 N. A. M. Rodger, *The Wooden World: An Anatomy of the Georgian Navy* (London: Fontana Press, 1988), pp. 134–5.

4 N. A. M. Rodger, *The Command of the Ocean: A Naval History of Britain, 1649–1815* (London: Penguin, 2005), p. 407.

5 N. A. M. Rodger 'Recent Books on the Royal Navy of the Eighteenth Century', *Journal of Military History*, 63:3 (1999), 694. See Cindy McCreery, 'True Blue and *Black, Brown and Fair*: Prints of British Sailors and their Women during the Revolutionary and Napoleonic Wars', *British Journal for Eighteenth-Century Studies*, 23 (2000), 135–52; Louise Carter, 'British Women during the Revolutionary and Napoleonic Wars, 1793–1815: Responses, Roles and Representations' (PhD thesis, University of Cambridge, 2005); Margarette Lincoln, *Naval Wives and Mistresses, 1750–1850* (London: National Maritime Museum, 2007); Jennine Hurl-Eamon, 'The Fiction of Dependence and the Makeshift Economy of Soldiers, Sailors, and their Wives in Eighteenth-Century London', *Labor History*, 49:4 (2008), 481–501; Patricia Y. C. E. Lin, 'Caring for the Nation's Families: British Soldiers' and Sailors' Families and the State, 1793–1815' in Alan Forrest, Karen Hagemann and Jane Rendall (eds), *Soldiers, Citizens and Civilians: Experiences and Perceptions of the Revolutionary and Napoleonic Wars, 1790–1820* (Basingstoke: Palgrave Macmillan, 2009), pp. 99–117; Helen Doe, *Enterprising Women and Shipping in the Nineteenth Century* (Woodbridge: Boydell, 2009); Melanie Holihead, 'Cut Adrift or Towed Astern: Sailors' Wives in Mid-Nineteenth Century Portsea Island Considered in Perspective', *Journal for Maritime Research*, 17:2, 155–68 (accessed 13 July 2016). Similar concerns and economies of make-shift can be found among sailors' wives in Brittany as well: see Emmanuelle Charpentier's 'Incertitude et stratégies de (sur)vie: Le quotidien des femmes des «partis en voyage sur mer» des côtes nord de la Bretagne au xviiie siècle', *Annales de Bretagne et des Pays de l'Ouest*, 117:3 (2010), 39–54, http://abpo. revues.org/1812 (accessed 13 July 2016). Amy Lynn Smallwood's unpublished MA dissertation, 'Shore Wives: The Lives of British Naval Officers' Wives and Widows, 1750–1815' (MA diss., Wright State University, 2008) also bears note for its focus on women of higher status.

6 Hurl-Eamon, 'The Fiction of Female Dependence', 482; Lin, 'Caring for the Nation's Families', pp. 100–3. For modern studies identifying similar factors, see Padden, Connors and Agazio, 'Stress, Well-being and Coping in Military Spouses during Deployment Separation', 255–60; Helen Mederer and Laurie Weinstein, 'Choices and Constraints in a Two-Person Career: Ideology,

Division of Labour, and Well-Being among Submarine Officers' Wives', *Journal of Family Issues*, 13:3 (1992), 334–50.

7 Erin E. Dimiceli, Mary A. Steinhardt and Shanna E. Smith, 'Stressful Experiences, Coping Strategies and Predictors of Health-Related Outcomes among Wives of Deployed Military Servicemen', *Armed Forces & Society*, 36:2 (2010), 352–73 (accessed 20 July 2016); Cherie Blank et al., 'Coping Behaviours used by Army Wives during Deployment Separation and their Perceived Effectiveness', *Journal of the American Academy of Nurse Practitioners*, 24 (2012), 661 (accessed 20 July 2016).

8 Cecil Aspinall-Oglander (ed.), *Admiral's Wife: Being the Life and Letters of the Hon. Mrs. Edward Boscawen from 1719 to 1761* (London: Longmans, Green and Company, 1940); Godfrey Mundy (ed.), *The Life and Correspondence of the Late Admiral Lord Rodney*, 2 vols. (London: John Murray, 1830).

9 Hurl-Eamon, 'The Fiction of Female Dependence', 482; Lin, 'Caring for the Nation's Families', pp. 100–3.

10 'Tussy', a nickname derived from Thusnelda, the patriotic German heroine whose romanticised tragic love story with Arminius (Germanicised to Hermann) was popular in plays, poetry and operas through the eighteenth century. Special thanks to Professors Matthew Philpott and Stuart Parkes for their assistance on tracing the nickname. See also Lauren Nossett, 'Changing Ideals of Femininity: Representations of Thusnelda in Klopstock, Kleist and Grabbe' (unpublished MA thesis, University of Georgia, 2010).

11 Thomas Francis Fremantle (hereafter TFF) to Elizabeth 'Betsey' Wynne Fremantle (hereafter EWF), HMS *Ganges*, Bearhaven, 14 December 1803. Unless otherwise specified, the quotations in this snapshot are taken from this letter.

12 The reconstruction of this scene is based upon EWF to TFF, Swanbourne, 4 February 1812.

13 The practice of numbering letters continued in naval families into the late twentieth century.

14 EWF, Journal, Sunbury, 23 November 1811.

15 EWF, Journal, 23 August 1800.

16 EWF, Journal, 24 August 1800.

17 EWF, Journal, 25 August 1800.

18 EWF to TFF, Swanbourne, 20 July 1803.

19 See for instance, EWF, Journal, Liphook, 1 November 1804.

20 TFF to EWF, [Portsmouth], 1805.

21 TFF to EWF, HMS *Ganges*, off Moon Island, 19, 23 April 1801.

22 TFF to EWF, HMS *Neptune*, off Ushant, 23 May 1805.

23 EWF, Journal, 20, 22 August 1810.

24 TFF to EWF, Portsmouth, 4 September 1810.

25 EWF to TFF, Swanbourne 21 October 1810.

26 EWF to TFF, Swanbourne, 30 October [1810].
27 TFF to EWF, 18 November [1810].
28 EWF to TFF, Swanbourne, 11 November 1810.
29 EWF to TFF, Swanbourne, 25 November, 16 December 1810, 18 January 1811.
30 TFF to EWF, HMS *Ganges*, Copenhagen, 5 April 1801.
31 *Ibid.*
32 TFF to EWF, HMS *Neptune*, off Cádiz, 1 October 1805.
33 EWF, Journal, 7 November 1805; Garlies to EWF, Admiralty, 6 November 1805; Buckingham to EWF, 7 November 1805.
34 EWF to TFF, Swanbourne, 29 December 1810.
35 EWF to TFF, Swanbourne, 16 December 1810.
36 EWF to TFF, Swanbourne, 29 December 1810.
37 EWF to TFF, Swanbourne, 1811.
38 EWF to TFF, Swanbourne, 18 November 1810.
39 EWF to TFF, Swanbourne, 16 November 1810.
40 EWF to TFF, Swanbourne, 18 November 1810.
41 EWF to TFF, Swanbourne, 2 December [1810].
42 EWF to TFF, Swanbourne, 16 December 1810.
43 EWF to TFF, Swanbourne [1811].
44 EWF to TFF, Swanbourne [1812].
45 EWF to TFF, Englefield Green, 2 November 1812.
46 D/FR/31/1/11/1–2, William Fremantle to TFF, Englefield Green 15 August 1811; D/FR/31/1/23, William Fremantle to TFF, Englefield Green, 1 November 1812.
47 D/FR/42/1/18, Buckingham to EWF, Stowe, 2 August 1811.
48 The Halifax station was naval shorthand for the Royal Navy's North American Station. The squadron was based at the Naval Dockyard in Halifax, Nova Scotia, and active in the waters along the American East Coast and down to Bermuda.
49 EWF to TFF, Swanage, 17 October 1812; Englefield Green 2 November 1812; Stowe, 28 November 1812.
50 TFF to EWF, HMS *Ganges*, 7 leagues due south of Elsinore, 21, 22 March 1801.
51 EWF to TFF, Swanbourne, 18 November 1810.
52 EWF, Journal, 26 August 1800.
53 EWF, Journal, 28 August–2 September 1800.
54 EWF, Journal, 2–22, 27 August 1810.
55 EWF, Journal, 12–13 October 1810.
56 EWF to TFF, Swanbourne, 9 December [1810].
57 EWF to TFF, Swanbourne, 19 January [1812].
58 Connexion: in eighteenth-century usage this word reflected close ties and interdependence between people, but, most relevantly here, it had a specific political meaning, indicating a group of people connected by shared interests,

especially political, religious or commercial. See *Compact Edition of the Oxford English Dictionary*, 2 vols. (Oxford: Oxford University Press, 1987), vol. 1, p. 839.

59 EWF, January 1801.

60 TFF to EWF, 1801.

61 EWF to TFF, Brook Street, 3 June 1813.

3

The Admiralty's gaze: disciplining indecency and sodomy in the Edwardian fleet

Mary Conley

It is difficult to imagine that a historical study about homoerotic practices in the navy represents a new naval history – when it has been a site for naval research for forty years, yet the approach to engaging in studies of maritime sexualities has changed since Arthur Gilbert's initial studies on disciplining sodomy cases in the eighteenth- and early nineteenth-century Royal Navy.[1] Within the past twenty years, there has been a growing scholarly literature about homoerotic activity in the navy that still relies heavily upon court martial records, but that analyses them in new ways to draw out histories of consensual desire, sexual violence and institutional power.[2] Those developments, which have expanded what we know about same-sex intimacies afloat (even if refracted through disciplinary records), themselves benefited from the maturation of maritime masculinity studies and the ascendancy of the histories of gender and sexualities, which provided methods not only to capture the lived experiences of seafarers but also to assess social, institutional and imperial power relations from the testimonies, commentaries and sentencing associated with courts martial boards.[3] This newer scholarship has put to rest any older interpretations that questioned the extent of intimate relations between men either because 'a ship at sea was about the most difficult possible place to commit sodomy' or that charges for sodomitical acts seldom came before a court martial board.[4] Perhaps the most influential of these new trends has been to connect the navy with the broader field of maritime history, which requires that analysis travels from wooden worlds to port towns and to capital cities through networks of ideas, goods and peoples.[5]

This chapter on sodomitical charges in the Edwardian navy benefits from this recent scholarship, recognising that these charges offer us both glimpses into intimate life below decks in the navy – albeit translated through disciplinary charges – and into the disciplinary intentions of naval officers and the Admiralty who oversaw these cases. Extending what Philippa Levine has argued in her studies of the British Empire to the navy, sexuality in the fleet became an 'invaluable tool' for officials to 'regulate sexual behaviour', to define gendered norms of masculinity and femininity, and to discipline 'proper and improper sexual practices'.[6] This was perhaps most true within the all-male confines of the pre-war navy, where disciplining sexuality required elaborate classificatory schemes. For clarity in this chapter, I am using the contemporary term 'sodomitical' to refer to a whole host of homoerotic acts that were punishable by court martial, and 'sodomy' to refer to the specific charge of anal penetration.[7] While one intent of the chapter is to shed more light upon the nature of consensual intimate relations between men, another is also to reveal the extent to which trial records, which could privilege allegations of coercion, could reveal the features of disciplining non-consensual acts, particularly when charges involved boy ratings and their superiors. The half-dozen cases that exist from the early twentieth century reveal a navy that was particularly apprehensive about the possibilities that sodomitical practices would enervate the fleet whether in terms of discipline or disease.

Often, the detection of a venereal disease was enough to warrant an investigation. On 18 January 1902, Admiral Charles Hotham, Commander-in-Chief of the Portsmouth Station after consultation with Captain Edward H. Gamble, the Inspecting Captain of Boys Training Ships, called a court of inquiry to investigate the unusual cases of three naval boys who had recently been treated at Haslar Hospital for syphilis.[8] Five days earlier the Fleet Surgeon had first reported to the Inspector General and the Commander of the training ship HMS *St Vincent*, that two boys from that ship had been admitted for treatment for anal ulceration and syphilitic sores that were the result of a 'contagious disease' that suggested sodomy. Directed to find out how the boys became infected, the first court of inquiry could initially find no explanation for infections, nor perpetrators of an offence, until three more boys were admitted to the hospital three days later. Then James Peel, the father of David Peel, one of the patients, reported that his son recently admitted that he had been sexually assaulted by a man at a Portsmouth music hall in 1900, three months before entering the navy. In testimony before the court, David Peel, who had sold programmes at the Empire Music Hall before volunteering for the navy, noted how a man had propositioned him by the stage door, asking for a 'snack' in exchange for ten shillings. The boy Peel argued that he broke free to escape the assault by his assailant after an interruption by a passerby. Peel had also maintained that 'no one else had ever "interfered with" him' but that he had heard 'constant conversation on this and similar subjects amongst the boys', though he had 'never seen anything happening'. Owen Beezley, another of the syphilitic patients, had asserted in his testimony that 'no one had ever actually taken liberties with him', but a Marine Private had invited him to let him 'have a "snack"'. Although the curiosity of the court was piqued by the boys' testimonies, particularly the boys' casual references to 'snacking', a medical examination of the accused private convinced the court that he was falsely accused. Without evidence to explain the origin of the syphilitic cases, on 25 January 1902 the court recommended that four of the boys, including Peel, be discharged with the note 'services no longer required'; and that two other boys, including Owen Beezley, be assigned to separate training ships with commanding officers advised to watch them closely.

However, the case was not closed. In the wake of the inquiry, David Peel's father forwarded a letter from his son to the naval authorities that provided a new version of events alleging he had been assaulted by three different men on the ship: one of them a quartermaster who had already transferred ships, and two corporals still on board ship.[9] The corporals had denied the allegations, and physical inspections revealed no signs of syphilis. One of the corporals, John Roadley, had also been extensively questioned about his relationship with Peel to determine whether he had threatened him to stay quiet when Peel was in the hospital. While the court admitted that the medical evidence from the boys raised 'the suspicion of sodomy', it ended its inquiry without a finding because Peel's allegations could not be corroborated, and because Peel himself was considered an unreliable witness giving contradictory confessions. Although this was not a court martial, the investigation ended with the reiteration that Peel be discharged from the service.

What was originally intended as a week-long inquiry turned into a sputtering three-month investigation that involved three different courts of inquiry. In the following weeks, two more naval boys, Joseph Rogers and Ralph Edwards from the *St Vincent* were treated at Haslar for syphilis, leading to further allegations against Corporal Roadley and a new accusation of sodomy and assault against Petty Officer James Cheeseman. In addition, another boy rating – Christopher Morris from the same mess – alleged that a petty officer had attempted to assault him in his hammock in the middle of the night. While other boys testified to witnessing an intruder, their inability to verify the assailant because of the dimly lit deck meant that Morris's identification was ignored by the new court of inquiry. Joseph Rogers and Ralph Edwards were asked whether they could 'have resisted Corporal Roadley's criminal assault on you in the cell'. Rogers replied that he could have but he would have continued to have been 'bothered' by him. According to Edwards, Corporal Roadley had coerced him to engage in sex after threatening that it was 'better to have a snack than have a birching'. When Edwards was asked how he knew what Roadley meant by 'snack', Edwards noted that he 'had heard it talked about by boys and men in the ship; the expression "snack" meaning an unnatural assault'.

For clarification, the court asked for medical advice from Deputy Inspector General James Porter who affirmed that the cases in this set of boys indicated 'a strong suspicion that it has been contracted by unnatural intercourse' that was the result of a 'habit of unnatural gratification' because 'the anus in each case is funnel shaped'.[10] The court also wanted to clarify some of the basic features of syphilis, the nature of sexual desire and the likelihood of consent. In questioning, Porter mistakenly argued that it was impossible for men to be non-symptomatic carriers of syphilis, which bolstered exculpating Roadley because he showed no signs of the disease.[11] In addition, Fleet Surgeon Charles Buchanan-Hamilton replied that he did not believe 'an unnatural assault' could 'be made on boys of the age in the service without their consent', which contradicted the boys' claim of coercion. While the term 'rape' was never used in the questioning, the wider inquiry revealed a court interested in determining whether the boys were victimised or culpable.

Countering the victims' allegations against Roadley and Cheeseman, Petty Officer George Smith was one of the last to be interviewed by the court on 4 April, and he testified that most of the boys in question had taken frequent leaves to Portsmouth's 'low disreputable bad places' like the French Maid near Agnes Weston's Sailors' Rest when on afternoon leave. Smith encouraged another boy rating, Albert O'Hagan, who had also been admitted to Haslar with syphilis to share with the court that he had gone on leave in Portsmouth. Information from other boys whose names George Smith supplied to the court suggested that O'Hagan had not only frequented the French Maid but also had been propositioned by men on the street in uniform. The court learned of the proximity of these disreputable entertainments to the Sailors' Rest, which reserved rooms for naval boys on leave, and that Edwards and Rodgers had had frequent leaves into the city, while Morris had not. The suggestion was that their syphilis could have been acquired ashore, perhaps during encounters with older men from these establishments. As a consequence of this new circumstantial evidence about their suspected recreation ashore, the boys' allegations about assaults by petty officers aboard ship were thrown out as deceitful fabrications.

While still no one perpetrator was named as the source for the infections, the court contented itself that the boys were 'willing agents' whose infections were the result of their onshore recreations. Despite the boys' alleged complicity, by the end of 4 April, the court argued that it made no sense to try them by court martial. Instead, based upon the accrual of evidence over three months and three courts of inquiry, the last court made a series of concrete recommendations to the commander-in-chief of the Portsmouth Station and to the Admiralty. It recommended that married men be selected for posts of instructors at training establishments; that Portsmouth be out of bounds for afternoon day leaves and weekend overnight leaves; that medical examination of all *St Vincent* boys needed to take place regularly as a precaution against boys' desires for concealment; that given the scandal all present petty officers and any type of instructor or member of the ship's police of *St Vincent* needed to be replaced and drafted to another ship; that boys be given regular hammock billet assignments on-board ship to ensure that they were accounted for; and that training ships should be better lit. It also recommended that the two boys, Edwards and Rogers, be both ceremoniously birched with twenty-four cuts aboard *St Vincent* and dismissed with disgrace. O'Hagan was discharged in August from the service for medical reasons because of syphilis, Morris was reassigned to HMS *Partridge* and stayed in the service until his discharge after the war in 1919. In the wake of the report to the Admiralty, conversations among admirals from the different training establishment agreed in principle to most of these recommendations, like the hammock assignment, but cautioned against hiring based upon marriage rather than upon the qualifications of the men.

While the *St Vincent* investigation reveals how naval boy ratings could become prey to those in power afloat or those with access to them ashore, the questioning of witnesses revealed that the court used the setting to learn more, even if misinformed, about the parameters of consent and the nature of sodomy and syphilis. In the three different investigations, the court was consistently pleased by the explanations provided by ship's officers and corporals who denied the charges and testified that no indecent language was even heard in the mess, despite the boys' candid accounts of frank discussions of sex among the boy ratings. Although the court rejected the claims against the individual privates, corporals and petty officers, the court still recommended sweeping changes to be made in the oversight and the training of boys to minimise the chances for abuse – whether it was in the kind of man who would be right for the job or in the provision of better lighting in the messes to reduce concealment. The testimonies also revealed that the language of these homoerotic encounters – of having a 'snack' – were similar whether at the naval station or ashore. Importantly, the judicial procedures, court recommendations and use of medical expertise helped to inform an Admiralty that was physically distant from the ever-changing cultures of shipboard life. Perhaps more than any other disciplinary offence, sodomitical offences, those comprising an alleged indecency that involved same-sex sexual encounters, attracted Admiralty attention because even one scandal of 'immorality' helped to serve as a harbinger of the state of naval discipline in the entire fleet.

The *St Vincent* cases served as a bellwether for the kind of sodomitical offences that would come to trial in the early 1900s, and that often occurred in home waters and in training establishments. The cases frequently raised issues of consent, coercion, as well as conspiracy (as the defence of the defendant) – and a significant number of cases involved boy ratings (typically between sixteen and eighteen years old) and older petty officers. As with the *St Vincent* cases which made recommendations about hammock billeting, recommendations from courts martial could entail wider fleet recommendations. While the *St Vincent* cases raise questions about the vulnerability of new recruits aboard ship and within port towns, the cases also highlight how the language used in the testimonies can illuminate the nature of wider social relations afloat and ashore.

To contextualise the *St Vincent* inquiry, then, requires a fuller understanding of archival challenges, naval discipline, homoerotic desire, venereal disease and shipboard hierarchies. There has been surprisingly little written either about the extent of intimate same-sex relations or the surveillance of men's sexual lives in the Royal Navy and in the maritime world in the period after 1861.[12] In part, the explanation for the silences is straightforward. First, few ratings or officers who served in the late Victorian and Edwardian navy left contemporary, candidly written accounts about the prevalence and nature of homosexual relations in the navy. This is hardly revelatory given the increasing social reproach for homosexuality by the 1880s and 1890s, as evidenced by scandals like the Cleveland Street and Oscar Wilde trials.[13] Social fears cast homosexuality as a danger to the very foundations of Victorian virtues of domesticity, work and duty. John Tosh notes that in late Victorian society, the figure of the homosexual represented 'someone who struck at the roots of the family, flouted the work ethic and subverted the camaraderie of all-men association'.[14]

Anecdotal remembrances of British ex-servicemen who had served in the early twentieth-century navy were gathered in a general oral history project from the 1970s where men recalled, among other topics, the existence of same-sex relations aboard ship that were described as 'homosexuality' in the questioning.[15] While none of the elderly interviewees admitted to engaging in relations with other ratings when they were in service, anecdotal commentaries ranged from a recognition that such relationships existed aboard ship, a resignation that some of these relations occurred within a situational context and an outrage when these relationships involved petty officers and boys.[16]

There are real archival challenges for the historian who wants to extend the narrative into the twentieth century because detailed record keeping of court martial cases in the archives actually tails off dramatically in the late Victorian period. Admiralty records contain only a handful of cases for the Victorian and Edwardian periods. Moreover, court martial returns are difficult to access, Admiralty digests (annual ledgers that briefly detail and organise correspondence to the Admiralty) are unwieldy, and naval punishment returns to Parliament lack detail about sodomitical offences after 1867. Yet, despite these challenges, Laura Rowe's recent work on court martial returns in the First World War suggest that sexual offences were the fourth most common charge for ratings after drinking, violence against a superior and disobedience and comprised nearly 9 per cent of the total charges between 1914 and 1919.[17] Of course, the frequency of disciplinary charges did not reflect the frequency of the occurrence of these acts but rather reflected the willingness of officers and the Admiralty to pursue disciplining these acts. Nor did the absence of a charge reveal the absence of intimate relations.

Although the Admiralty historically considered sodomy as one of the gravest threats to the maintenance of naval discipline, it was difficult for the Admiralty and its officers (never mind the public) to name intimate acts between men, whether consensual or not, beyond sodomy. While charges of sodomy were often interchangeable with buggery in the eighteenth and nineteenth centuries, buggery disappeared from early twentieth-century charge sheets. From the nineteenth to the twentieth centuries, allusions of uncleanliness and indecency could hint at a range of alleged improper relations between men or could also entail concealing a venereal disease from the ship's surgeon. Earlier euphemistic charges of 'lewd' and 'nasty' acts, were replaced by the turn of the century with a codification of offences enumerating sodomy, indecent assault (almost always involving men or boys rather than women), gross indecency and indecent conduct. Despite the regularisation of the allegations, the public charges remained nondescript.

The Admiralty's reticence to categorise these acts uniformly did not deter it from imposing decisive punishment when sodomy was proved. Sodomy had been a capital offence since the 1533 Act of Henry VIII. The Articles of War of 1661 had specifically stipulated punishment of death 'without mercy' for 'the unnaturall and detestable sin of Buggery or Sodomy'.[18] The number of cases and convictions connected with sodomy and indecency contracted considerably in the nineteenth century in the wake of the French Revolutionary and Napoleonic Wars.

Most writings about sodomy and the maritime world concentrate upon the long eighteenth century, ending in the post-Napoleonic years of the 1830s. While the last naval rating was hanged for a proven charge of sodomy in 1829, the 1861 Naval Discipline Act replaced this capital punishment with new sentences from five years to life imprisonment.[19] The effect upon naval law of the 1885 Criminal Law Amendment, which recriminalised homosexual acts between men whether in public or private and adjusted the sentencing, led to the new Naval Discipline Act of 1889, which laid out five years' imprisonment for sodomy charges and enumerated the possible sentencing of between two and five years' imprisonment for men found guilty of other charges that included indecent assault and gross indecency. The threshold to prove sodomy remained high – there needed to be a witness not only to the act taking place between the two parties but also to the specific act of anal penetration. Even in the case of assault, the testimony of the alleged victim was not enough to convict without corroboration. Admiralty court martial boards were wary of the possibilities of conspiracy, retribution and retaliation in these cases, given the severity of the punishment. The standard for proof probably explained why few cases went forward and likely led many captains to put forward lesser charges or to avoid court martial proceedings altogether and mete out their own summary punishments (that is without a formal trial) to the sailor suspected of alleged misconduct. By the early Edwardian period, an offence of sodomy was often accompanied by subordinate indecency or assault charges to help ensure a proven verdict on at least one of the counts.

Court martial records offer an unusual and productive archive for understanding how naval men's sexual lives were caught within the balance of a hierarchical naval justice system that could mete out justice summarily aboard ship, locally through the court martial, and centrally through the oversight of the Admiralty. At all these levels, naval leadership exerted its power over lower ranks through policing and defining the boundaries of alleged normative and deviant sexual identities. Histories of naval mens' sexualities have been influenced and defined against Foucauldian approaches that have considered the ways in which laws both regulated and produced 'sodomite' and 'homosexual' identities.[20] Rather than seeing these naval men as a world apart, gender and cultural historians examining sailor identities afloat have increasingly tried to connect these men's lives to subcultures ashore as well as to general British historiographies of homosexuality. While British historians of sexuality like Randolph Trumbach and H. G. Cocks have questioned the birth of the so-called 'homosexual' type as a consequence of the infamous Labouchere Amendment, there has been little response to thinking about how civil law affected the ways that sodomy and 'indecent acts' were punished in the post-1861 and -1885 period, or the ways that naval ratings used courts martial to defend themselves against such charges. In a reappraisal of the transformative reach of the 1885 Labouchere Amendment, H. G. Cocks notes that by the eighteenth century all homosexual acts became liable to prosecution as an 'assault with intent to commit sodomy', adhering to a common law principle that an intent to commit a crime was in itself criminal.[21] Punishments from naval court martial records from the eighteenth through to the nineteenth century support Cocks's conclusions. In his study of nineteenth-century law, Cocks concluded that, despite Labouchere's claims to the contrary, 'his efforts did not change the law in a dramatic fashion'.[22] Sean Brady argues that late Victorian civil laws continued to punish criminal acts rather than to define a 'vilified "type"'.[23] Rather than see the navy and naval discipline as a world away from civilian society, a study of disciplining sodomy and indecency in the navy may reveal that the navy was not so far removed from the realities of policing same-sex intimacies ashore.

Although it seems reasonable to conclude that homoerotic relations occurred throughout the fleet no matter the prohibition or punishment, what they signified in terms of men's own self-identities is complicated.

George Chauncey cautions against resorting to 'hetero-homosexual bina-rism', noting that 'men's identities and reputations simply did not depend on a sexuality defined by the anatomical sex of their sexual partners'.[24] Similarly, Matt Houlbrook's *Queer London* reminds us that 'forms of understanding that we often assume to be timeless – the organisation of male sexual practices and identities around the binary opposition between "homo" and "heterosexual" solidified only in the two decades after the Second World War'.[25] Long commissions combined with all the things that a ship lacked – privacy, leave and women – probably fostered male intimacies that transcended the bounds of typical male camara-derie. Despite the methodological challenges of the 1970s oral history project, the testimonies were filled with pensioners' memories that intimate homosexual relations were not unusual but remained secretive, that naval men often did not report fellow ratings engaged in such acts because they felt in their words that, 'It's not my business', acknowledged that 'there's a lot more goes on than is ever caught' and that officers were reticent to bringing a sexual offence to trial if the offence would detract from the reputation of the ship.[26] What is ever-present in these records is how former naval ratings vividly recalled the role that naval discipline had in policing the boundaries of sexual relations afloat.

Systematic searching of court martial records in the National Archives yields far fewer case studies than earlier periods. Only around half a dozen courts martial for charges of indecency and sodomy exist in the Edwardian navy. Of the six case studies that I reviewed that involved charges of sodomy or indecency, all were kept because they engaged Admiralty review and set precedent for future cases. When used along-side the statistics from court martial returns for the period, a clearer picture emerges about the kinds of cases that concerned commanding officers across the fleet and Admiralty officials in particular.

Between 1900 and 1913, naval court martial boards tried around 137 cases involving alleged 'indecency' that could range from charges of sodomy, gross indecency and uncleanness, to having a hand in another man's hammock.[27] It is difficult to compare judicial statistics between different periods because of different classification cultures for offences and because of the different intensity of charges during wartime. While Seth LeJacq notes that there were at least 490 trials for sodomitical offences between 1690 and 1900, Laura Rowe has noted that 229 men were charged with 374 general 'sexual offences' that occurred during wartime between 1914 and 1919.[28] In this study, I have chosen to examine the figures from trials, where a prisoner could face multiple charges, rather than to group all of the offences together. And, with contextualisation from remaining case studies, these court statistics reveal interesting patterns about the nature of the charges, where they originated and who comprised the ranks charged. A deeper examination of the Edwardian naval court martial figures and cases highlight the kinds of cases that came to trial and received punishment as well as the stations in which these cases took place. In particular, the numbers also speak to the kinds of men brought to trial for crimes, and whether there were meaningful distinctions between the main charges of sodomy, indecent assault, gross indecency and other miscellaneous charges that spoke of 'indecent conduct'. When paired with more qualitative data from the case studies that exist within Admiralty court martial records, from service certificates, or from the gleanings of courts of inquiry, a better picture of naval discipline towards sodomitical offences emerges at a time of naval expansion and reorganisation. While the range of charges could result in a range of punishments, summary punishments and discretionary actions by commanding officers highlight that much more was caught than came to trial and likely more activities took place afloat and ashore than were caught. In addition, it is evident from the treatment of boys and men who were either acquitted of crimes or listed as a named party in an offence that officers could still wield discretionary powers over personnel matters through discharging officers with a 'services no longer required' (SNLR) designation that left no stigma on a man's service certificate but removed him from naval service. And when discretionary powers of the court martial board appeared too provocative, the Admiralty stepped in with oversight to annul or ameliorate a sentence.

In examining the kinds of cases that came to trial between 1900 and 1913, it appears that there was a regularity to the charges and often to the punishments. Court martial returns distinguished between three main offences of 'sodomy', 'indecent assault' and 'gross indecency'. Indecent assault was the most frequent charge, with over fifty-eight men charged while forty-seven men and boys were charged for sodomy. With only thirteen of the 137 main charges made, gross indecency was a charge rarely levelled on its own (only four charges came in the first decade), most likely because of the tradition in a court martial to try a specific offence rather than a behaviour.[29] The fourth major category could be lumped together as miscellaneous offences, although the offences named ranged from being very specific – 'making improper proposals to boys', 'improperly interfering with a stoker in his hammock', and 'sleeping with a boy' – to more general offences that were to the 'prejudice of good order and naval discipline' or 'indecent conduct' and 'uncleanness', both of which stood as euphemisms for a range of alleged offences from masturbation, improper fraternisation, bad language to venereal disease. To ensure a punishment, prisoners would often be charged with multiple offences that could in one charge include 'attempted sodomy' and 'indecent assault' through to an 'act to the prejudice of good order and naval discipline in forcibly taking a boy first class behind a screen in a sail loft'.[30]

The main charges were often proved and when they were not, secondary charges often were. Service certificates for over half of these men and boys charged revealed, even when acquitted, that all men were reassigned ships if they were involved in a case involving alleged sexual offence. And it was frequent practice that, even in courts martial where boys were charged but acquitted or where boys were named, that they were dismissed from the service as SNLR as had happened in some of the *St Vincent* cases. Roughly half the sodomy cases were proved (twenty-three of forty-seven), with typical sentences of five years' penal servitude and dismissal with disgrace from the navy. Of the twenty-four cases that were not proven for sodomy, fourteen were proven for lesser charges of attempted sodomy, indecent assault and gross indecency, and the average charge was either eighteen or twenty-four months' hard labour with dismissal with disgrace. Together, over 79 per cent of all sodomy cases were proved and led to punishments of at least eighteen months hard labour and dismissal with disgrace from the service.

It was routine for at least two individuals to be tried together on sodomy charges even if the second defendant had claimed that he was assaulted.[31] In March 1902, Walter Cannell, an able seaman, and William Vincent, a stoker, were tried in a court martial proceeding in HMS *Pembroke* at Chatham for committing an act of sodomy in their ship, HMS *Northumberland*.[32] While Cannell had argued that the charge was the result of a conspiracy against him, Vincent had pleaded guilty to committing sodomy with Cannell, clarifying to the judge advocate who had asked what he had meant by stating, 'he fucked me'.[33] Although his defence had rested upon repeated refusals of his advances, Vincent's admission of guilt was enough to prove the charges against him and Cannell. Both were sentenced to ten years' penal servitude. The sentence gained the attention of the Admiralty who appeared surprised by its length and had admitted that there had been no cases proved for sodomy in the navy since disciplinary and criminal reforms in 1891. Upon review, Vincent's sentence was reduced to three years' penal servitude but Cannell's remained at ten years, with the First Naval Lord, Admiral Walter Kerr, defending the decision, holding that he did 'not regret that a sentence of 10 years was inflicted by the court', and hoping that its effect would be a 'deterrent' for the 'benefit of the service'.[34] Of the 137 cases reviewed, Cannell's ten-year sentence was the only punishment granted of more than five years.

In the cases of charges of indecent assault, lone defendants or pairs of defendants often faced charges of assaulting another unnamed witness. Despite the lack of a co-defendant, 50 per cent of indecent assault cases were proven for indecent assault, with the percentage increasing to around 74 per cent when lesser charges of gross indecency were also proved. The average imprisonment for indecent assault, if proven, was two years' hard labour and dismissal with disgrace, while punishments for lesser charges were typically between six and twelve months' hard labour with dismissal. Of cases where gross indecency was specifically charged, only seven of thirteen were proven, with an average of twelve months' hard labour, and for the various specific miscellaneous charges nine of the nineteen charges were proved, and the punishments ranged from disrating (from petty officer to able seaman) and loss of good conduct badges to two years' hard labour. For cases involving gross indecency or the miscellaneous charges of indecent conduct, there were no lesser charges to prove, although there were accompanying charges of violence and prevarication.

In reviewing the cases, a few patterns emerge. Rather than courts martial resulting from sexual offences occurring when men were far from home, they were more likely in home stations, and were more frequent in training establishments at Devonport, Portsmouth or the Nore. Yet the overall number of boys charged was comparatively small, with just around ten boys in total brought up on charges. While six boys were charged with sodomy, no boy ratings were charged with indecent assault, a striking absence given there were fifty-six cases. A closer look at the offence descriptions of the court martial returns reveals that boy ratings were the most common rank to be noted victims of indecent assaults. Of thirty-three indecent assaults where the victim's rank was noted, one-third of the victims were boy ratings.[35] Some 20 per cent of the miscellaneous sexual offences either charged boys or named boys in the charges, while 13 per cent of the men charged were petty officers for whom the majority were charged for relations with boys. Given the findings of previous studies such as Burg's *Boys at Sea* or the reminiscences of men who had served recalled in McKee's *Sober Men and True*, it is perhaps unsurprising to find that many of the cases involved boy ratings and petty officers. Boys, who could enter the navy as young as fifteen, and into the marines as young as fourteen (if entered as a bugler), often found themselves the object of attention of older men who took them under their wing to mentor them in the ways of shipboard life. While older sailors provided young sailors with useful knowledge about naval life, these relationships could transgress the bounds of friendly camaraderie, and mentors could exploit the vulnerability of newly engaged boy recruits. Despite efforts to segregate boys physically from older ratings to protect them from possible dangerous liaisons, these predatory 'winger' relationships were common in the anecdotal remembrances of former naval ratings.[36] It is difficult to know how to assess offences where boy ratings of sixteen or seventeen were either charged or named. While fourteen represented the age of consent, ship hierarchies distorted young men's abilities to thwart an advance or an assault and provided a superior with the power to coerce. The Admiralty did pay attention to these cases – of the twelve court martial cases in which the Admiralty intervened, eleven involved boy ratings and men of petty officer rank, with the punishments often annulled based on incomplete evidence or irregular court procedures. While petty officers often had the prospect of returning to service, a boy rating who was acquitted or who was named in an assault was most likely to be dismissed from service, as in the *St Vincent* cases.[37] Since it was common for boy ratings to be weeded out of navy when they had been named – even as a victim – in a sexual offence, there was little incentive to implicate a superior in a sexual offence when either informal retribution or official discharge was likely.

A case from 1913 highlights both the difficult position of boy ratings on ships and the degree to which court martial cases could reconnect Admiralty Lords to the realities of shipboard culture. In August 1913, three men and one first-class boy from the cruiser HMS *Gloucester*, stationed in the Mediterranean, were charged with sodomy.[38] The charges that these individuals engaged in acts in 'derogation of god's honour' developed initially from medical evidence provided by the ship's doctor who connected multiple cases of gonorrhea to a boy rating's own case. The doctor was already suspicious that the men were engaging in indecent conduct because he argued that they had sought treatment in the sick bay for venereal disease 'at a time long after it would have developed if contracted on shore'. The prosecution of all the cases depended upon the testimony and confession of Charles Herbert, the sixteen-year-old boy rating implicated, and charged three other stokers and seamen with engaging in consensual sexual acts with him. During witness testimony, one stoker witness testified that he had overheard one of the defendants, William Sutton, an ordinary seaman, admit to acquiring gonorrhea from having 'a lump of ass of a boy'. When asked by the court whether such a comment was unusual to make, the stoker admitted that 'it was a sort of a remark made in the head night after night'.[39] The court testimony disturbed the court martial board for many reasons. Not only did the culture of *Gloucester* seem to foster such 'immorality' aboard ship, but Herbert's youth was cause for worry. More vexing was Herbert's confession that he engaged in sexual acts afloat for money and that he had also conducted such business on his previous ship, HMS *London*. When the Admiralty reviewed the case, it speculated whether Herbert's frequent ship changes as a boy (he had been drafted to no less than seven vessels since his training on *Impregnable*) prevented the development of proper discipline befitting a seaman and perhaps played a part in his alleged abysmal conduct. Herbert's captain on *Gloucester* fretted that 'such an unsettled existence when first joining the service must be very bad for the boy, and makes it impossible for the Officers or Petty Officers to know anything about him or to properly look after him'.[40] The case would lead the Admiralty board to issue a weekly order in early January 1914 about discouraging 'the frequent change of ships in the case of boys' to prevent boys from becoming 'seriously demoralised'.[41] In the case of the four defendants, the court martial board had initially recommended that offenders receive ninety days' imprisonment with hard labour and dismissal with disgrace. Though charges were proven for all defendants, sentencing took a different course. Two of the men received sentences of two years' imprisonment, Sutton received a three-year prison term and Herbert was awarded the maximum of five years' penal servitude, indicating that the board saw him more as the provocateur of the crime rather than as its unfortunate victim.

The Herbert case also caused enough alarm within the Admiralty for it to issue a confidential memorandum entitled 'Unnatural Offences' in December 1913, which was circulated to the commanding officers in the fleet.[42] The Admiralty strongly advised that officers attend to the 'moral well-being of the ship's companies' by emphasising 'the horrible character of unnatural vice and its evil effects in sapping the moral fibre of those who indulge in it', as well as the physical dangers to those who submitted themselves 'to the desire of vicious men'.[43] In addition, the Admiralty advocated for a clearer classification of crimes of indecent relations involving men. Where charges of assault could not be proved but the presence of venereal disease suggested intimate male relations, the Admiralty suggested that officers bring forth charges of 'uncleanliness' that would lead to a sailor's dismissal from service. Since the sentences were so grave, the Admiralty also cautioned officers to conduct thorough investigations and to be wary of potential problems where the case rested upon the testimony of one witness or the possibility of blackmail existed. The Admiralty's reliance upon ship's officers and medical staff to oversee more vigilantly the sexual behaviours of naval men aboard ship represented a shift in dealing with the problem, suggesting that the Admiralty increasingly perceived that indecency was a more prevalent problem than it had previously admitted and that recourse to court martial was ineffective in preventing such incidents.

An examination of these court martial cases and the returns reveals a world not only distant to modern readers but in many ways distant to the Admiralty boards that reviewed the cases. Although the nature and length of sentencing lessened by the Edwardian period, anxieties had not abated and the consequences remained severe. While the Admiralty warned in 1913 that the dangers of 'unnatural vice' would sap the 'moral fibre' of the men who 'indulged', the message could also be taken as a eugenicist harbinger that sodomy's spread had the power to 'sap' the efficiency of the entire fleet, and ultimately the Empire, if it were left unchecked. A decade of cases revealed to the Admiralty that boy ratings were crucial to stemming the spread of this immoral pathogen. In the 1902 *St Vincent* cases, the Admiralty understood that boys on training ships could need protection from attack from potentially predatory petty officers afloat or civilians ashore. Ten years later, the *Gloucester* cases led Admiralty officials to believe that entrepreneurial boys, misled in their training, were now the catalyst for vice as they engaged ratings afloat for profit in exchange for sex. The brazen confession of Herbert in the *Gloucester* case likely unhinged Admiralty officials who worried that a sodomitical culture involving naval boy ratings as 'rent boys' might be more prevalent throughout the fleet. However, the involvement of boys in these cases was most often as victims of assault. As courts-martial returns revealed, boy ratings were more likely to be named within the charges of a sodomitical offence brought before a court martial between 1900 and 1913. Yet it remained difficult throughout the period for the Admiralty to distinguish between consent and coercion.

Notes

1 See Arthur N. Gilbert, 'The *Africaine* Courts Martial: A Study of Buggery and the Royal Navy', *Journal of Homosexuality*, 1 (1976), 111–22; and 'Buggery and the British Navy, 1700–1861', *Journal of Social History*, 10 (1976), 72–98.
2 Among the long list of scholarship on courts martial and naval sodomy, see

Hans Turley, *Rum, Sodomy, and the Lash* (New York: New York University Press, 1999); Isaac Land, '"Sinful Propensities": Piracy, Sodomy, and the Empire in the Rhetoric of Naval Reform, 1770–1870' in Anupama Rao and Steven Pierce (eds), *Discipline and the Other Body: Correction, Corporeality, Colonialism* (Durham, NC: Duke University Press, 2006), pp. 90–114; B. R. Burg, *Boys at Sea: Sodomy, Incest, and Courts Martial in Nelson's Navy* (New York: Palgrave Macmillan, 2007); Seth S. LeJacq, 'Buggery's Travels: Royal Navy Sodomy on Ship and Shore in the Long Eighteenth Century', *Journal for Maritime Research*, 17:2 (2015), 103–16. Matthew Seligman's recently published *Rum, Sodomy, Prayers and the Lash* (Oxford: Oxford University Press, 2018) appeared too late to incorporate into this study.
3 For a review of recent literature on gendered maritime history, see the introductory essay by Quintin Colville, Elin Jones and Katherine Parker, 'Gendering the Maritime World', *Journal for Maritime Research*, 17:2 (2015), 97–101. For gender's impact upon the broader field of British imperial history, see Philippa Levine (ed.), *Gender and Empire* (Oxford: Oxford University Press, 2004). For a sophisticated primer on the history of sexuality, see Matt Houlbrook and Harry Cocks (eds), *Palgrave Advances in the Modern History of Sexuality* (Basingstoke: Palgrave Macmillan, 2005).
4 N. A. M. Rodger, *The Wooden World: An Anatomy of the Georgian Navy* (New York: Norton, 1986), pp. 80–1.
5 Isaac Land, 'The Many-Tongued Hydra: Sea Talk, Maritime Culture, and Atlantic Identities, 1700–1850', *Journal of American and Comparative Cultures*, 25 (2002), 412–17; Quintin Colville, 'Enacted and Re-enacted in Life and Letters: The Identity of Jack Tar, 1930 to Date', *Journal for Maritime Research*, 18:1 (2016), 37–53; Andrew S. Thompson, *Writing Imperial Histories* (Manchester: Manchester University Press, 2016); Brad Beaven, Karl Bell and Robert James (eds), *Port Towns and Urban Cultures: International Histories of the Waterfront, c. 1700–2000* (New York: Palgrave Macmillan, 2016).
6 Philippa Levine, 'Sexuality and Empire' in Catherine Hall and Sonya O. Rose (eds), *At Home with the Empire: Metropolitan Culture and the Imperial World* (Cambridge: Cambridge University Press, 2006), pp. 139–40.
7 LeJacq, 'Buggery's Travels', 105.
8 The National Archives (hereafter TNA), ADM 1/7578 1902, 'HMS *St. Vincent*, cases of syphilis amongst boys'.
9 *Ibid.*, 11 February 1902.
10 *Ibid.*, 31 March 1902.
11 *Ibid.* In reality, syphilis can remain infectious in its latent dormant stages. See 'Syphilis-CDC Fact Sheet' from https://www.cdc.gov/std/syphilis/stdfact-syphilis-detailed.htm (accessed 1 December 2017).
12 Christopher McKee, *Sober Men and True: Sailor Lives in the Royal Navy, 1900–1945* (Cambridge, MA: Harvard University Press, 2002); Paul Baker and Jo Stanley, *Hello Sailor: The Hidden History of Gay Life at Sea* (London:

Longman, 2003), and more recently, Matt Houlbrook, *Queer London: Perils and Pleasures in the Sexual Metropolis, 1918–1957* (Chicago: University of Chicago Press, 2006).

13 H. G. Cocks, *Nameless Offences: Homosexual Desire in the Nineteenth Century* (London: I.B.Tauris, 2003), pp. 114–54.

14 John Tosh, *Manliness and Masculinities in Nineteenth-Century Britain: Essays on Gender, Family and Empire* (Harlow: Pearson, Longman, 2005), p. 43.

15 Imperial War Museum (hereafter IWM) Sound Archive, *Oral History Recordings: Lower Deck, 1910–22*, 1982.

16 For an overview of these interviews see McKee, *Sober Men and True*, pp. 192–204.

17 Laura Rowe, '"Step This Way, Please!": Gender Transgression and Normative Behaviour in the Royal Navy in the Early Twentieth Century', unpublished paper delivered at Northeast Conference on British Studies, Storrs, Connecticut, October 2013. Also see her book *Morale and Discipline in the Royal Navy during the First World War* (Cambridge: Cambridge University Press, 2018), which was published after the chapter's completion.

18 'Charles II, 1661: An Act for the Establishing Articles and Orders for the regulateing and better Government of His Majesties Navies Ships of Warr & Forces by Sea', in *Statutes of the Realm*, vol. 5: *1628–80*, ed. John Raithby (s.l, 1819), p. 313. *British History Online*: http://www.british-history.ac.uk/statutes-realm/vol5/pp311–314 (accessed 3 August 2018).

19 Gilbert, 'Buggery and the Royal Navy', p. 85. Initially directing sentences of at least three years penal servitude, the Naval Discipline Act was amended in 1865 to require not less than five years' imprisonment. See Eugene Rasor, *Reform in the Royal Navy: A Social History of the Lower Deck, 1850 to 1880* (Hamden, CT: Archon, 1976), p. 117; Theodore Thring, *A Treatise on the Criminal Law of the Navy* (London: Stevens & Sons, 1877), p. 235.

20 Michel Foucault, *History of Sexuality*, vol. 1: *An Introduction*, trans. Robert Hurley (New York: Vintage Books, 1980); Randolph Trumbach, 'Modern Sodomy: The Origins of Homosexuality, 1700–1800' in Matt Cook (ed.), *A Gay History of Britain: Love and Sex between Men since the Middle Ages* (Oxford: Greenwood Press, 2007), pp. 77–105; Isaac Land, 'Sinful Propensities', pp. 90–114.

21 See H. G. Cocks, 'Trials of Character: The Use of Character Evidence in Victorian Sodomy Trials' in R. A. Melikan (ed.), *Domestic and International Trials, 1700–2000*, vol. 2 (Manchester: Manchester University Press, 2003), p. 38; Cocks, *Nameless Offences*, p. 31.

22 Cocks, *Nameless Offences*, p. 17.

23 Sean Brady, *Masculinity and Male Homosexuality in Britain, 1861–1913* (Basingstoke: Palgrave Macmillan, 2005), p. 12.

24 See George Chauncey, *Gay New York: Gender, Urban Culture and the Making of the Gay Male World, 1890–1940* (New York: Basic Books, 1994), p. 97.

25 Houlbrook, *Queer London*, p. 7.
26 Mckee, *Sober Men and True*, p. 194; Albert A. Heron, Leading Seaman, 000681/20, IWM Sound Archive.
27 *Return of Naval Courts-Martial* (London: HMSO, 1900–13), accessed from the Admiralty Library in Portsmouth (my appreciation to Laura Rowe for alerting me to the library's complete collection of returns).
28 LeJacq, 'Buggery's Travels', p. 105; and research from Rowe, 'Step This Way'.
29 Nine of the thirteen charges for gross indecency came in 1912 and 1913. See *Return of Naval Courts-Martial*; William Hickman, *A Treatise on the Law and Practice of Naval Courts-Martial* (London: John Murray, 1851), p. 168. Hickman noted, 'It is a rule that "every indictment must charge a man with a particular offence, and not with being an offender in general"'.
30 *Return of Naval Courts-Martial*, p. 3.
31 See *Return of Naval Courts-Martial*: around forty of the forty-eight individuals tried for sodomy were charged alongside another individual.
32 TNA, ADM 1/7608, 'Courts Martial for the trial of Walter Cannell, AB of HMS *Northumberland* also William John Vincent, Stoker HMS Northumberland, 26 March 1902'.
33 TNA, ADM 1/7608, William Vincent's testimony from courts martial, line 152.
34 TNA, ADM 1/7608.
35 See *Return of Naval Courts-Martial*: of the twenty-three cases where no rank of the victim was named, four more cases are likely to have involved a boy because the ship of the defendant was a training ship.
36 Albert Heron and James Cox, IWM Sound Archive.
37 TNA, ADM 1/7537, 'Minutes of Court Martial held on G. R. Murphy, Sick Berth Attendant, HMS *Duke of Wellington*, 14 June 1901'.
38 TNA, ADM 156/9, 'Court Martial on Charles Henry Herbert, Boy First Class, 18 September 1913'.
39 *Ibid.*
40 *Ibid.*
41 TNA, ADM 156/9, weekly order, 788, 9 January 1914.
42 TNA, ADM 105/104/NL5773, circular letter 'Unnatural Offences', 18 December 1913.
43 TNA, ADM 105/104, secret circular letter, N.L. 5773, 18 December 1913.

4

Navy, nation and empire: nineteenth-century photographs of the British naval community overseas

Cindy McCreery

This volume provides a timely opportunity to reconsider how we define and approach British naval history. Ships and war are of course a fundamental part of this history, but so too are people – civilians as well as officers and sailors. This is particularly true in periods of 'peace', such as the second half of the nineteenth century, when the Royal Navy depended on a diverse range of personnel on the spot as much as its warships to manage local relations. The navy thus needs to be understood from the perspectives of these individual officers, sailors and civilians on foreign stations as much as those based in Britain, and on junior as well as senior staff. Examining how these diverse individuals constituted naval communities overseas and how these functioned (their leisure pursuits as well as their work routines) provides further insight into the navy's day-to-day operation as well as its impact on the wider world. This chapter provides a further step in this direction.

Why photographs? Jan Morris's evocative study of Admiral Jacky Fisher, perhaps the most iconoclastic as well as influential British naval officer of the late nineteenth and early twentieth centuries, begins with a photograph. In *Fisher's Face: Or Getting to Know the Admiral*, Morris recalls how, in the late 1940s, seeing a studio portrait photograph of the admiral sparked a forty-year quest to understand Fisher the man as well as the officer.[1] Morris's discussion of Fisher and his fellow naval officers, sailors and auxiliary members of the naval community (wives, children, civilian employees) helps us better understand the Edwardian navy. In turn, it provides a model of how we might use photographs to help us comprehend the cultural world of the Victorian navy. Most importantly, though, photographs deserve attention because they mattered to the nineteenth-century naval community.

From the development of photography in the late 1840s, photographs became an important means of both recording nineteenth-century naval life and communicating it to others. This chapter employs photographs taken mostly at Simon's Town, South Africa, in the 1860s to trace the links between Victorian naval officers and the wider community. It is based largely on photographs from two nineteenth-century albums, produced for and by individual families. One is the most famous family of the age – Britain's royal family – while the other, the Waymouth family, is more obscure.[2] Thanks to the increased digitisation of family records and the work of amateur as well as professional historians, the histories of even 'ordinary' naval families such as the Waymouths can now be studied alongside the more famous Windsors; then known as the Saxe-Coburg-Gothas. What is missing from much family history, however, is a comparative approach, and this chapter pays attention to the similarities as well as differences between the photograph albums to make broader claims about the naval community.

In his influential book *Queen Victoria: First Media Monarch*, John Plunkett emphasised the significance and sophistication of the Queen's engagement with the new media of the nineteenth century, including photography.[3] Queen Victoria and her husband Prince Albert were quick to realise the value of portrait photography as one tool for promoting loyalty among their subjects. They also employed photography to record private family moments, and several members of their family, including their second son Prince Alfred, Duke of Edinburgh (1844–1900), became keen photographers in their own right. Yet Alfred's use of photography, and indeed Alfred himself, remain virtually unknown. This is curious, for nineteenth-century audiences, particularly those overseas, had plenty of opportunities to see Alfred. When he sailed around the world in HMS *Galatea* from 1867 to 1871, more people saw Alfred than ever set eyes on his mother, father or siblings.[4] Through visual representations such as paintings, lithographs and, in particular, photographs, Alfred's image reached even more viewers.

Nineteenth-century Royal Naval officers' use of photography is even less familiar to us today. Certainly there has been important scholarship on nineteenth-century photography and its links with the British Empire. James R. Ryan has drawn our attention to the ways in which various agents of empire, such as the Royal Corps of Engineers in Abyssinia in 1867 and Christian missionaries in India, used photography to both extend and justify their own particular versions of British imperialism.[5] So too there has been some attention from historians of photography, although this tends to focus on the work of individual professional photographers, for example the itinerant British photographer John Thomson, who did so much to introduce mid to late nineteenth-century British audiences to scenes of Siam (now Thailand) and China. Later, Thomson introduced these same audiences to another exotic urban scene – the streets of London. Felice Beato performed a similar function in Japan and India, though he also rewrote (or rather, rephotographed) history by recreating, and embellishing, scenes from the Indian Rebellion of 1857.[6]

Yet if nineteenth-century photography within the British Empire and Asia more generally has received some scholarly attention, photography within the nineteenth-century Royal Navy has received much less. Here scholars could learn from the authors of popular histories who have done much to record and reproduce historical photographs of the Royal Navy. These well-illustrated volumes make clear just how often the Royal Navy was a subject of photography in the nineteenth century. In turn, this provides some evidence, though it is usually little commented on, of Royal Naval personnel's own interest in photography.[7] Royal Naval officers were in fact early and eager adaptors of photographic technology, both within and beyond the British Empire. A recent volume on the history of early Western photography in China acknowledges the important role played by individual junior British naval officers, for instance lieutenants, in taking many of the first known photographs of Chinese port cities.[8] But it does so only in passing, without really considering why naval officers turned to photography and what this practice tells us about the navy itself. Conversely, histories of naval bases often include historic photographs but comment little on the production of these images – who took them, for what purpose, and where were they displayed?[9]

Naval officers' use of photography can be understood, in part, as a logical extension of their training in the art of observation. Midshipmen and other junior officers were taught to look closely at land formations and sea and weather conditions. They were expected to keep detailed logbooks which not only recorded the ship's passage but included detailed sketches of land elevations, harbour entrances and other features. These logbooks frequently contained extra material, including sketches of ports and their inhabitants as well as shipmates, both on and off duty.[10] So too, some naval officers began to photograph such scenes, albeit for private, not official, use. By the mid-nineteenth century, Royal Naval personnel were regular visitors to at least the coastal areas of all six inhabited continents – and some visited Antarctica. Officers with the requisite funds to purchase equipment and receive training in its use (and it must be stressed that this was a tiny minority until the invention of cheaper and simpler cameras at the end of the century made photography a popular middle-class hobby) photographed not only the places they visited, but people. In particular, they photographed themselves and their fellow officers (less often ordinary sailors, except as part of a group on the deck of a warship) as well as family members aboard ship and ashore.

If taking photographs of landscapes or ports from a distance was in some ways just another way for naval officers to keep a logbook, or create casual souvenirs, taking (or, much more often, purchasing) photographs of people close to them implies additional meaning. In her classic study *On Photography*, Susan Sontag notes that: 'memorializing the achievements of individuals considered as members of families (as well as of other groups) is the earliest popular use of photography'.[11] Naval communities are an excellent example of 'individuals considered as members of families'. More than most nineteenth-century workers, naval officers and sailors lived and socialised 'on the job', with years at a time spent aboard ship and on foreign stations. Such physical isolation from their own families and home communities was extreme even by the standards of mass European migration. This also made relations with officers and civilians abroad all the more meaningful – a substitute family. Photographs provided a convenient and durable means of recording these relationships.

Most nineteenth-century photographs of naval officers (and, indeed ordinary sailors, who became keen consumers of individual photographs to send to family members) were taken in commercial photographic studios by professional photographers. At major bases such as Halifax and Malta, local firms specialised in naval photographs. Two decades after his visit to the Cape, Prince Alfred, now commander-in-chief of the Mediterranean Fleet based in Malta, appointed the Ellis family 'Photographers to the Fleet'.[12] While many photographs depict naval officers in some version of their naval uniform – from the smart 'dress' uniform worn on ceremonial occasions to the everyday long coats and caps worn aboard ship, others show them in civilian dress, occasionally sporting local and/or exotic accoutrements.[13] James E. Bowly of HMS *Racoon* is depicted in his sub-lieutenant's uniform in photographs in the Wits Album taken at Simon's Town in 1867. A few years later, after his promotion to lieutenant, Bowly features in another, very different photograph. Here Bowly wears a three-piece suit, plus thick fur gloves and fur hat and stands, along with a similarly dressed lieutenant from

Figure 3   Lieutenant Bowly and Lieutenant Bridges, R.N., 1870–2

another Royal Navy ship, next to a bearskin, in a photograph taken in the Notman Studio in Halifax, Nova Scotia.

But even in small naval bases like Simon's Town, photographs played an important role in helping to define and record the naval community. Both

Figure 4 Officers of HMS *Racoon*, 1859–61

sailors and officers sat for individual carte-de-visite portraits in Cape Town studios like Lawrence & Selkirk. Copies were sent to family and friends 'at home' as well as exchanged with local friends and colleagues – including crews of visiting foreign warships. Group photographs were also taken. The Wits Album described below contains a series of twenty-three individual carte-de-visite portraits, each depicting one or two officers, which have been pasted together over two pages of the album to form a group. Headings in the album indicate that this depicts 'Officers H.M.S. "Racoon" – 1859–1861'.[14] One photograph includes an officer, J. Bremner, with a woman who was probably his wife; another depicts the wife of the captain (Captain J. A. Paynter was depicted separately in another photograph on the next page); and two photographs show the same dog lying at an officer's feet. The overall impression is of a close-knit group, which included women and pets, who turned to photography to memorialise their community.

Other group photographs were taken outdoors, especially on board ship. Indeed, group photographs of officers, sometimes with sailors and often with pets such as dogs, arranged on the quarterdeck of a warship, became an iconic means of commemorating a ship's commission.[15] Finally, group photographs were taken outside in or near the grounds of overseas naval stations, often near a recognisable landmark. In Simon's Town, for example, photographs were often taken on the verandah or on the lawns surrounding Admiralty House. The Wits Album includes a photograph of a man, woman and child (perhaps Silas Waymouth, his wife Jane and young son Arthur) sitting on a bench just outside Admiralty House.[16] As well as a place where Royal Navy officers entertained visiting officers and dignitaries such as Prince Alfred, Admiralty House and its environs appears to have functioned as a space where naval officers and their families could relax whilst off duty – or at least served as an attractive venue for photographs.[17] Outdoor photography was technically more difficult as well as more expensive than studio photography. It required specialist equipment, training (or else the funds to pay professional photographers) and time – the latter perhaps more available to naval officers on overseas stations in peacetime than to many others.

But just as important as the fact that naval officers commissioned and took photographs of the naval community is what they did with them. In addition to being exchanged with or posted to colleagues (including officers from foreign navies), friends and relations, naval photographs were often preserved in albums.[18] Sometimes these albums were devoted to a single naval career, or even, a single voyage; other albums displayed naval photographs as part of a broader family history.[19] Wives and daughters appear to have played an important role in creating and arranging albums, which often included not only photographs but sketches and dried plants. Moreover, elite women often acted as local hostesses, entertaining visiting naval officers and including them within family gatherings. An album in the State Library of South Australia made up by Caroline Louisa Turton, the daughter of Sir Dominick Daly, governor of South Australia 1862–8, and his wife Caroline Maria (née Gore) provides a good example.[20] It is inscribed in pencil: 'Mother's book of Naval friends when in S. Australia, officers of the Galatea &c – Prince Alfred, Queen Victoria's son who visited Adelaide in HMS "'Galatea" in Nov 1867'. In addition to photographs of these distinguished naval visitors, the album contains cartes-de-visite of wives of officers as well as Turton's husband's relatives serving in the Royal Navy.[21] Such albums reveal the great overlap between nineteenth-century family and naval life. In turn these albums were often passed down through the generations, and many remain today in family collections. Arranging photographs in albums (including in sections organised by career posting, for example by ship command and/or naval base) signals the importance of these people and places to naval officers. It helped them to retain connections with people over vast segments of both space and time, and, in later life, served as an aide-mémoire for themselves, their family and friends to reflect on a busy and well-connected naval career.

Two naval photograph albums, what I call here the Windsor and Wits Albums, help to illuminate this naval community in the 1860s.[22] While these albums display important and revealing differences, they share a focus on the Royal Naval community in and around Simon's Town, South Africa. While they are remarkable in some ways – the Windsor for the quality of its photographs and the Wits for the number and variety of naval photographs – both are broadly representative of the many other photograph albums compiled by naval officers in the second half of the nineteenth century.

As my name for it suggests, the Windsor Album is very much a royal album. It was created on the instructions of Prince Alfred, Duke of Edinburgh, and was presented to his mother, Queen Victoria, as a birthday present in 1869.[23] It depicts Alfred's first global voyage in HMS *Galatea* from 1867–8. In mid-1867, the *Galatea* left Portsmouth and visited Gibraltar, Marseille, Madeira, Brazil, Tristan da Cunha and the Cape of Good Hope, as well as the Australian colonies, before returning to Portsmouth in June 1868.[24] This and the subsequent voyages, which lasted until 1871, took Alfred and the rest of the 540-member crew around the world and served as an important prototype for later British royal tours.[25] While Alfred's royal status certainly gave him special treatment in the places he visited (everyone he met was aware that he was Queen Victoria's second son), Alfred's role as captain of HMS *Galatea* was no mere courtesy title. Alfred had entered the navy as a fourteen-year-old in 1858 and served as a professional naval officer for thirty-five years, attaining the highest rank in the navy, admiral of the fleet, in 1893. Only with the death that year of his uncle, Ernst II, did Alfred reluctantly leave the navy, and Britain, to become Duke of Saxe-Coburg and Gotha in Germany. Throughout the *Galatea* voyages, Alfred saw himself, and was seen by others, as a professional naval officer as well as a prince.

The second album, here called the Wits Album because it is held in the historical papers section of the William Cullen Memorial Library at the University of the Witwatersrand ('Wits') in Johannesburg, South Africa, is not a royal album. Yet there are numerous royal references within it, starting with the highly collectable carte-de-visite photographs of members of various continental European royal families as well as photographs of and by Prince Alfred himself.[26] The album is better understood, though, as a naval family album, compiled probably by Silas Waymouth and his family, who were based at Simon's Town in the late 1860s.

Silas Waymouth provides another example of a distinguished nineteenth-century naval career – albeit, unlike Alfred's, not in the executive (seagoing) branch. Born the seventh son (and tenth of twelve children) of John Waymouth and Eliza (née Glanville) in Wales in 1837, Waymouth entered the accounting branch of the navy in 1853 and was promoted to paymaster in 1866. He served as secretary to commanders-in-chief and other officers at Royal Navy bases at the Cape of Good Hope, and in the Mediterranean and Ireland. Waymouth's career coincides with the greater professionalisation of 'civilian' officers and also a concomitant rise in status. No longer automatically associated with money-grabbing pursers who made a profit through selling goods to sailors aboard ship, the late nineteenth-century paymaster, responsible for the payment of wages, was increasingly valued as a skilled accountant. In 1867, the year of Prince Alfred's visit to Simon's Town, the navy announced 'that a Paymaster of 15 years' seniority should rank with a Commander'. Waymouth achieved this in 1881, when he held a rank equivalent to that held in Simon's Town in 1867 by Acting Commodore Richard Purvis. In 1885, Waymouth retired from the navy as fleet paymaster, and became secretary of the Orient Company, in which capacity he helped deploy its vessels as troopships during the Egyptian Campaign (1896–98) and Second South African War (1899–1902) – where his previous experience of Simon's Town no doubt came in useful. He died in Malta in 1911.[27]

Aside from the general improvement in paymasters' status, Waymouth's steady promotion within the navy suggests his high individual reputation. Waymouth apparently developed close personal ties within the

Royal Navy, both among fellow paymasters but also, significantly, with sea officers. The Wits Album is full of both individual as well as group photographs of naval officers, usually captioned below in ink with the officer's name, rank and, sometimes, the year the photograph was taken. Both junior and senior officers feature, and appear to include both colleagues Waymouth considered as personal friends (for instance, officers on the *Racoon*, or paymasters he had served with earlier) as well as officers he worked under or knew of via the global naval network. These include well-known admirals such as Rear-Admiral F. A. Campbell of the Detached Squadron, who Waymouth probably served under in Ireland, and who is depicted in a large indoor group photograph with some of his officers.[28] In addition, a page in the album is devoted to photographs of Captain H. T. Burgoyne (captain) and Captain Casper Coles (designer) along with their ship, HMS *Captain*.[29] Both men, along with most of the crew, perished when the controversially designed, top-heavy *Captain* sank in a gale on 6 September 1870. This tragedy affected the broader naval family, and as such was recorded in the journals and diaries of a diverse range of officers across the globe.[30] It is thus not surprising to find it commemorated in Waymouth's album. The death date of many individuals is handwritten under their photograph in the album. For Victorian naval officers as well as the wider population, death loomed large in their imagination – as it did in their daily lives.

If Alfred provides an example of the elite family background of many senior Royal Navy officers in the Victorian period, Waymouth provides an example of loyal service rewarded. Both men enjoyed a long and successful career in the navy and, in turn, both developed an apparently deep commitment to the service, which is illustrated in their albums. In turn, they may have inspired younger family members' naval careers; Alfred's nephews Albert Victor and George, later George V, as well as Waymouth's eldest son Arthur, served together in the navy aboard HMS *Britannia*.[31] Still, as neither the prince nor the paymaster came from aristocratic naval families like the Keppels, both men may have felt somewhat outsiders. Their perceived need to demonstrate that they 'belonged' in the service may help to explain the prominence of naval photographs within their albums.

There are important differences between the albums which naturally reflect the royal and non-royal status of their respective owners. The Windsor Album is physically much larger, has been expertly bound in expensive green leather and marbled boards and contains approximately 100 high-quality black-and-white photographs. These are mostly large, 'cabinet' size professional photographs as well as some large panoramic stock photographs, for example of the environs of Simon's Town and Cape Town, some of which fold out from the album pages.[32] Most of the photographs are captioned below in elegant copper-plate handwriting. An index of the main contents is given at the front of the album, which contributes to its professional air.[33] This was an album created as a presentation object, yet it contains images which were personally important to its creator.

The Wits Album is smaller and made of cheaper quality materials. It lacks the Windsor Album's solid provenance and records, and, like so many family albums which have become separated from their original family, we cannot be sure that it is in its original binding. It contains approximately 173 photographs, along with some pen-and-ink sketches (which often serve as section dividers) as well as a few pressed plant leaves or fronds. The photographs are mostly small and include many of the carte-de-visite portraits which became a global hit from the late 1850s until the early twentieth century.[34] Like the Windsor Album, many of the Wits Album photographs are captioned, but in ordinary cursive script, not formal calligraphy as in the Windsor Album.

Most importantly, the Wits Album appears to have been arranged somewhat piecemeal. In contrast to the Windsor Album's single focus on the first *Galatea* voyage 1867–8, with distinct start and end points and precise geographical coverage which follows the ship's itinerary from Britain to the Cape of Good Hope and then on to Australia, the Wits Album meanders. It includes both royal and naval portraits from the 1850s to the 1870s, as well as landscape scenes and ship portraits corresponding to naval tours of duty at Simon's Town, Malta and the west coast of Ireland. This corresponds to what we know of Silas Waymouth's service at the Cape of Good Hope naval station, with the Mediterranean Fleet and the Reserve Detached Squadron in Ireland. But there are many miscellaneous photographs as well, for example portraits of European royalty, including a studio portrait of Prince Alfred wearing civilian dress, dated 1869 and taken during the *Galatea* voyage.[35] So, while the Windsor Album was designed formally to commemorate a single journey, and formed part of a broader set of visual and textual records of Alfred's *Galatea* voyage, the Wits Album was designed to record a career naval officer's interests over two decades – a substantial chunk of an entire career, and life. This album may also reflect the interests and contacts of Silas Waymouth's wife, Jane, who, like many wives and daughters, may also have had a hand in arranging the photographs and pressed plants in the album and writing the photograph captions.

Despite these differences in scope, there is much that connects these two albums. Both include many individual portraits, the small cartes-de-visite as well as larger photographs. In particular, they depict naval life at Simon's Town naval base at the time of Prince Alfred's 1867 visit there in HMS *Galatea*.[36] Simon's Town in the second half of the nineteenth century was small and somewhat isolated. The base of the Royal Navy's modest Cape of Good Hope Station, Simon's Town, in False Bay, South Africa, lacked the facilities and panache of more prominent foreign stations such as Malta, headquarters of the Mediterranean Fleet. While geographically separate from the commercial, political and population hub of Cape Town in Table Bay (over a mountain range, 22 miles distant), Simon's Town struck many visiting naval officers in the 1860s as a friendly community.[37] Certainly the albums suggest the effort naval officers went to make their own time there, and that of visitors, enjoyable.

Naval sociability is at the heart of both albums' coverage of Simon's Town, and there is much overlap. The two albums contain almost identical photographs of several local scenes. For example, both contain versions of 'Officers of H.M.S. Racoon'.[38] This overlap between the two albums indicates the ready availability of photographs to visiting and resident naval officers in Simon's Town, as well as a shared interest in recording naval life. It also suggests a personal connection between the royal captain, Prince Alfred, and the local paymaster, Silas Waymouth.

One photograph depicts the acting head of the Cape of Good Hope station with his senior officers, including, according to the hand-written caption below some of the versions: R. M. Sperling (acting commander), J. Bowly (sub-lieutenant) and R. C. Jolliffe (flag lieutenant).[39] Another version includes 'S. Waymouth (Sec.)'.[40] Wearing naval dress uniform and arranged in a group on the verandah of Admiralty House, Simon's Town, they represent the Royal Navy on duty. But their smiles and somewhat relaxed manner, suggest that, while staged, the photograph reflects the group's colleagiality and personality. This is clearly a group of men who not only work but enjoy moments of relaxation together. That this photograph was specially commissioned (it was taken by professional photographers Lawrence & Selkirk of Cape Town) reflects its importance, at least for its first customer – perhaps Prince Alfred, Commodore Purvis or one of the other officers photographed. Moreover, the fact that multiple versions of this photograph exist, in both the Wits and Windsor Albums, suggests that it mattered to Prince Alfred and Silas Waymouth. Numerous similar examples of shared photographs of Simon's Town officers exist, including

Commodore Purvis and Four Officers of H.M.S. "Racoon".

The "Signalman". Cape Town

Commodore Purvis &c with Signalman.

The "Racoon" and "Galatea" in Simons Bay

Commodore Purvis

Figure 5 Officers of HMS *Racoon*

one showing Alfred with Acting Commodore Purvis.[41] Here photographs serve as a means of recording and maintaining naval friendships.

More than just opportunities to take photographs of groups of officers, Alfred's presence in Simon's Town allowed him to record moments of relaxation. Throughout his *Galatea* voyages, Alfred demonstrated his preference for informal social gatherings over the endless round of formal civic celebrations.[42] Just as Simon's Town represented a welcome respite from lengthy sea voyages for many Royal Navy crews, it also provided an opportunity for private recreation for Alfred. In South Africa as elsewhere on his world voyages, it was within the naval community, not the vice-regal community, where Alfred felt most at home. On his previous visit to the Cape in 1860, as a midshipman aboard HMS *Euryalus*, Alfred brought along a carte-de-visite camera, the first in the Cape. At the end of his visit he presented it as a gift to local commercial photographer Frederick York, which in turn further stimulated local photography.[43] So too, in 1867 Alfred seems to have spent a fair amount of his limited free time in Simon's Bay photographing (or having others photograph) members of the station in informal and humorous re-enactments of their naval duties. Of the thirty-nine pages of photographs of the Cape of Good Hope in the Windsor Album, almost a third (twelve) are devoted to Simon's Town, and at least three pages contain photographs taken by Prince Alfred himself. Overall, at least forty-three photographs out of 100 in the album depict the Cape, signalling the importance of this visit to Alfred.[44]

In turn, the photographs Alfred took emphasise the collegiality of the local naval community. Series of similar photographs appear on pages in both the Windsor and Wits Albums. In 'Hoisting the Affirmative', for example, naval personnel watch a black signalman (identified in other photographs as 'Charles') raise a signal flag.[45] Another image shows Acting Commodore Purvis leaning against a fence with the harbour beyond, the ships *Racoon* and *Galatea* at anchor in the background. Signalman Charles stands to the left of Purvis, his telescope apparently trained on the ships.[46]

Charles was possibly one of the 'Kroomen', members of the Kru people of Liberia in West Africa who were recruited by the Royal Navy from the late eighteenth century. Alternatively, he may have been one of the freed slaves or 'Seedies' employed by the Royal Navy in Indian Ocean ports, or else an African of other origins. By the 1860s, almost 100 Kroomen served aboard Royal Navy vessels in East Africa.[47] In Simon's Town, according to a history of Admiralty House, Kroomen were accommodated in a building near the secretary's residence – in other words Silas Waymouth's house.[48] The compact site meant that executive officers, the paymaster and Kroomen lived close to one another. One photograph in the Wits Album is captioned, from left to right: 'Admiralty Cottage in Simon's Town The Sect. Residence SW & Arthur Mrs S.W. Charles The Black Signalman.'[49] While Charles's presence in the two albums may suggests his importance within the naval community, there is another possible explanation. Contemporary albums often featured photographs of Africans and other non-white people as curiosities. In the Wits Album, for example, a page of photographs of African men and children wearing native dress (or, in one case, only trousers) appears under the derogatory heading 'Kafirs'.[50] On two other pages, a photograph of an African child was placed at the centre of a page, surrounded by conventional carte-de-visite portraits of European males. These are mostly identified as naval officers; one appears to be a very young midshipman. On the first of these pages, the African child wears what looks like a blanket; the photograph is captioned 'A South African nigger'.[51] In the other, by contrast, the child wears a white suit and carries a cane; a hat and briefcase are placed nearby. His dress recalls that of a contemporary showman.[52] It is possible that Charles may fulfil a similar exotic role in the photographs of Simon's Town naval base. But the fact that he appears well integrated into naval culture, wearing uniform and carrying out naval duties, makes it more likely that he was seen as part of, rather than apart from, the Simon's Town naval community.

The repeated reference to Charles by his first name may indicate his perceived inferior status. Like a servant or a child (e.g. 'Arthur'), Charles is distinguished in the album from local naval officers who were referred to by their surname ('Jolliffe, Sperling'), while distant officers were referred to by both first and surname and also, often, naval title ('Captain Cowper Coles'). Superior officers in Simon's Town, or distinguished visitors like Prince Alfred, were referred to their title and surname 'Commodore Purvis', 'HRH Prince Alfred'. Still, while certainly represented in an inferior position within the naval and social hierarchy, Charles was still acknowledged by name, as an individual. Jane Waymouth (*née* Sutherland Miller), wife of Silas, lacked even this acknowledgment of her individuality. She appears throughout the album as 'Mrs. S.W.'.[53] Other married women were referred to by their full surname in the album, for example 'Mrs Henderson'. But unmarried women were often identified by both first and last names, perhaps to distinguish members of the same family, for instance: 'Miss Harriet Cloete', 'Miss Bella Cloete', 'Miss Josephine

Cloete.[54] The presence of these women, along with other members of well-known Dutch (Boer) families at the Cape (e.g. Myburgh, Dupruet) suggest both the prestige associated with British naval officer circles at Simon's Town – and the fact that relations between elite Dutch and British residents were perhaps closer than historians have assumed. Explanations such as 'of Cape Town' were added in pencil to several of these entries – suggesting that details were added, perhaps at a later date, to jog viewers' memories – or to provide the necessary context for those viewers unfamiliar with the album's content. We must be cautious, however, in assuming that this, or any other photograph album, provides a full and accurate picture of local life. Many groups who we know were an important part of Simon's Town (and indeed the broader Cape community), such as 'Malays' and sailors, make no appearance in the album. We also lack precise information about who arranged these albums, and when. The Wits Album, in particular, lacks clear provenance information, and it is possible that images were added, removed or moved after the original owner's death.

Nor should we make too much, perhaps, of Alfred's photographs. Certainly they should be understood partly as a hobby – a way to pass the time whilst overseas. Photography may have been particularly appealing to Alfred when he found himself in small communities with limited entertainment options. It is perhaps significant that in Australia, his next stop after the Cape, Alfred apparently preferred to attend the theatre and enjoy other urban forms of sociability than to take photographs.[55] Still, the navy long remained important to Alfred after his interest in taking photographs seemed to wane. It is thus significant that while at the Cape Alfred chose the naval community as his photographic subject. He personally took many of the photographs of Simon's Town which ended up in the Windsor Album. By contrast, the photographs in the album recording his official visits to Government House, Cape Town, were apparently the work of others.[56] So, too, while Waymouth would almost certainly have included Alfred's photographs in his album whatever their subject (there was clearly prestige associated with photographs taken by Queen Victoria's son), their naval flavour fits with the Wits Album's wider interest in recording local naval life.

For Silas Waymouth, even more than the globe-trotting Prince Alfred, the naval community was his 'home'. As a resident rather than a visitor to Simon's Town, moreover, Waymouth's naval community included civilian local residents. A photograph of approximately twenty-eight men (in civilian dress), women and children standing and seated on the grass,

Figure 6 Photographs taken by the Duke of Edinburgh, Simon's Bay, 1867

may depict a group picnic in the environs of Simon's Town.[57] While some of the identifying captions are hard to decipher, they appear to include names of civilian as well as naval families. Indeed, the line between naval and civilian life, work and family was evidently somewhat blurred for the Waymouth family. Several group photographs in the Wits Album include Arthur, Silas Waymouth's young son. Some are individual portraits but others show Waymouth with a range of adults, an apparently welcome member of the local naval community. In the picnic photograph described above he is described as 'on Hon Chas Butterworth's shoulder'.

A page of the album devoted to photographs by Prince Alfred includes the 'Hoisting the Affirmative' photograph and the photograph of Purvis and Charles with the telescope.[58]

It also includes two photographs of young Arthur, dressed in a kilt, seated outside on the grass under a tree, next to HMS *Racoon*'s officers Sperling and Jolliffe and two puppies. This early naval camaraderie may have influenced Arthur's subsequent choice of a career and possibly even fostered a later royal connection; as we have seen, Arthur served as a naval cadet along with Prince Alfred's nephews Albert Victor and George. Arthur became a rear-admiral, and gained fame for his role in inventing the Waymouth-Cooke rangefinder used by the navy.[59]

As well as describing the broad range of members of the Simon's Town naval community, the Wits Album displays the links between past and present, natural and human history. A two-page spread provides a good example. The left-hand page includes two photographs of Simon's Town with cottages, a photograph of a sketch of Napoleon's tomb '*Valle[sic] du Tombeau*' at St Helena, one dried fern and some other remnants of plants.[60] The reference to the site of Napoleon's original tomb may have held particular reference for Silas Waymouth; more generally it was a popular tourist spot for nineteenth-century naval officers even after 1840, when Napoleon's remains were reinterred at Les Invalides in Paris. The right-hand page contains another photograph (taken, according to its mount, by the Cape Town studio Lawrence & Selkirk) of the officers of HMS *Racoon* with the names of the officers handwritten in ink underneath.[61] Near this is a photograph of the *Racoon*. A caption handwritten in pencil notes that this was the ship Alfred sailed in to shoot elephants at Knysna during his 1867 visit. A smaller photograph of another warship, HMS *Marlborough*, is placed on the right. Also included on the page are leaves from three dried plants, like the others these were possibly collected in the Simon's Town area.

While this selection and arrangement reflects the interests of the album's owners, and the dried plants may reflect a female hand, these items would also have been of interest to other naval officers. For Prince Alfred, for example, HMS *Racoon* was significant not only as the ship in which he sailed to Knysna in 1867 but as the ship in which he had been promoted to lieutenant in 1863.[62] HMS *Marlborough* was a first rate which had served as flagship of the prestigious Mediterranean Fleet from 1855 to 1864. As such, she represented the pride of the Royal Navy and an appropriate choice for a naval photograph album. So, too, images of Simon's Town would have appealed as souvenirs to both visiting and resident officers. Finally, references to the great French leader Napoleon's incarceration by the British on the island of St Helena, guarded by that ultimate defence system, the Royal Navy, were bound to please civilian as well as naval British viewers alike. This concerted effort to record and remember naval colleagues, both living and dead, speaks to the strong sense of identity which naval officers developed with colleagues, especially on overseas stations.

These two albums suggest the importance of photographs for nineteenth-century British naval officers, particularly those overseas. Purchasing, exchanging and posting individual photographs such as the small cartes-de-visite provided a ready means of keeping up with family, friends and colleagues around the world. Group photographs enabled individual ship's companies, groups of officers as well as local naval communities to be commemorated. While most naval photographs were taken indoors in professional photographic studios, some were taken outdoors, and by amateurs such as Prince Alfred. Many photographs were included in albums which were preserved within families and usually passed down to subsequent generations. Women may well have played an important role in selecting and arranging photographs, sketches and dried plants in albums, and more broadly albums help us to recover the important role women and children played in the British naval community. As we have seen, there was much overlap between the family and the naval community. The Windsor and Wits Albums reveal important differences in focus, scope and quality but they share an interest in and affection for the naval community, broadly conceived. In turn they help us to understand the interests and preoccupations of two successful yet very different types of nineteenth-century naval officer: the traditional seagoing officer and the modern paymaster of the accounting branch.

This discussion of their shared use of photographs taken during Prince Alfred's 1867 visit to Simon's Town has drawn attention to the way in which naval officers, their wives and children engaged both with other naval personnel but also civilians as part of their daily routine. Furthermore, photographs help to document attitudes to race; here, in particular, to Africans encountered both within the naval community, such as Charles the signalman, as well as more stereotyped views of 'Kafirs'. Less problematic are images of Dutch inhabitants of the Cape, who appear to have been well integrated into British social networks. Contemporary photographs thus help us to understand better the complex web of networks – with senior officers, colleagues, sailors, civilians of different racial and ethnic backgrounds, wives and children – which constituted and enriched nineteenth-century British naval life overseas. There is, of course, much more to be learned from nineteenth-century naval photographs. They deserve a closer look.

Notes

1 Jan Morris, *Fisher's Face: Or Getting to Know the Admiral* (New York: Random House, 1995), p. 10.

2 My identification of the Waymouth family as the probable creators of this photograph album has been greatly assisted by information from geneao-logical websites such as Ancestry.com and Genes Reunited.com.au, which reproduce documents such as newspaper obituaries and service records but also depend on family trees and other unique biographical information con-tributed by family historians.

3 John Plunkett, *Queen Victoria: First Media Monarch* (Oxford: Oxford University Press, 2003). See also Anne M. Lyden, with contributions by Sophie Gordon and Jennifer Green-Lewis, *A Royal Passion: Queen Victoria and Photography* (Los Angeles, CA: J. Paul Getty Museum, 2014).

4 This is the subject of my current book project, 'Queen Victoria's Sailor Son and the First Global Royal Tour: Prince Alfred's Voyages on HMS *Galatea*, 1867–71' (forthcoming).

5 James R. Ryan, *Picturing Empire: Photography and the Visualization of the British Empire* (London: Reaktion Books, 1997).

6 Anne Lacoste, with an essay by Fred Ritchin, *Felice Beato: A Photographer on the Eastern Road* (Los Angeles, CA: J. Paul Getty Museum, 2010).

7 Popular photographic histories include Basil Greenhill, *A Victorian Maritime Album: 100 Photographs from the Francis Frith Collection at the National Maritime Museum* (Cambridge: Patrick Stephens Ltd, 1974), and Wilfrid Pym Trotter, *The Royal Navy in Old Photographs* (London: J. M. Dent & Sons Ltd, 1975).

8 Terry Bennett (author), Anthony Payne and Lindsey Stewart (eds), *History of Photography in China: Western Photographers, 1861–1879* (London: Quaritch, 2010).

9 Boet Dommisse, *Admiralty House Simon's Town* (Simon's Town: J. Dommisse, 2005).

10 See, for example, National Maritime Museum (hereafter NMM), CUR/2: the logbooks of HMS *Galatea* and HMS *Hercules* kept by Midshipman Harry R. Moore.

11 Susan Sontag, *On Photography* (London: Penguin, 1977), p. 8.

12 From 1869 until the 1920s, the Notman Studio in Halifax, Nova Scotia, produced many photographs of Royal Navy officers and sailors, see

https://novascotia.ca/archives/royalnavy/ (accessed 8 July 2016); Morris, *Fisher's Face*, p. 146.

13 Nova Scotia Archives, accession no. 1983–310 40854, Notman Studio, 'Lt. Bowly & Bridges, R.N.', 1870–2, Figure 3.

14 University of the Witwatersrand, historical papers, Cape Town, photograph album, A1552, 1860–77 (hereafter Wits Album). This album is fully search-able online (www.historicalpapers.wits.ac.za), and I give the page numbers as they are listed online, e.g. 'A1552-1-01.jpg'. 'Officers H.M.S. "Racoon" – 1859–2861', A1552-1-61–62.jpg. A1552-1-61, Figure 4.

15 For a good example see: State Library of South Australia, http://collections. slsa.sa.gov.au/resource/PRG+280/1/33/244 (accessed 8 July 2016), photo-graph of officers, including Alfred, Duke of Edinburgh, on board the *Galatea*.

16 Wits Album, A1552-1-033.jpg.

17 The Simon's Town Museum (www.simonstownmuseum./com/museum/stm. htm) contains numerous examples of such photographs, and I thank the staff and volunteers for their kind assistance.

18 See Wits Album, A1552-1-026, 055 and 061.jpgs respectively. The album includes photographs of Ottoman, Russian and Swedish naval officers.

19 Naval officers sometimes filled multiple albums. See, for example, NMM, BRO/16–21 and NMM, HEN/16–19: the Brown and Henderson series of albums.

20 Marjorie Findlay, 'Daly, Sir Dominick (1798–1868)', *Australian Dictionary of Biography* (Canberra: Australian National University, 1972), http://adb.anu. edu.au/biography/daly-sir-dominick-3359/text5065 (accessed 10 July 2016).

21 State Library of South Australia, Daly Family, PRG 1513/3/1–51, 'photo-graph album relating to the visit of Alfred, Duke of Edinburgh and Naval officers to South Australia in 1867, and the visit of H.M.S. "Falcon" in April 1865'.

22 I provide a preliminary overview of these albums in my 'Telling the Story: HMS *Galatea*'s Visit to South Africa, 1867', *South African Historical Journal*, 61:4 (2009), 817–37.

23 Royal Collection Trust, Windsor (hereafter Royal Collection). The title on the volume reads: 'Cruise of Her Majesty's Ship Galatea 1867–1868 Presented by His Royal Highness the Duke of Edinburgh', and inside the date of presenta-tion is 24 May 1869. I thank senior curator Sophie Gordon and former curator Lisa Heighway for their assistance.

24 The first voyage was commemorated in a published volume written by the *Galatea*'s chaplain and illustrated by the artist who accompanied Alfred: Revd. J. Milner and O. W. Brierly, *The Cruise of HMS Galatea, Captain H.R.H. The Duke of Edinburgh, K.G., in 1867–1868* (London: W. H. Allen and Co., 1869).

25 See my *Royals on Tour: Politics, Pageantry and Colonialism* (Manchester: Manchester University Press, 2018), pp. 56–79.

26 Contemporary albums often contained cartes-de-visite of European royalty among portraits of other celebrities; see, for example, Auckland War Memorial Museum, PH-ALB-92: the Lush Album.

27 The National Archives (hereafter TNA), ADM 13/71/195, ADM/196/11/578, ADM/196/76/1154, ADM/196/79/994; Ancestry.com, 'Silas and Jane Waymouth, children and grandchildren' family tree (accessed 7 July 2016); Michael Lewis, *England's Sea Officers: The Story of the Naval Profession* (London: George Allen & Unwin, 1939), pp. 250–1.

28 Wits Album, A1552–1–083.jpg.

29 Wits Album, A1552–1–080.jpg.

30 Thus, midshipman Marcus McCausland of HMS *Liffey*, Flying Squadron, noted hearing of the loss of the *Captain* in his journal entry made in Bahia, Brazil, on 5 October 1870: Charles Fountain (ed.), 'The Cruise of the Flying Squadron 1869–1870, A Midshipman's Diary by Marcus McCausland', www.pbenyon.plus.com, 2002 (accessed 12 June 2018).

31 Royal Collection, RCIN 2584339, 'Arthur W Waymouth', 1878, albumen print.

32 The Windsor Album prints are contact prints, which indicate that they were produced using cumbersome, professional equipment – information from Sophie Gordon, private correspondence, 6 February 2009.

33 This album has also apparently been fumigated at some point. I thank Frances Dimond, former Curator of Photographs at the Royal Collection, for this information.

34 *Carte-de-visite* photographs measured 2.125×3.5 inches, and were often mounted on card measuring 2.5×4 inches. See William C. Darrah, *Cartes de Visite in Nineteenth-Century Photography* (Gettysburg, PA: Darrah-Smith Books, 1981). In the Wits Album, however, most have been cut down in size, perhaps to fit more images on the page.

35 Wits Album, A1552–1–010.jpg; A1552–1–011–13.jpg.

36 A third, de-mounted album, held in the Veste Coburg in Germany (one of Alfred's residences as Duke of Saxe-Coburg and Gotha) contains photographs from the *Galatea* tour, 1867–71. It includes two photographs from Alfred's visit to Simon's Town which are similar to photographs in the Windsor and Wits albums.

37 See, for example, McCausland, 'Flying Squadron', 3 and 8 October 1869. So, too, the officers and crew of the Confederate raider CSS *Alabama* enjoyed their visit in 1863, see Dommisse, *Admiralty House*, p. 32. For other naval officers' responses, see McCreery, 'Telling the Story', and S. M. Jones, *Personal Accounts of Visitors to Simon's Town, 1770–1899* (Cape Town: University of Cape Town School of Librarianship, 1964).

38 This is folio 26 in the Windsor Album, and A1552–1–031.jpg in the Wits Album (Figure 5).

39 The commander-in-chief of the station was Commodore Henry Caldwell. A photograph in the album notes that he died in 1868. From approximately

late June 1867, he was recorded as sick and presumably absent, see NMM, WQB/14, Purvis, captain's letter book, 'Transmitted Quarterly & Half Yearly returns to 30 June 1867 … Cap. Ricd Purvis Senior Officer. Commdore Sick', 5 July 1867. Several photographs of Caldwell (in civilian dress as well as naval uniform), his wife and young child appear in the Wits Album, suggesting a close personal as well as professional relationship with Silas Waymouth.

40 Wits Album, A1552-1-035.jpg.

41 Royal Collection, Windsor Album, folio 25.

42 See Cindy McCreery, 'Two Victorias? Prince Alfred, Queen Victoria and Melbourne, 1867–68' in Robert Aldrich and Cindy McCreery (eds), *Crowns and Colonies: European Monarchies and Overseas Empires* (Manchester: Manchester University Press, 2016), pp. 51–76.

43 Marjorie Bull and Joseph Denfield, *Secure the Shadow: The Story of Cape Photography from Its Beginnings to the End of 1870* (Cape Town: Terence McNally, 1970), p. 77.

44 This is the only section of the Windsor Album which contains photographs labelled as having been taken by Prince Alfred. Most of the photographs appear to have been taken by professional photographers, or possibly Alfred's friend Lord Newry (see note 56).

45 Royal Collection, Windsor Album, folio 26; Wits Album, A1552-1-021, 32.jpg; and see McCreery, 'Telling the Story'.

46 Royal Collection, Windsor Album, folio 26; Wits Album, A1552-1-032.jpg.

47 Daniel Owen Spence, *A History of the Royal Navy: Empire and Imperialism* (London and New York: I.B.Tauris, 2015), p. 54.

48 Dommisse, *Admiralty House*, p. 143.

49 Wits Album, A1552-1-043.jpg.

50 Wits Album, A1552-1-067.jpg.

51 Wits Album, A1552-1-016.jpg.

52 Wits Album, A1552-1-040.jpg.

53 Jane Waymouth may well have written the captions for the photographs in this album, which may explain these brief references to herself. Similarly, Silas Waymouth is identified as 'S. W.' throughout the Wits Album.

54 See, for example, Wits Album, A1552-1-025.jpg.

55 There are numerous photographs of Alfred's visit to Australia in the Windsor Album, but none of them were apparently taken by Alfred.

56 Some photographs taken at Government House, Cape Town, may have been taken by Alfred's friend and travel companion Lord Newry. See McCreery, 'Telling the Story', endnote 39.

57 Wits Album, A1552-1-046.jpg.

58 The page is captioned in pencil 'Photographed by H.R.H. the Duke of Edinburgh Simons Bay Novr. [*sic*] 1867'. In fact, Alfred was at Simon's Town on and off between mid-August and early October 1867. Wits Album, A1552-1-032.jpg (Figure 6).

59 TNA, ADM/196/20/458, ADM/196/42/139, ADM/196/87/137. Arthur's younger brothers Ernest and Charles, born after the family left the Cape, became majors in the army; Ancestry, 'Silas and Jane Waymouth'.
60 Wits Album, A1552–1–030.jpg.
61 Wits Album, A1552–1–031.jpg.
62 Milner and Brierly, *Cruise of HMS Galatea*, p. 59.

5

Salt water in the blood: race, indigenous naval recruitment and British colonialism, 1934–41

Daniel Owen Spence

First World War centenary commemorations have attempted to raise greater awareness and recognition of the important contribution that colonial servicemen played in that conflict. Another significant anniversary has been overshadowed, however – the seventy-five years since the start of the Second World War, which witnessed an even greater participation from Britain's colonial empire in services beyond the army. Excepting the imperial jewel, India, not until 1933 was the first locally manned Asian or African naval force established, followed within eight years by another fourteen other British colonies, protectorates and mandate territories who would contribute over 40,000 men to the naval war effort.[1] Yet this element of Britain's Senior Service continues to be overlooked by the historiography.

Their formation was a response to internal as much as external threats to British imperial power during the 1930s. Growing nationalism meant local naval forces served as bulwarks for preserving imperial prestige and colonial order, fortifying the empire physically and psychologically. Imperial discourses of power proliferated from the late nineteenth century, influenced by anthropological studies of indigenous peoples, to provide a moral and ideological justification for a British colonialism built upon systems of racial hierarchy and control. Colonial naval forces were indoctrinated in these discourses, with ideas of 'Anglo-Saxonism' and 'Orientalism' delineating a chain of command where paternalistic British officers instructed 'native' ratings as part of a 'civilising mission' to 'develop' the 'character' of a 'modern' navy.[2] Martial race theory, where certain ethnic groups were considered naturally predisposed to military service, heavily influenced colonial army organisation after the 1857

Indian Uprising. It served to divide and rule by promoting imperially loyal ethnic groups over anti-colonial ones. For naval recruiters, a distinctive 'seafaring race' theory evolved around maritime semantics but with a similar imperial purpose. Utilising transnational research that reconciles official records with subaltern sources from across the Caribbean, South and South-East Asia, this chapter examines the intersections between indigenous and European histories, maritime communities and naval culture, the discourses of power and identities that emerged from these relationships, and their impact upon colonial societies and imperial power at the twilight of the British Empire.

From the mid-nineteenth century, British recruitment of indigenous soldiers for its colonial armies became shaped by what was termed 'martial race' theory. This racial discourse of power contributed to Britain's 'colonisation of the mind',[3] legitimising the acquisition of empire upon the basis that the British had earned the right to rule in India by defeating the conquering races that formed the martial classes there, considered to be among the best natural soldiers in the world. This, by extension, confirmed Britain's status as the pre-eminent military power.[4] The rise of this theory following the 1857 uprising, when 'martial' became a byword for those Indians who had remained loyal to the British, has advanced David Killingray's argument that the belief that 'certain peoples or societies had a special capacity for military service – was largely a colonial construct'.[5] In response, Douglas Peers has shown that depictions of martial Indians were actually in evidence as early as thirty years before the rebellion had even taken place.[6] British officers serving in the Indian Army, such as George MacMunn, whose book *The Martial Races of India* helped disseminate the theory beyond the subcontinent, were 'invested in the truth of the martial race ideology'[7] as, for them, this was experiential knowledge gained from their operations on the ground, not an imperial imagining imposed by officialdom.[8]

Instead of being passive subjects of this theory, colonial peoples exerted agency to shape their own identities and take advantage of the opportunities that being perceived as martial races opened up to them. The work of David Omissi lends credence to the importance of indigenous military heritages by showing the 'customs and self-image of Indian communities who had a martial tradition quite independent of the colonial encounter'.[9] The majority of ethnic groups who were recorded by the colonial, military and anthropological authorities as exhibiting martial characteristics were already aware of this and believed in their own fighting abilities, based upon personal or collective participation in past battles.

These exploits were celebrated, and possibly exaggerated, in order to gain access to the economic and social benefits offered by colonial military service. This has been described as 'Gurkha syndrome' by Cynthia Enloe, where impoverished rural communities developed reputations for strong military discipline, as otherwise they would lose access to one of the few avenues for employment available to them.[10] It was thus in the interests of all parties, the army, colonial administrators, and the 'martial races' themselves, to develop and live up to that identity, resulting in what has been described by John M. Mackenzie as 'a circular, self-replicating effect' in which 'supposed martial races became more warlike precisely because it was expected of them'.[11]

This pressure to perform also originated from the indigenous community below the colonial apparatus, as recalled by Jaswant Singh Gill, the first Sikh to join the Malayan Royal Naval Volunteer Reserve and inaugural commander of Singapore's post-colonial navy:

> I'm from the Punjab ... My grandfather was the ADC [aide-de-camp] to King George V, my grandfather fought in the First World War, my uncles fought in the Second World War ... as a community, we are a martial race ... it comes naturally to us ... Our community says you are a martial race ... you are a soldier, you fight ... The British never said 'you are a martial race' and therefore you become a martial race ... we were already a martial race, the only thing the British realised was that we were a martial race ... soldiering comes to us naturally.[12]

In her own book on martial races, Heather Streets argued that: 'the power of martial race ideology stemmed from its very flexibility and ambiguity: it was adaptable to a variety of historical and geographical situations and functioned alternatively to inspire, intimidate, exclude, and include'.[13] The experience of Jaswant Singh Gill shows that this geographic fluidity transcended the terrestrial boundary of the coast, begging the question of how martial race theory was applied to serve the very distinct nautical requirements of colonial navies. John M. MacKenzie has even suggested that while 'we are all familiar in imperial history with the theory of martial races ... what of the notion of maritime races?'.[14] This idea is supported by scholarship examining Kru naval service on the West African coast,[15] and the maritime employment of South Asian Lascars in the Indian and Pacific Oceans,[16] while Frances Steel has shown that in early twentieth-century India, stokers who 'belonged to the northern and warlike races' impressed the Mercantile Marine Committee 'with their manly character'. As mercantile ships were likely to be requisitioned for fighting forces, questions of loyalty and strength were paramount.[17]

There was a limit to how useful 'martial races' could be for the navy, however. While colonial naval recruiters were still influenced by this ideology, they naturally had a preference for coastal communities who had a long tradition of working the sea, which gave them not just the skills but a culture of seafaring, compared to the more rural martial races. The relationship with the natural environment was thus essential in shaping these ethnic identities and instilling a special call of the sea among lifelong sailors that their landlubber equivalents could not always share or understand. These 'seafaring races' still had to be disciplined and obedient, both to their superior, usually British, officers, and to the colonial regime they were expected to defend against both external aggressors and internal dissidents. As well as being a practical solution to problems of manpower and finance facing Britain at this time of imperial overstretch and geopolitical tensions,[18] seafaring race theory was also an ideological fortification to the rising tide of anti-colonial sentiment, allowing Britain to identify, train and equip armed bodies of loyal indigenous subjects to sustain its declining imperial power.

This occurred in Britain's most important colony, India, where the proud heritage of the Indian Army has often overshadowed an even longer naval history in the subcontinent. India's modern navy has roots in the Honourable East India Company's Marine, a local auxiliary established by the British East India Company in 1613. This force went through several name changes, becoming the Bombay Marine in 1686, His Majesty's Indian Navy in 1830, again the Bombay Marine in 1863, Her Majesty's Indian Marine in 1877, before receiving the title Royal Indian Marine in 1892. In all this time was there not one Indian naval officer, until Engineer Sub-Lieutenant Dijendra Nath Mukerji received his commission in 1928. While the Indian Army was a more attractive proposition offering better prospects for young Indian men (which limited the pool for naval recruiters) there were also British prejudices concerning Indians' seafaring abilities, motivations and reliability:

> Since India has not been a sea-going nation, the recruits, both officers and men, will for some time not join the Navy merely for the love of the sea, but for what the Navy has to offer them in the way of a career. I think this is bound to result in more failure and wastage than if the call of the sea was inherent.[19]

Naval aptitude and maritime sentiment were thus believed to be racially inherent by the British, who of course saw themselves as the paramount seafaring race, having acquired the largest maritime empire. In contrast, Indians were seen to require Britain's naval paternalism, as part of a maritime 'civilising mission' to develop the nautical potential of the colonised while reinforcing their psychological domination.[20]

Not all Indians were viewed in the same way, however, and most of the Royal Indian Marine's recruits were Ratnagiri Muslims from the Konkon coast. This community possessed a long maritime heritage of oceanic trade and fishing, as one British officer reflected upon:

> I had a very good example of this old seafaring instinct on the long passage from Mombassa to Cochin with seven ships in company ... the Boys Training Ship *TIR* using every stitch of canvas was some two miles ahead of the rest ... Her old Commissioned Boatswain was Mr. Ali Mohaddin, a Konkani Muslim whose ancestors had sailed in the trade winds to Africa for about 2000 years.[21]

The Royal Indian Marine was reorganised again in 1934 as the Royal Indian Navy (RIN), at which point the traditional martial races were sought to fill a more combatant role. Punjabi Muslims began to replace the Ratnagiris, as it was believed that 'as a gunnery signal or any other kind of specialist the Punjabi Mussalman was way ahead of the Ratnagiri',[22] and while they were still 'good seamen', Ratnagiris were considered to be 'of a low standard of education and with few natural martial qualities' in comparison.[23] More important was the 'better I.Q. plus guts',[24] and the 'instinct for leadership which [was] implicit in the men from the Punjab'. The chief of the RIN, Admiral John Henry Godfrey, even preferred Punjabis over British seamen in some instances:

> Given good leadership and training he can withstand the sun and climate better, he is more easily fed, he is not at prey to skin diseases, and gastric troubles, he needs little comfort, and his sleeping arrangements are extremely simple.[25]

Crucially though, it was believed here that Punjabis still required 'good leadership and training', demonstrating a need for the predominantly white officer class to remain in their positions of authority, with Indians deemed unready to take over for the foreseeable future: a microcosm for the British Raj and its ongoing 'civilising mission' in India.

Godfrey was also particularly taken with the idea that climate affected character. The Enlightenment philosophers Hume, Montesquieu and

Kant thought that northern Europeans possessed greater industry, discipline and intelligence because of the 'temperate' climate they inhabited, as opposed to the hotter, more humid tropics, which instead sapped energy and incited uncontrollable passions.[26] By the mid-nineteenth century, this discourse had evolved to assess the 'inherent' climatic suitability of different races, and to emphasise British biological superiority to justify its colonial governance.[27] Naval and military officers serving in the subcontinent were influenced by this, particularly naval surgeon James Johnson of the *Caroline*, who published *The Influence of Tropical Climates on European Constitutions* in 1818, and General Sir O'Moore Creagh, commander-in-chief of the Indian Army between 1909 and 1914, who believed that 'where the winter is cold, the warlike minority is to be found'.[28] This was then echoed in a booklet written by Godfrey, which prepared new British officers for the 'Creeds and Customs' of Indian sailors:

> The people of the North are fairer of skin than those of the South and the climate in which they live, generally speaking, is more conducive to energetic modes of living than that of the south. In South India, the majority of people are dark in countenance and inclined to be less martial minded … Modern education is very much further developed in South India. The climatic conditions of Assam and Bengal are not conducive to strenuous or energetic work.[29]

In 1935, the Government of India passed an act under its name decreeing that 'no subject … in India shall on grounds of religion, place of birth, descent, or colour be prohibited from … any occupation'.[30] This legislation forced the RIN to become more representative of the country's ethnic demography by recruiting Hindus who had previously been neglected because they were not seen to belong to seafaring or martial races.

The navy's racial ideology had not fundamentally altered. Enlistment of higher educated Hindu castes from the south of India was dictated by this political motivation but also by perceived operational necessity, as the force expanded and acquired increasingly sophisticated warships requiring technically skilled personnel:

> Courage must remain doubtful in the case of the 'soft' races – Madrassi, Bengalis and South Indians from Travancore-Cochin – until it has been proved in modern action. No one has any doubt about the known fighting qualities of the Sikhs or Rajputs, or the seamanship of the Konkani Muslims, but unfortunately these races generally do not have the brain to compete with electronics, radar, fire control.[31]

The Hindu recruits had to deal with prejudiced superior officers who doubted both their fighting ability and their loyalty to the service and the colonial state. In Godfrey's words, 'it was always realised that [southern Hindus] were Nationalist minded … on account of the higher standard of education'.[32] Commodore James Wilfred Jefford, who had served in India since 1922, was similarly suspicious of these matriculates and their 'veneer of book learning overlaying their gullible nature' which made them, in his eyes, 'God's gift to the unscrupulous politician'.[33] For these British naval officers, an education, by its nature, developed one's ability to think independently and critically, a notion that went against the indoctrination and obedience demanded for the chain of command, and the colonial system, to function effectively. Any exposure to political thought was seen to render such men susceptible to the preachings of Indian nationalist leaders, which might result in a conflict of personal and professional loyalty. Though other factors were involved, to an extent these fears were realised when the RIN experienced a major mutiny in 1946 involving over 10,000 Muslim and Hindu personnel from sixty-six ships and shore establishments, an event that triggered the start of Britain's Indian withdrawal.[34]

Elsewhere, the sole colonial naval force in the Caribbean, defending Britain's largest oil-producing colony, was the Trinidad Royal Naval Volunteer Reserve. Insufficient numbers of Trinidadians volunteered, however, fuelling a belief that 'most Trinidadians do not like the sea'.[35] In reality, they preferred higher-paid construction work on the American bases established there following the 1940 Destroyers for Bases agreement, while colonial officials also feared subversive labour 'agitators' on the island after the Butler riots of 1937.[36] Recruits were therefore drawn from ten other West Indian territories,[37] with special maritime preference given to men from the Cayman Islands. Over 1,000 Caymanians from a population of just 6,500 volunteered for naval service during the Second World War, two-thirds of the islands' male adults,[38] and the highest contribution per capita of any Allied country. Roger C. Smith has argued that while other West Indians 'remained tied to the land even in post slavery times and … viewed their coastlines as boundaries or barriers', the Caymans' few terrestrial resources dictated that its people 'depended on the sea as a resource and an avenue for survival'.[39] The islanders were predominantly occupied in turtling, sharking, rope-making and boatbuilding, with the 1934 census recording 50 per cent of Caymanian men as being engaged in the seafaring industry.[40] From an early age, boys would learn to sail, and by 'their teens [they could] handle the local cat boats, craft about 20 feet long ... and built of island timber'.[41]

On the eve of the Second World War, 'large numbers of people of all classes of the community anxious to serve their KING and COUNTRY in the present crisis' stepped forward.[42] In the words of one volunteer:

> The old and young alike from Cayman offered their services to go and fight for their mother country, including myself ... I was a young boy, still in my teens, proud to go and fight for my country.[43]

Though most Caymanians had never visited Britain, they still felt that it was their country and must be defended. They are an example of what Alex Law calls 'island nationalism', which draws its power from 'the imaginary relationship of the collective group to the sea', creating 'an open tension between the strong centripetal pull of settlement and rootedness and the centrifugal push of mobility and migration'.[44] Largely descended from shipwrecked British mariners,[45] Caymanians still felt an urge that 'all they had in their life ... on their mind, is to go to sea', leading many to sign up for the navy,[46] at a time when 'a quasi-biological British "island race" discourse' was being used by Winston Churchill to stimulate wartime sentiment.[47]

As with martial race theorists in India, naval recruiters were influenced by environmental determinism and anthropological studies which marked Caymanians out from other West Indians:

> The average Caymanian is probably of better physique, is healthier, and has a better intelligence than ... the inhabitants of any other island in the West Indies and the countries bordering the Caribbean. This is attributable primarily to his energetic life. Other factors are his higher moral standards and the absence on the island of the usual tropical diseases.[48]

Caymanians exhibited an 'unusually good intellect', were considered 'hard-working' and 'honest', characteristics which then became racialised:

> Most of the people are hardy and healthy, tall, and wiry, like their seafaring forefathers from the east coasts of England and Scotland ... The proportion of whites and mixed to blacks is considerably higher than in most of the other islands of the West Indies. Roughly ... 40 per cent each, blacks 20 per cent.[49]

Many Caymanians had a lineage that could be traced back to the British Isles, emphasised through their noticeably lighter skin colour, particularly when viewed next to prospective recruits from other Caribbean colonies. Remarks about Caymanians' 'noticeably fair' complexion, which displayed 'strong traces of Scandinavian origin',[50] linked to the martial race theory that lighter-skinned northern Indians drew their 'superior military capabilities' from Aryans who had conquered them.[51] It was similarly believed that Caymanians inherited their maritime skill from those early British settlers.

It was the appointment of Allen Wolsey Cardinall, commissioner of the Cayman Islands between 1934 and 1941, which promoted the colony's sailors in the eyes of the Admiralty.[52] An official who 'takes a great interest in the Native customs and habits', he recognised and institutionalised the island's maritime heritage in the aid of economic and social progress. He put the Caymans Islands on the regional map by founding an annual sailing regatta in January 1935, which attracted competitors from across the West Indies and America, as well as the Royal Navy who recognised that 'Cayman Islanders … would make fine material on which to draw in time of war, in the same way as the Newfoundland fishermen were in the last'.[53] They lent a cup for the race winners in the hope that 'the presentation of such a prize would stimulate interest in the Royal Navy that might be invaluable in the event of hostilities'.[54] The sentimental bonds formed by visiting warships preserved an uncritical and patriotic relationship between the civilian public and the navy when war did break out, which:

> created much interest in Cayman … not only because of knowing the [cruiser HMS] *Orion* when she attended Cayman's 1938 regatta but also because we had great faith in the mother country's naval fleet, the most formidable in the world.[55]

Such displays of 'naval theatre', which Jan Rüger argues were 'one of the principal factors in promoting and maintaining the unity of Empire' and the 'fostering of imperial sentiment',[56] enhanced the prestige of the Royal Navy for Caymanians, inculcating a belief and pride in British imperial and naval power that encouraged volunteers like Harry McCoy: 'It had been grounded in us that … "Britannia ruled the waves", and "Britons never shall be slaves" … we just felt that Britain was invincible'.[57]

Commissioner Cardinall devised another way in which to culturally ground this sentiment, by starting the Trafalgar Day school essay competition in 1935, which like imperial literature, encouraged Caymanian youths to admire and emulate the chivalric qualities encapsulated by British naval heroes such as Horatio Nelson. One child again echoed 'Rule Britannia' by asserting that: 'when we study the lives of such men as Lord Nelson, we are proud to know that we form a part of the British Empire, and with the spirit of Nelson we can truly sing: "Britons never shall be slaves"'. Another declared that, '[Nelson] has left us his mantle of inspiration which is inspiring thousands of youths of the British Empire today'.[58] Several of these pupils would later volunteer for the navy after war broke out. Two troops of Sea Scouts were created to help channel these youths. They were given tours of visiting warships, exposing them first-hand to British naval culture, and providing a pool of loyal, disciplined recruits for the navy when war broke out,[59] such as McCoy: 'I was a Sea Scout, and being a Caymanian, I already had the salt water in my blood ... so I volunteered when the opportunity came'.[60] That this identity was so readily embraced by Caymanians also presents another naval example of 'Gurkha syndrome'. The Cayman Islands were poor before naval remittances became available, and the professional reputation of its sailors helped earn them employment with international shipping companies after the war, most notably National Bulk Carriers. It was in their economic interest to embrace their identification as a 'seafaring race', and once they did, like the Gurkhas, they became more 'amenable to discipline'.[61]

Such behaviour also evinced itself in South-East Asia. On the eve of the First World War, Britain's inspector-general of its overseas forces suggested that 'a loyal and patriotic Malay nation, trained to arms might well prove in future a fitting guardian for the western portal to the Pacific'.[62] Yet his idea was not initially taken forward, as there was a belief that Malays did not represent one of the martial races, instead being seen to be 'soft', 'indolent' and too 'easy going', having not opposed British rule as Indians had.[63] Arthur Henderson Young, British high commissioner in Malaya and governor of the Straits Settlements, added that Malays would 'resist routine and also prolonged barrack life with continual discipline', but as an alternative he proposed that:

> a naval unit would appeal to the Malay, he would feel perfectly at home on the water. His objection to discipline and hard work on land would not be the same when on water.[64]

Their maritime traditions were inherited from Malay merchants and pirates who had long performed a fundamental role in regional trade and power politics up to the extension of British colonialism in the nineteenth century. These included the Orang Laut, the 'People of the Sea' or so-called 'Sea Gypsies', a community of sailors who lived nomadic lives aboard their boats and used their nautical skills to make livelihoods as fishermen, traders or even tax collectors and fighting sailors for the region's sultans.[65]

It was not until April 1934 that the Admiralty established a Royal Naval Volunteer Reserve (RNVR) unit in the Straits Settlement of Singapore. Only European officers and Malay ratings were allowed into this force, disbarring the large Chinese and Indian communities that inhabited the Malay Peninsula. Maritime heritage was used to justify this racial prejudice, with the British claiming that the Malays constituted a 'seafaring people and along the coasts of the Peninsula there are hundreds of sturdy fishermen suitable for training'.[66] In his 1936 Annual Report for the RNVR (Singapore Division), the commanding officer, Commander L. A. W. Johnson, was delighted to confirm that 'the Malays are proverbially a seafaring race and the formation of a Naval Unit has appealed to them, and has certainly justified itself'.[67] A second RNVR branch was subsequently formed in Penang in October 1938, as well as a full-time Malay Section of the Royal Navy the following year, informally referred to as the 'Malay Navy', which relieved British sailors on warships stationed to the Far East. The commander-in-chief of the China Station, Admiral Sir Percy Noble, was reportedly impressed upon inspecting the new unit:

> The seafaring traditions of the Malays admirably adapt them to life in the new arm of the Empire fighting service ... Every Malay must be proud to feel that members of his own race have already proved their worth as seamen and are playing an important part defending their own land from the menace of Hitlerism.[68]

By November 1940, the first two Malays, Johari bin Haji Mohamed Saleh and Manoff bin Haji Yusof, had been promoted from seaman to petty officer.

Officials were quick to use this as further evidence of Malay wartime loyalty in the naval defence of the empire, which justified their racial recruitment:

> The rapid promotion of these seamen is indicative of the enthusiasm with which the Malays have seized the opportunity of displaying the seafaring tradition of their race in this new arm of the Royal Navy.[69]

The British clearly believed that nautical skill was something that was innate to Malays, just as it was with themselves, Caymanians and Ratnagiri Indians. Yet this did not preclude the need for Royal Navy doctrine and its 'civilising' effect in tempering and honing this raw ability, something emphasised in Ministry of Information propaganda which highlighted the Malays' transformation from 'fishing and peasant folk ... once famed as pirates. Today, they make fine seamen ... Under the supervision of

British officers'.[70] Just as the Zulus and Boers in South Africa were denigrated by British militarists because they failed to conform to Western conventions of warfare, so Malays were similarly lowered to legitimise Britain's policies on account of their piratical past. Thus, not only did local naval forces defend the empire from external threats, they also strengthened its moral and social fibre within, by providing an outlet for unemployed colonial labour:

> the pay is enough to satisfy the easy-going Malay, the work suits him, the discipline also apparently suits him – very much better than anyone expected it would – and he likes the sea and boats and everything associated with them.[71]

In comparison, the Royal Navy distrusted the Chinese, thinking them to be 'superstitious and stubborn', and linking them with socialism and protest following their involvement in the 1922 Hong Kong seamen's strike.[72] In 1930, the General Officer Commanding Singapore, Major-General Harry Pritchard, published a report investigating the 'Fighting Value of the Races of Malaya', where he concluded that while 'Chinese burglars stood up well in their brushes with the police', such 'fighting value' only materialised when the Chinese could profit from it.[73] While the British used the local sultans to keep the Malays in check, Chinese political and social ties were less reliable and could become anti-colonial, especially among those connected to the communists, nationalists, and triad secret societies.[74] Such discriminatory recruitment drew criticism from Straits Eurasians, who were fighting for greater political, economic and social justice:

> The Eurasian position is tragic, due to the fact that we are brought up in European environment, with European traditions and living standards. As a rule we are not an agricultural race, so we cannot go back to the land, as some suggest. Neither do we get a dole … The pro-Malay policy in Malaya as a whole has crushed our hopes, and we are being entirely 'cabined'. Our Malacca lads would jump at the chance, if given the opportunity to enrol in the navy or the RNVR, as they are on par with the Malays, where the sea is concerned, having come from a long line of seafaring forebears.[75]

Despite possessing a maritime heritage of their own, it was not enough to make Eurasians a 'seafaring race' for the navy. While they possessed similarities with the Caymanians in tracing an ancestry to European sailors, the Cayman Islands' geographic isolation and underdevelopment until the mid-1930s meant that culturally they remained distinctively 'inferior' which justified British colonial leadership. In comparison,

Eurasians were closer to their European forebears, maintaining a similar culture though they were viewed as an 'other' race. With Singapore being a much more ethnically diverse and strategically important imperial base, Eurasians stoked British fears about racial mixing and the danger it posed to their colonial authority which was built on systems of racial superiority. To allow Eurasians into the navy would undermine the chain of command by blurring the racial distinction between the European officer class and their Asian ratings.

By the time the Pacific war broke out in December 1941, the Malay Navy had recruited 1,430 Malays from the Straits Settlements, Malaya and Sarawak,[76] with a waiting list numbering thousands more.[77] Its popularity was seen as proof of and reinforced maritime racial stereotypes:

> The sea attracts the Malay like water does a duck. He joined the SSRNVR [Straits Settlements Royal Naval Volunteer Reserve] when the call for volunteers came – and he and his friends are still joining ... there were whispers in the Bazaars and the Kampongs that Malays would be wanted in a unit of their own in the RN. Before the naval authorities in Singapore could fully appreciate the work of the whispers, they were inundated with applications.[78]

As with Caymanians, the Malays' affirmation of their 'seafaring race' identity can be seen as another expression of 'Gurkha syndrome', as they were traditionally the more economically deprived of the Straits communities and the navy offered them an opportunity to elevate themselves out of poverty.[79] This progress was used to justify Britain's 'civilising mission' and demonstrate the positive transformation of Malays under colonial rule:

> It is another step towards employing the 'sons of the soil' in the defence of their own country. First ... came the SSRNVR which confirmed the belief that coffee-shop loungers and office peons could be turned into good sailors, and that in the country there was plenty of material that could be absorbed into the RN.[80]

Ultra-imperialists feared that without an Empire to govern, British 'civilisation might decline and that a kind of Oriental torpor might descend upon the nation'.[81] It was hoped that this 'civilising duty' would reinvigorate European officers suffering 'tropical inertia', and strengthen their moral fortitude. Under Britain's naval paternalism, the traditional 'lounger' or 'lazy Malay' was thus transformed into an alert, dedicated professional sailor, ready to defend the Empire:

On a visit to HMS *Pelandok* yesterday, we saw the ratings at their training, noticed the concentrated looks on their faces as they listened to lectures on boxing, the compass, anchor and cable work, and the rule of the road at sea; watched their nimble fingers making bends and hitches and splicing wires; heard the dots and dashes of an electronic 'buzzer' as they were being taught signalling and telegraphy, and appreciated their quickness at the guns.[82]

As with martial race theory, which had influenced British naval recruiters, their identification of 'seafaring races' was not a purely ethnographic observation, but evolved in response to a range of local, geopolitical, imperial and strategic concerns which varied across regions. 'Seafaring race' theory was one of several pseudoscientific racial ideologies used over the preceding century to reinforce the notion of the colonial 'other', and to reaffirm British primacy and legitimise their imperial authority. Within the armed forces, this implicit hegemony played an additional role in enforcing discipline and preserving a racially demarcated chain of command. 'Progress' under naval instruction reinforced the notion of a civilising mission, where colonial peoples still required Britain's paternal guidance in order to become developed enough to govern themselves, both politically and militarily. Seafaring race theory served to divide and rule, legitimising the exclusion of groups seen as threatening to British authority within this racial ordering, such as matriculates, nationalists, labour unionists, communists, secret societies and Eurasians, while buttressing colonial collaborators. In the Caribbean, Caymanians were given favoured status, officially on account of their seafaring qualities, though this masked the fact they were considered more reliable on account of their lighter skin colour and British ancestry than slave-descended West Indians who were expressing anti-colonial nationalistic sentiments at the time. As with the martial races, Caymanian and Malay ratings also exhibited characteristics of 'Gurkha syndrome', embracing seafaring identity and the naval employment it offered in order to alleviate their relative poverty. But ultimately for the British authorities, the perceived imperial loyalty of colonial naval recruits was considered more important than any seafaring ability they might possess, inherent or otherwise.

Notes

1 For more see Daniel Owen Spence, *Colonial Naval Culture and British Imperialism, 1922–67* (Manchester: Manchester University Press, 2015), from which elements of this chapter are drawn.
2 For these concepts see John Anthony Hilton, *Anglo-Saxon Attitudes: A Short*

Introduction to Anglo-Saxonism (Norfolk: Anglo-Saxon Books, 2006); Edward W. Said, *Orientalism* (New York: Pantheon, 1978); Harald Fischer-Tiné and Michael Mann (eds), *Colonialism as Civilizing Mission: Cultural Ideology in British India* (London: Anthem Press, 2004); Joseph M. Hodge, Gerald Hödl and Martina Kopf (eds), *Developing Africa: Concepts and Practices in Twentieth-Century Colonialism* (Manchester: Manchester University Press, 2014); Peter J. Cain, 'Empire and the Languages of Character and Virtue in Later Victorian and Edwardian Britain', *Modern Intellectual History*, 4:2 (2007), 249–73; C. J. Wan-ling Wee, *Culture, Empire and the Question of Being Modern* (Oxford: Lexington Books, 2003).

3 First coined by Ngugi wa Thiong'o, *Decolonising the Mind: The Politics of language in African Literature* (London: Heinemann Educational, 1986).

4 George MacMunn, *The Martial Races of India* (London: Low, Marston and Co., 1933), p. 353.

5 David Killingray, 'Guardians of Empire' in Killingray and David Omissi (eds), *Guardians of Empire: The Armed Forces of the Colonial Powers, c. 1700–1964* (Manchester: Manchester University Press, 1999), pp. 1–24, 15.

6 Douglas M. Peers, '"Those Noble Exemplars of the True Military Tradition"; Constructions of the Indian Army in the Mid-Victorian Press', *Modern Asian Studies*, 31:1 (1997), 109–42.

7 Heather Streets, *Martial Races: The Military, Race and Masculinity in British Imperial Culture, 1857–1914* (Manchester: Manchester University Press, 2004), p. 2.

8 First coined by Ronald Robinson, John Gallagher and Alice Denny, *Africa and the Victorians: The Official Mind of Imperialism* (London: Macmillan, 1961).

9 David Omissi, *The Sepoy and the Raj: The Indian Army, 1860–1940* (London: Palgrave Macmillan, 1998), pp. 24–5.

10 Cynthia H. Enloe, *Ethnic Soldiers: State Security in a Divided Society* (Athens, GA: University of Georgia Press, 1980), p. 25.

11 John M. MacKenzie, in Streets, *Martial Races*, pp. viii–ix.

12 Interview by author with Jaswant Singh Gill, 10 July 2009, Singapore. First cited in Spence, *Colonial Naval Culture*, p. 5.

13 Streets, *Martial Races*, p. 4.

14 John M. MacKenzie, 'Lakes, Rivers and Oceans: Technology, Ethnicity and the Shipping Empire in the Late Nineteenth Century' in David Killingray, Margarette Lincoln and Nigel Rigby (eds), *Maritime Empires: British Imperial Trade in the Nineteenth Century* (Woodbridge: Boydell and Brewer, 2004), p. 125.

15 See George E. Brooks, *The Kru Mariner in the Nineteenth Century: A Historical Compendium* (Newark, NJ: Liberian Studies Monograph Series No. 1, Liberian Studies Association in America Inc, 1972); Diane Frost, *Work and Community among West African Migrant Workers since the Nineteenth Century* (Liverpool: Liverpool University Press, 1999).

16 See Aaron Jaffer, *Lascars and Indian Ocean Seafaring 1780–1860: Shipboard Life, Unrest and Mutiny* (Woodbridge: Boydell and Brewer, 2015); G. Balachandran, *Globalizing Labour? Indian Seafarers and World Shipping, c.1870–1945* (Oxford: Oxford University Press, 2002); Rozina Visram, *Ayahs, Lascars and Princes: Indians in Britain, 1700–1947* (London: Routledge, 1986).
17 Frances Steel, *Oceania under Steam: Sea Transport and the Cultures of Colonialism, c. 1870–1914* (Manchester: Manchester University Press, 2011), pp. 109–10.
18 See Spence, *Colonial Naval Culture*, pp. 13–25.
19 National Maritime Museum (NMM), MLS/10/1, MS 81/006, D.O.61, G Miles to Sir Claude Auchinleck (C-in-C, India), 24 September 1946.
20 Daniel Owen Spence, 'Imperial Ideology, Identity and Naval Recruitment in Britain's Asian Empire, c. 1928–1941' in Duncan Redford (ed.), *Maritime History and Identity: The Sea and Culture in the Modern World* (London: I.B.Tauris, 2013), pp. 294–315: 296.
21 The National Archives (TNA), ADM 205/88, 'India and the Sea', 1953, p. 1.
22 NMM, GOD/34, MS 80/073, Jefford, para. 34.
23 Godfrey cited in Patrick Beesley, *Very Special Admiral: The Life of Admiral J. H. Godfrey* (London: Hamilton, 1980), p. 266.
24 NMM, GOD/34, MS 80/073, Jefford, para. 34.
25 NMM, GOD/41, MS 80/073, Godfrey to Somerville, 29 August 1943, p. 4.
26 Daniel Owen Spence, 'Imperial Transition, Indianisation and Race: Developing National Navies in the Subcontinent, 1947–1964', *South Asia: Journal of South Asian Studies*, 37:2 (2014), 323–38.
27 George C. D. Adamson, '"The Languor of the Hot Weather": Everyday Perspectives on Weather and Climate in Colonial Bombay, 1819–1828', *Journal of Historical Geography*, 38:2 (2012), 144–5.
28 Chris Smith, *India's Ad Hoc Arsenal: Direction or Drift in Defence Policy?* (Oxford: Oxford University Press, 1994), p. 46.
29 NMM, RIN/74, MS 81/006, John H. Godfrey, V.Adm. FOCRIN, *Creeds and Customs in the RIN*, Naval Headquarters (India), 1 January 1945, pp. 6–7.
30 'Government of India Act 1935', 2 August 1935, Legislation.gov.uk, http://www.legislation.gov.uk/ukpga/Geo5and1Edw8/26/2/enacted (accessed 26 June 2012).
31 TNA, ADM 205/88, India and the Sea, p. 5.
32 NMM, GOD/43, J. H. Godfrey, Naval Headquarters, 'Future of the RIN: First Impressions', India 1943–1946, vol. 3, 8 March 1946, p. 2.
33 NMM, RIN/5/3 (6), MS88/043, Jefford to Mr Justice Ayyangar during Commission of Inquiry, *The Times of India*, 24 April 1946; NMM, RIN/74, MS 81/006, Godfrey, *Creeds and Customs in the RIN*, 1 January 1945, pp. 1–2; NMM, GOD/43, Godfrey, 'Future of the RIN', 8 March 1946, p. 1.
34 See Daniel Owen Spence, 'Beyond *Talwar*: A Cultural Reappraisal of the

1946 Royal Indian Navy Mutiny', *The Journal of Imperial and Commonwealth History*, 43:3 (2015), 489–508.

35 Norman Rudolph McLaughlin, *The Forgotten Men of the Navy* (Miami, FL: N. R. McLaughlin, 2002), prelude.

36 TNA, ADM 1/10969, 'Defence of Trinidad Oil Refineries, Note of a Meeting held at the Colonial Office on Monday, 8th May', 1939.

37 Guyana, Barbados, Grenada, St Vincent, Antigua, Montserrat, St Kitts, St Lucia and Dominica.

38 Michael Craton, *Founded Upon the Seas: A History of the Cayman Islands and Their People* (Kingston: Ian Randle Publishers, 2003), p. 291.

39 Roger C. Smith, *The Maritime Heritage of the Cayman Islands* (Gainesville, FL: University Press of Florida, 2000), p. 51.

40 Cayman Islands National Archive, 'Colonial Report 1937', p. 13.

41 A. J. A. Douglas, 'The Cayman Islands', *The Geographical Journal*, 95:2 (1940), 128–9.

42 Cayman Islands National Archive, 'Government Notice, No. 98/39', 30 August 1939.

43 McLaughlin, *Forgotten Men of the Navy*, prelude.

44 Alex Law, 'Of Navies and Navels: Britain as a Mental Island', *Geografiska Annaler. Series B, Human Geography*, 87:4 (2005), 267–77: 267.

45 James H. S. Billmyer, 'The Cayman Islands', *Geographical Review*, 36:1 (1946), 33.

46 Interview with T. Ewart Ebanks (1), p. 20.

47 Law, 'Of Navies and Navels', 269.

48 James H. S. Billmyer, 'The Cayman Islands', 41–2.

49 *Ibid.*, 34–5.

50 Douglas, 'The Cayman Islands', 127.

51 Thomas Metcalf, *Imperial Connections: India in the Indian Ocean Arena, 1860–1920* (London: University of California Press, 2007), p. 72.

52 Cayman Islands National Archive, Interview with Harold Banks, Carley Ebanks and Harvey Ebanks, conducted by Liz Scolefield, 18 May 1996, transcript p. 20.

53 TNA, ADM1/9749, 'H.M.S. "Dundee's" No.2/37', 28 February 1938.

54 TNA, ADM 1/9749, 'Cayman Islands Regatta – Proposed Presentation of a Cup', 4 May 1937.

55 Sir Vassel Johnson, *As I See It: How Cayman Became a Leading Financial Centre* (Sussex: Book Guild, 2001), p. 60.

56 Jan Rüger, *The Great Naval Game: Britain and Germany in the Age of Empire* (Cambridge: Cambridge University Press, 2007), pp. 175–6.

57 Cayman Islands National Archive, Interview with Harry McCoy, tape 2, side A, p. 7.

58 Cayman Islands National Archive, 'Trafalgar Day', Central Registry File 706/35, 5 October 1935.

59 Cayman Islands National Archive, Interview with Ernest Panton, conducted by Iva Johnson-Good and Roger Good, 1979–80, transcript p. 2.
60 Cayman Islands National Archive, Interview with Harry McCoy, tape 2, side A, p. 10.
61 Enloe, *Ethnic Soldiers*, p. 25.
62 Nadzan Haron, 'Colonial Defence and British Approach to the Problems in Malaya 1874–1918', *Modern Asian Studies*, 24:2 (1990), 275–95: 286–7.
63 Metcalf, *Imperial Connections*, p. 77; Kevin Blackburn, 'Colonial Forces as Postcolonial Memories: The Commemoration and Memory of the Malay Regiment in Modern Malaysia and Singapore' in Karl Hack and Tobias Rettig (eds), *Colonial Armies in Southeast Asia* (London: Routledge, 2006), p. 302.
64 Haron, 'Colonial Defence', p. 287.
65 Cynthia Chou, *The Orang Suku Laut of Riau, Indonesia: The Inalienable Gift of Territory* (London, 2010), p. 1; Geoffrey Benjamin, 'On Being Tribal in the Malay World' in Geoffrey Benjamin and Cynthia Chou (eds), *Tribal Communities in the Malay World: Historical, Cultural and Social Perspectives* (Singapore: Institute of Southeast Asian Studies, 2002), pp. 7–76: 41, 45.
66 *The Straits Times*, 26 January 1937, p. 11.
67 *Ibid.*, 26 October 1936, p. 13.
68 *The Singapore Free Press and Mercantile Advertiser*, 13 September 1940, p. 7.
69 *Ibid.*, 22 November 1940, p. 7.
70 Imperial War Museum, K 1430, 'Malays in British Navy, Malaya, c. 1942'.
71 *The Straits Times*, 23 May 1937, p. 2.
72 Liew Kai Khium, 'Labour Formation, Identity, and Resistance in HM Dockyard, Singapore (1921–1971)', *International Review of Social History*, 51:3 (2006), 415–39.
73 Quoted in W. David McIntyre, *The Rise and Fall of the Singapore Naval Base, 1919–1942* (London: Macmillan, 1979), p. 225.
74 *Ibid.*, pp. 225–6.
75 *The Straits Times*, 25 May 1937, p. 12.
76 Royal Malaysian Navy Museum, Malacca, 2 July 2009.
77 *The Straits Times*, 28 September 1940, p. 11.
78 *Ibid.*
79 Enloe, *Ethnic Soldiers*, p. 25.
80 *The Straits Times*, 28 September 1940, p. 11.
81 Charles Dilke, 1872, quoted in Peter J. Cain, 'Empire and the Languages of Character and Virtue in Later Victorian and Edwardian Britain', *Modern Intellectual History*, 4:2 (2007), 249–73: 270, 279.
82 *The Straits Times*, 28 September 1940, p. 11.

Part II
Representations of the Royal Navy

6

Memorialising Anson, the fighting explorer: a case study in eighteenth-century naval commemoration and material culture

Katherine Parker

That the navy and national identity are intricately connected and mutually constitutive is attested to by the work of several historians.[1] Such connections are also evident in the ample presence of naval and maritime themes in surviving material culture ranging from wine coasters to figurines to fans, to name but a few examples. A particularly rich, yet understudied, material culture source that chronicles the connections between navy and nation are commemorative medals. The Royal Navy both commissioned and served as subject matter for medals, the domestic production of which exploded in the eighteenth century. To buy or commission a medal was to participate in the creation and consumption of a legacy – a simplification process born of a specific historical context.[2] By examining one medal in particular, it is possible to analyse one such legacy in the making and, more broadly, to expose the embedded nature of the navy within British culture.

In looking at a medal depicting George Anson's circumnavigation of the globe between 1740 and 1744 and his victory at the First Battle of Finisterre in 1747, several questions arise. First, which acts were chosen to be commemorated, and how? This begs the further question, which acts were not chosen, and why not? Second, what is the role of long-distance navigational feats (henceforth referred to as exploration), in the career structure of the Royal Navy in the eighteenth century? How does exploration fit into the (re)making and remembering of a naval hero? This chapter argues that exploration is best understood as an activity not separate from or peripheral to a naval career, but as one central to the eighteenth-century naval career structure, starting especially with Anson's circumnavigation. By examining Anson's achievements as they were struck for posterity, it is possible to glimpse the intricate webs of meaning that artisans and admirals alike used to confer value on certain actions in a nation defined by global maritime activity.

The Royal Navy was an institution upon which the public could fix patriotic nationalism, both celebratory and critical, in the eighteenth century. As increased participation in extra-parliamentary politics created a public sphere focused on trade, liberty and empire at the local level, British forces at the international level were involved in near-constant wars.[3] It was in the eighteenth century that Britain transformed itself into a more efficient, bureaucratic, fiscal-military state. Indeed, the state was only able to attain its superpower status by successfully commanding the logistics, administration and fund-raising necessary to manage the considerable resources needed for prolonged conflict.[4]

Such an emphasis on war led to public appreciation for those leaders who could bring victory, and therefore power, to the emerging British nation. It has also led to a focus by historians on the role of battle in making naval warrior-heroes. Nelson and his fellow officers of the French Revolutionary and Napoleonic Wars have dominated the field of naval heroism, not least because the bicentenary of Nelson's death spurred growth in an already burgeoning field of popular interest.[5] Scholars of naval heroism have focused on the political ramifications of naval victory in the public reaction to the volatile Admiral Vernon.[6] For the mid-eighteenth century, Stephen Moore argues that the celebrity of admirals mitigated public experience of naval defeat and victory.[7] All of these works underline that naval battles were without a doubt the main way for officers to gain promotion quickly, and were certainly the most lauded acts in the press and in material culture. However, they were not the only acts worthy of commemoration and promotion.

Long-distance voyages to little known areas – an activity the Admiralty increasingly controlled in the eighteenth century – also offered to increase the prestige of the navy and therefore the nation. Although several schol-ars have emphasised the importance of exploration in defining naval heroism, much of this scholarship has focused on Captain Cook or nineteenth-century Arctic exploration.[8] This latter period has also been problematically elided with the earlier, eighteenth-century context – an era in which a community interested in geographic knowledge, and led in part by the Admiralty, struggled to learn how to gather and dissemi-nate information from long-distance expeditions. In addition, the precise definition of exploration was expanding during the eighteenth century from an emphasis on military reconnaissance to include the gathering of knowledge about the natural world.[9] Thus, while the Anson expedition was bellicose in intention – it was part of the global strategy to attack Spanish trade in the War of Jenkins' Ear and resulted in the rare capture of a treasure galleon – the completion of a circumnavigation marked Anson's voyage as singular for its time. It therefore offers an opportunity to analyse the interplay of combat and exploration in the commemoration of a naval career.

Commemoration not only depended on acts deemed heroic, but on the media in which such acts were preserved. Whereas print sources have proven a rich bank of information about the wider representation and reception of the Royal Navy in British society, other material culture sources, like medals, have been less studied. Between the 1540s, when the first English medals were struck, and 1800, English and British engravers made 720 medals. Of these, 570 were made in the eighteenth century alone, making this a particularly fertile period to study. Prior to 1740, the majority of medals were made by engravers of the Royal Mint, who took private commissions when not working on state projects. However, military victories in the 1740s, especially Vernon's at Portobello, marked a sudden increase in privately manufactured medals produced outside of the Mint, and signalled a shift in production from state to private industry.[10] For the first time medals, especially those struck in cheaper pinchbeck, were available to a wider audience, although those struck in silver and gold were still considered luxury items.[11]

On the small space of two medal faces, engravers chronicled a variety of cultural milestones for diverse audiences, including royal marriages and coronations, the passage of acts and bills and, especially in the last third of the eighteenth century, scientific and artistic achievements. After royal events, the largest category of medals was those commemorating military victories, particularly those at sea. Whether commissioned for elite distribution or made of lesser metals for sale to the masses, the medals represent a distillation of cultural achievements into commodity form. They were carefully designed symbols of national achievement at a time when Britons were consolidating a national identity.[12] Those depicting Lord Anson show this selection process by highlighting certain parts of his career at the expense of others, and simultaneously reveal the centrality of certain maritime achievements in eighteenth-century British culture.

George Anson, a second son, was born in 1697 and entered the navy in 1712. His family had strong political connections via his uncle, Thomas Parker, later Lord Macclesfield, who served as Lord Chief Justice and

Lord Chancellor while Anson rose to his first command in 1722. Anson saw action at Cape Passaro under Admiral Sir George Byng and spent the majority of his early command career protecting the shores of the Carolinas. In 1737, he was assigned to the *Centurion*, and it was in this ship that he circumnavigated the globe as part of an effort to harass Spanish trade. After his famous voyage, Anson was promoted rear-admiral of the white and served, with the exception of a few months, on the Admiralty Board for nearly two decades. Partnered with Lord Sandwich, he achieved many reforms to ship design, signalling and shipyard maintenance, while spearheading the organisation of the Western Squadron and the creation of the Royal Marines. These reforms are considered his most important achievements by naval historians today.[13] Stints of active command explain his victory at the First Battle of Finisterre in 1747, after which he received a barony. Early patrons and admirers included naval officers like Sir Charles Wager and Sir John Norris and, later, Lord Hardwicke, Macclesfield's protégé. In 1748, Anson married Lord Hardwicke's daughter, Lady Elizabeth Yorke, cementing political ties. Though Anson served as an MP for Hedon in Yorkshire from 1744 to 1747, he never spoke in Parliament and was far less pugnacious and public in his politics than his contemporary, Vernon. Anson died, childless, in 1762.[14]

Although Anson was far from a stranger to the British public, in the late 1760s his brother, Thomas Anson – MP for Lichfield, Fellow of the Royal Society, amateur architect and medal collector – sought to create a commemorative medal that would craft his brother's image as an active naval hero whose achievements were still relevant. According to announcements in the 13–16 May 1769 issue of the *St James's Chronicle* and the *Whitehall Evening Post*:

> We hear a great Quantity of Gold, Silver, and Copper Medals, are now distributing to the Nobility, Gentry, &c. in Commemoration of Lord Anson's sailing round the World, engraved by Mr. Pingo, and designed by James Stuart, Esq. F.R.S. The Face represents Victory crowning the Head of the late Lord Anson. On the Reverse is a Figure representing Circumnavigation; round it are disposed six Crowns of Laurel, in which are inscribed Saunders, Brett, Dennis, Campbell, Keppel, and Saumarez, being the Names of the principal Officers who served with his Lordship in the Expedition round the World.[15]

To understand better the construction of Anson's legacy, it will be helpful to explore first the manufacture of this medal, then the events recorded on its faces, spending particular time on the circumnavigation.

Figure 7 Obverse of medal commemorating the Battle of Cape Finisterre, 1747, and Admiral George Anson's voyage, 1740–4

The Mr Pingo mentioned in the papers refers to Thomas Pingo Jnr, engraver at the Royal Mint and the Assay Office and member of the Pingo metallurgy family. The combined output of the Pingo family accounts for 30.3 per cent of the attributable medals struck in London and 12.28 per cent of those struck in Britain during the eighteenth century. The productive period of the Pingos began in 1742, when Thomas Jnr received his first known commission from the Admiralty to commemorate the taking of five Spanish ships by Captain Smith Callis.[16] The last medal that his family created – his sons Lewis and John continued the private business and served in their father's positions at the Mint and Assay Office respectively – was also an Admiralty commission, this time

Figure 8 Reverse of medal commemorating the Battle of Cape Finisterre, 1747, and Admiral George Anson's voyage, 1740–4

to reward the fourteen captains and seven admirals involved in Lord Howe's victory on 1 June 1794.[17] The Pingo family was an artisan business allied specifically with the navy and with government more broadly. Such partnerships and combinations of private and state manufacture were vital to any artisan wishing to gain wealth and prestige in the mid-eighteenth century.[18]

The designer of the medal, James 'Athenian' Stuart, had already engraved several medals as part of wider artistic interests. Other medals of his design include the military victories at Gorée, Louisburg, Montreal and Quebec.[19] Most famous for *The Antiquities of Athens Measured and Delineated by James Stuart, F.R.S. and F.S.A., and Nicholas Revett, Painters and Architects* (1762), the classical references on the Anson medal may owe to Stuart's enduring interest in Greek and Roman art and architecture. However, the Pingo medals, and commemorative medals more broadly, often employed laurels, wreaths, gods and goddesses as part of a shared cultural lexicon based on classical symbolic representations. Stuart designed the Anson medal and then sent it to Pingo for striking, although it seems Stuart was also involved in the distribution of the medals. The Pingo accounts record the standard charge of £80 for the dies, as well as fifty gold and eighty silver medals. In addition, Pingo struck forty medals in copper. As the newspaper account references, the medals were distributed to friends and influential people in high society including, possibly, Voltaire.[20]

What would the valued recipients of such a gift have seen? Starting on the obverse, they would see Anson's bust being crowned with a laurel by Victory. Her left foot touches the prow of a galley, referring to the nautical nature of this particular legacy. The text reads 'George Lord Anson' and 'Vict. May III, MDCCXLVII'. 3 May 1747 was the date of Anson's most famous victory at sea, the First Battle of Finisterre, where his superior force took six French ships. Although no Trafalgar – one nineteenth-century biographer described the battle as a 'most timely little action' – it served as a rare bright spot in the War of the Austrian Succession.[21] Anson took command of the fledgling Western Squadron in 1746, two years after he was appointed to the Board of Admiralty under Bedford. After the battle, Anson returned to administration and stayed there, with one brief stint of active command in 1758. As mentioned above, Anson was highly successful at the Admiralty, overseeing many important reforms, but one learns nothing of this from his medal.

Although contemporaries in government and in the Royal Navy applauded his efforts, it is interesting that the medal makes no mention of Anson's service on the Board.[22] Instead, it depicts Anson as a younger man, mid-career, just after his two great successes at sea. This revealing selectivity of commemoration shows a high value placed on action and virility, not administration and policy. Thomas Anson and 'Athenian' Stuart both knew that the small space of a commemorative medal was no place to try to argue for the importance of administrative work, nor did they seek to make such an argument. Rather, they viewed the two round faces of a blank medal as opportunities to tie Lord Anson to other medals recalling great victories, signalling British strength and national achievement. A ballad written just after Anson's triumph at Finisterre explicates the point:

> Long had the French Navy with that of proud Spain,
> Insulted our Coasts & rode Lords of the Main,
> Look'd into our Ports with a Show to invade,
> Our Castles defy'd & half ruin'd our Trade;
> Britannia amaz'd at this Signal disgrace,
> Vents awful a Sigh and in Clouds veils her Face;
> But rouz'd on her naval Sons fixes her Eyes
> and bids with a Smile two lov'd Admirals Rise…
> Overjoy'd they sail forth and come up with the Foe,
> Determin'd like Britons to strike a bold Blow…[23]

In order to bring pride to disgraced Britannia, 'lov'd Admirals' Anson and Peter Warren had to *sail* and *strike* a bold blow. Action is what restores national vigour, not administration.[24] Ballads such as these throw into relief the tension between active duty and clerical or secretarial work. The Royal Navy was the 'largest industrial unit of its day in the western world' and it is during Anson's tenure on the Admiralty when clerks and administrators were professionalising the running of the navy ashore.[25] However, the celebratory culture preserved in medals did not recognise this vital part of naval work. The rise of a bureaucratic class was perhaps accepted socially and even viewed as an opportunity for many educated men of the middling sort, but clerical and managerial duties do not seem to have been integrated into contemporary material culture of military commemoration.

Moving onto the reverse, those who received the medal would find a familiar event blazoned in gold, silver or copper. Anson's circumnavigation was a culturally salient point of reference not just for the privileged gifted with this medal but for British, and European, society at large. In 1740, and as part of the hostilities that would broaden into the War of the Austrian Succession, Anson was sent to 'annoy and distress the Spaniards, either at sea or land, to the utmost of your power'.[26] Due to the limited geographic knowledge of the Pacific region, the Admiralty gave the commander immense freedom to land and sail where he would; the Admiralty was in search of ports, trade partners and bullion to expand their realm and enrich the home island.[27] Anson did eventually harass the Spanish on land by sacking the town of Paita, and at sea by taking the Acapulco treasure galleon, although he lost five of his six ships and around 1400 of his 1900 men in the process.[28] The first expedition to be updated upon continuously by newspapers while it sailed, Anson returned home to an avid public eager to celebrate the first British victory of consequence since Vernon at Porto Bello in 1739.[29]

Much of the voyage's enduring fame was due to Anson's published account. Although planned as a combative mission, the account reframed the expedition in light of the geographic knowledge it gathered; it also suggested the creation of an exploratory programme planned by the Admiralty and manned by trained naval engineers. Compiled from Anson's and his officers' papers and written by the chaplain of the *Centurion*, Richard Walter, and Benjamin Robins, Fellow of the Royal Society and military engineer, the book became an instant bestseller. Released in 1748, it was serialised in *The Gentleman's Magazine*, and went through four editions in its first year of publication.[30] The account was in its sixteenth edition by 1781, and nineteenth-century biographers of Anson remark that the account was still well-known and widely read.[31] As the first voyage account endorsed by the Admiralty, it began a tradition of official accounts of exploratory missions that promised authority and credibility to the reading public while also establishing the Admiralty as the main arbiter of information about the South Seas. Numerous engravings, pocket globes and paintings popped up to ride the wave of popularity caused by the circumnavigation.[32] Lauded as one of the first Englishmen to circle the globe since Drake, Anson's success was based on the combination of navigational prowess and the taking of a rich prize.

The point here is not to argue that long-distance navigational feats had not previously been recognised as achievements – quite the contrary. However, they had not heretofore been such an integrated part of Royal Navy activity. The Anson circumnavigation was one of the first of its kind to be organised by the Admiralty, as opposed to the Admiralty granting approval to privateers willing to fund their own voyages to the Pacific. Thus Anson personally, and the Royal Navy as an institution, benefited from public interest in the expedition. Too often in popular exploration literature, and lingering still in some scholarly works, exploration is treated as an enlightened, lone-wolf activity meant to expose the objective reality of an area.[33] While much of this imagery comes from the romanticisation of a later explorer, James Cook, his apotheosis should not dominate historians' understanding of earlier exploration in English and British, or European, society.[34]

The medal's date of creation reveals the saliency of the circumnavigation twenty-five years after its completion. Thomas Anson ordered the medal struck in 1768, just as the Admiralty selected the aforementioned Cook to observe the transit of Venus in the Pacific. The implication of forging a medal in the middle of a new Pacific craze by harking back to earlier Pacific missions shows that Cook is but a part in a longer and more complex story of Pacific naval exploration. Indeed, it seems that Thomas wanted to remind society that his brother's legacy was embedded in current events; and that Anson lived on by inspiring additional exploration. Furthermore, 1768 witnessed the emergence of a new kind of empire. After the Seven Years' War, British overseas territories stretched around the globe. The geopolitical situation demanded a new administrative approach that sought to correct and expand geographic knowledge.[35] As Britain's imperial interactions changed, so too did the navy's role within the imperial nation. Building on the increased need for sufficiently accurate geographic knowledge to better plan and manage colonial possessions, the Anson medal presents the voyage, and by extension the Royal Navy, as a centre of imperial knowledge.

To return to the medal, the circumnavigation side of the coin is an interesting combination of images and names to invoke one of the most famous voyages of the century. Indeed, without the word 'circumnavigation' round the interior circle, a viewer might have difficulty discerning which event is being commemorated. At the centre is Victory, again, this time wearing armour, holding a trophy and standing atop a sea monster. The monster may represent the conquering of the dangers of the sea generally, or the Spanish who controlled the Pacific coasts more specifically. The presence of armour seems to suggest that circumnavigation is akin to a fight, thus elevating navigational feats to the level of battle as heroic act. Under the monster lies an orb, perhaps a globe, which Anson had shown to be but a track for man to traverse. Victory also holds a laurel wreath, as if to share Anson's crown on the obverse with the wreathed names that ring the outer rim. The inclusion of the officer's names – Keppel, Campbell, Saunders, Saumarez, Brett and Dennis – shows that the Admiralty valued experience in long-range expeditions when considering promotions, but also reveals one further facet of the Anson legacy, the importance of followers.

Anson certainly profited from preferment from superiors in his early career – indeed no aspiring officer could hope for promotion without strong backers higher in the command structure. After returning from his circumnavigation, the officers with whom he travelled all received rapid promotion based both on Anson's reports and from the continuing War of the Austrian Succession. Sir Peter Denis, lieutenant in the *Centurion*, was promoted to post-captain in February 1745 and eventually served as MP for Hedon, just as Anson had. In 1761, he served as flag captain to Lord Anson, received a baronetcy in 1767 and ended his career as a vice-admiral of the red. Sir Charles Saunders left with Anson in 1740 as third lieutenant in the *Centurion*. Anson promoted him to post rank while at sea. Saunders also served as a MP through Anson's influence, became a lord of the Admiralty in 1765 and served as First Lord, briefly, in 1766. Philip Saumarez, another *Centurion* third lieutenant who became a first lieutenant during the voyage, commanded the ship when Anson was away. When the *Centurion* was blown out to sea with a quarter complement, he navigated his way back to the stranded Anson and the rest of the crew, though it took nineteen days. Promoted captain after the circumnavigation, Saumarez died at the Second Battle of Finisterre. However, he is credited with the design of the uniform adopted for naval officers in 1748, an Anson-backed reform.

Perhaps the best known of the officers cited on the medal, Augustus Keppel was a midshipman when he sailed with Anson. He became acting lieutenant at sea. Upon returning and passing his lieutenant's exam, Keppel quickly rose through the ranks with Anson's patronage, making post rank at the age of nineteen, and becoming one of the most popular captains in the Royal Navy during the Seven Years' War. Keppel served with Saunders at the Admiralty. He also enjoyed a lively political career and was raised to the peerage as Viscount Keppel and Baron Elden in 1782. Sir Peircy Brett, who provided the drawings for Anson's 1748 account, was a second lieutenant to Anson and led the sacking of Paita. He was posted after the return of Anson, participated with him in the First Battle of Finisterre, served as captain of the fleet with Anson in 1758 and ended his career as an admiral, a knight of the realm, lord commissioner of the Admiralty from 1766 to 1770 and long-time MP for Queenborough, Kent. Finally, John Campbell, whose name is misspelled here but was corrected on later strikings, was promoted from midshipman to master while on the circumnavigation, and made post-captain in 1747. With Anson's approval, Campbell was selected to lead an expedition to the Pacific in 1749, a voyage aborted to avoid provoking the Spanish in the new peace. Campbell's interest in astronomy led him to organise sea trials of new lunar tables and instruments, a command granted by the Board of Longitude. Exploration and experimentation were major markers of his career. In the 1760s, Campbell would try Harrison's chronometer, and his later career was furthered, and stalled, by his close friendship with Keppel.[36] Participation in the circumnavigation was a boon to all these men's careers, perhaps most interestingly in the case of Campbell, who continued to explore and innovate for the Admiralty.[37]

The design of the medal is meant to tie Anson not only to the circumnavigation itself, but to link Anson's successes to those of his fellow officers. His legacy is made stronger and more long-lasting by associating his greatest success in action, the circumnavigation, to the numerous careers he shaped later in life. After returning to England, Anson was offered the rank of rear-admiral, a commission he returned when the Admiralty refused to date Brett's captaincy to his promotion at sea, as opposed to the date of Brett's return to Spithead. Brett's commission was eventually post-dated and Anson was vindicated when he foiled the invasion of Bonnie Prince Charlie in 1745.[38] The deeper significance of this episode is etched in the medal: one's naval heroism depended not only on one's own acts, but also on one's professional connections. In this way, perhaps Anson's administrative duties are being commemorated, albeit indirectly, for without his seat at the Admiralty he could not have rewarded those officers still active in the field. The eighteenth-century Royal Navy's success, and by extension Britain's success, depended on generations of officers training each other and recognising excellence in the lower ranks. The medal attests to Anson's supreme ability to identify and reward such excellence, without which he could not have slain the sea monster of circumnavigation trodden underfoot so triumphantly on the medal's face. Thus the medal ties the deceased Anson not only to contemporary Pacific exploration, but to naval officers still in service. Anson lived on in material and immaterial ways, all of which are referenced on the medal.

To return to the questions that shaped this inquiry, medals such as this represent the cultural solidification of certain events and acts that are deemed worthy of commemoration. Thus, these medals serve as a final product in a cultural distillation of the definition of naval heroism.[39] Whereas the navy made up a large part of government expenditure and employed many men in clerical and administrative duties, it was only a limited swath of activity that was preserved for posterity. Taken together, the two faces of the medal highlight that a naval hero was supposed to amass examples of courage in action. Although it would never be the primary way that officers could make their names, exploration was a celebrated activity in which officers could show bravery under pressure – if the expedition proved successful. Officers were also defined by those they helped to promote; this medal is a genealogy of naval heroism. Overall, the Anson medal makes clear that action in many forms was central to attaining commemoration, and that Anson's circumnavigation was a critical event in the development of the concept of naval heroism.

The diarist John Evelyn suggested that '*Decus Et Tutamen*' – 'an ornament and a safeguard' – be engraved on the first milled crown coinage of

1662.[40] Thomas Anson's commissioned medal was also meant to ornament and safeguard his brother's reputation as a naval man of action while applauding his devotion to his fellow officers who had protected the imperial nation. The Anson medal attests to the role of the navy in the British national imagination, a military service that in turn was meant to ornament and safeguard an expanding nation.

Notes

1 For a sampling of work on just the eighteenth century, see James Davey, 'The Naval Hero and British National Identity 1707–1750' in Duncan Redford (ed.), *Maritime History and Identity: the Sea and Culture in the Modern World* (London: I.B.Tauris, 2013), pp. 13–37; Margarette Lincoln, *Representing the Royal Navy: British Sea Power, 1750–1815* (Aldershot: Ashgate, 2002); Isaac Land, *War, Nationalism, and the British Sailor, 1750–1850* (New York: Palgrave Macmillan, 2009); N. A. M. Rodger, *The Command of the Ocean: A Naval History of Britain, 1649–1815* (New York: W. W. Norton, 2005), chapters 11–31; Gerald Jordan and Nicolas Rogers, 'Admirals as Heroes: Patriotism and Liberty in Hanoverian England', *Journal of British Studies*, 28 (1989), 202–24; Kathleen Wilson, *The Sense of the People: Politics, Culture and Imperialism in England, 1715–1785* (Cambridge: Cambridge University Press, 1995), chapter 3.

2 For more on the simplification process implicit in commemoration, as well as a discussion of the role of public historians in the face of the commercialisation of commemoration, see Ludmilla Jordanova, 'Marking Time' in Holger Hoock (ed.), *History, Commemoration, and National Preoccupation: Trafalgar, 1805–2005* (Oxford: Oxford University Press, 2007), pp. 7–19.

3 Wilson, *Sense of the People*, pp. 6–7, 67. Local political agitation and international warfare often intersected, as in the push in the periodical press for war in 1739. Rodger, *The Command of the Ocean*, p. 235; Philip Woodfine, '"Suspicious Latitudes": Commerce, Colonies, and Patriotism in the 1730s', *Studies in Eighteenth Century Culture*, 27 (1998), 37–8, 44.

4 John Brewer, *Sinews of Power: War, Money and the English State, 1688–1783* (London: Unwin Hyman, 1989), pp. xvi–xvii. See also Clive Wilkinson, *The British Navy and the State in the Eighteenth Century* (Woodbridge: The Boydell Press, 2004), pp. 13–19, 30–1, 36, 64.

5 Holger Hoock, 'Introduction' in *History, Commemoration, and National Preoccupation*, p. 1; Barry M. Gough, review article, *The Journal of Military History*, 70:3 (2006), 836; Jen Hill, 'National Bodies: Robert Southey's *Life of Nelson* and John Franklin's *Narrative of a Journey to the Shores of the Polar Sea*', *Nineteenth-Century Literature*, 61:4 (2007), 417–18; Tim Fulford, 'Romanticizing the Empire: The Naval Heroes of Southey, Coleridge, Austen, and Marryat', *Modern Language Quarterly*, 60:2 (1999), 161–96; Kathleen Wilson, 'How Nelson Became a Hero', *The Historian*, 87 (2005), 6–17; Jordan

and Rogers, 'Admirals as Heroes', 202. For more on the nuanced contemporary reactions to the death of Nelson, see Colin White, '"His Dirge Our Groans – His Monument Our Praise': Official and Popular Commemoration of Nelson in 1805–6' in Hoock (ed.), *History, Commemoration, and National Preoccupation*, pp. 23–48. On Nelson's effect on the study of naval leadership, see Richard Harding, 'The Royal Navy, History and the Study of Leadership' in Richard Harding and Agustín Guimerá (eds), *Naval Leadership in the Atlantic World: The Age of Reform and Revolution* (London: University of Westminster Press, 2017), p. 17.

6 Rogers and Jordan, 'Admirals as Heroes', 201–24; Kathleen Wilson, 'Empire, Trade and Popular Politics in Mid-Hanoverian Britain', *Past and Present*, 121 (1988), 74–109.

7 Stephen Moore, '"A Nation of Harlequins"? Politics and Masculinity in Mid-Eighteenth-Century England', *Journal of British Studies*, 49:3 (2010), 427–8. Periodicals and the press reductively presented admirals as either tarpaulins or gentlemen, those who rose through merit or through aristocratic ties. Individuals seldom fall easily into one category or another, as Anson's career bears out. Such socially constructed representations were also tied to competing masculinities within British society. As Wilson explains for Admirals Vernon and Nelson, the political and public spheres are primarily where these masculinities were created, changed, and circulated. Wilson, 'How Nelson Became a Hero', 1, 14, 17; Wilson, *Sense of the People*, chapter 3; Wilson, 'Empire, Trade and Popular Politics', 74, 108. In addition, masculinities were not explicitly naval. The gentleman officer type of masculinity described by Moore is very similar to that ascribed more generally to aristocrats, especially rich, idle young men involved in riotous acts. Rumours raged about such men, tapping into a larger cultural discourse about the nuances of eighteenth-century masculinity. Jason Kelly, 'Riots, Revelries, and Rumour: Libertinism and Masculine Association in Enlightenment London', *Journal of British Studies*, 45:4 (2006), 759–95.

8 For the Arctic, see especially Adriana Craciun, *Writing Arctic Disaster: Authorship and Exploration* (Cambridge: Cambridge University Press, 2016).

9 For more on the definition of exploration, see Katherine Parker, 'The Savant and the Engineer: Exploration Personnel in the Narbrough and Anson Voyage Accounts', *Terrae Incognitae*, 17:1 (2017), 6–20; Adriana Craciun, 'What Is an Explorer?', *Eighteenth-Century Studies*, 45:1 (2011), 29–51; Dane Kennedy, 'Introduction: Reinterpreting Exploration' in his *Reinterpreting Exploration: The West in the World* (Oxford: Oxford University Press, 2014), pp. 1–18; Marie-Noëlle Bourguet, 'The Explorer' in Michel Voelle (ed.) and Lydia G. Cochrane (trans.), *Enlightenment Portraits* (Chicago: University of Chicago Press, 1997), pp. 257–315.

10 Christopher Eimer, *The Pingo Family and Medal-Making in 18th-Century Britain* (London: British Art Medal Trust, 1998), pp. 6–7. For more on the

growth in the industry of attributable and unattributable medals, see appendices Table 1 (p. 36) and Table 3 (p. 38). 102 medals were made commemorating Vernon's victory between 1740 and 1743, more than any other figure in the eighteenth century. Wilson, *Sense of the People*, p. 146.

11 Pinchbeck was a cheaper alloy made of five parts copper to one part zinc. It is named after the engraver who created it. Christopher Eimer, *An Introduction to Commemorative Medals* (London: Seaby, 1989), p. 5. For example, there were over eighty types of pinchbeck medals made for the victory of Portobello alone. *Ibid.*, 76.

12 For more on this national identity creation process, see Linda Colley, *Britons: Forging the Nation, 1707–1837* (New Haven, CT: Yale University Press, 2005).

13 Andrew Lambert, *Admirals: The Naval Commanders who Made Britain Great* (London: Faber and Faber, 2008), pp. 137–40, 156; Daniel A. Baugh, 'The Eighteenth-Century Navy as a National Institution, 1690–1815' in J. R. Hill (ed.), *The Oxford Illustrated History of the Royal Navy* (Oxford: Oxford University Press, 1995), pp. 144, 156; Wilkinson, *The British Navy and the State*, pp. 10, 66, 94. Nineteenth-century biographers also appreciated Anson's administrative skills, even if they thought it peculiar how quietly Anson seemed to work for moderate reform. Sir John Barrow, *Life of George Lord Anson, Admiral of the Fleet, Vice-Admiral of Great Britain, and First Lord Commissioner of the Admiralty, Previous to, and During, the Seven Years' War* (London: 1839), p. v; 'Art. V. *Life of George Lord Anson, Admiral of the Fleet, Vice-Admiral of Great Britain, and First Lord Commissioner of the Admiralty, precious to, and during, the Seven Years' War. By Sir John Barrow, Bart., F. R. S. 8 vo. London: 1839,'* *The Edinburgh Review*, 69 (1839), 126; John Laughton Knox, *From Howard to Nelson: Twelve Sailors* (London: Lawrence and Bullen, Ltd., 1899), p. 161; Walter Vernon Anson, *The Life of Admiral Lord Anson, the Father of the British Navy, 1697–1762* (London: John Murray, 1912), pp. ix–x. For more on the changeable biographies of Anson, see Katherine Parker, 'Rewriting Admiral Anson as Naval Hero: Biographical Depictions of Sir George Anson from the Eighteenth to the Mid-Twentieth Century', *The Trafalgar Chronicle*, 24 (2014), 81–94.

14 Anson was placed on the Admiralty Board when Bedford became First Lord in November 1744. After this appointment, he became rear-admiral in June 1745, vice-admiral in 1746, full admiral in May 1749, and Vice-Admiral of Great Britain in 1750. He served as First Lord from 1751 to 1756, when the Newcastle government fell. In 1757 he became First Lord for the second time when Newcastle joined the Pitt government. He held that position until his death. All biographical information is from Lambert, *Admirals*, pp. 119–56; N. A. M. Rodger, 'Anson, George, Baron Anson (1697–1762)', *Oxford Dictionary of National Bibliography* (Oxford: Oxford University Press, 2004, online edn, May, 2008), http://www.oxforddddnb.com/view/article/574 (accessed 1 July 2016).

15 'London', *St James's Chronicle or the British Evening Post*, 1281 (London, England), 13–16 May 1769; 'London Intelligence', *Whitehall Evening Post or London Intelligencer*, 3610 (London, England), 13–16 May 1769.

16 Eimer, *Pingo*, 11, medal entry 1, p. 44. For the calculation of the percentages see Appendix 9, page 35.

17 *Ibid.*, 25, medal entries 69 and 70, p. 67. The private medal-making workshop of the Pingos was the first of its kind and contributed to the flowering of extra-Mint production that began in the 1740s. *Ibid.*, 28.

18 The Pingos were also beneficial to the state, which forged a closer relationship with artists and cultural projects in the latter third of the eighteenth century. Holger Hoock, *The King's Artists: The Royal Academy of Arts and the Politics of British Culture, 1760–1840* (Oxford: Clarendon Press, 2003), section III.

19 Eimer, *An Introduction*, 26. For the medal, see medal 69, plate 10.

20 Eimer, *Pingo*, 23; medal 38, p. 57. There were also at least some medals struck in Berlin Iron, as the personal collection of Mr Colin Paul attests. Berlin Iron was made almost exclusively in Germany and for use primarily with uniface medals. *Ibid.*, 15. Thus, the Anson Berlin Iron is an intriguing mystery as to provenance and manufacture.

21 Laughton, *From Howard to Nelson*, 192. Sir John Barrow, Fellow of the Royal Society, Second Secretary to the Navy, and Anson's first biographer, remarks on the importance of the battle for public morale. Barrow, *Life*, 168; 'Art. V', 147.

22 The appreciation for Anson's administrative abilities are most evident in his personal correspondence with Lord Sandwich. The correspondence reveals a deep friendship. It also reveals a great deal of admiration of Anson's knowledge and efficiency on Sandwich's part. Sandwich leaned on Anson heavily while away from the Admiralty. British Library, London (hereafter BL), MS Add 15957, fol. 57.

23 'Anson and Warren: A Song the Words by Mr. Lockman, Set to Music by Lewis Granom Esqr. 1747, Printed for J. Simpson in Sweetings Alley Royal Exchange'. BL G.316.a. (27.).

24 Frank Felsenstein, 'Unravelling Ann Mills: Some Notes on Gender Construction and Naval Heroism', *Eighteenth-Century Fiction*, 19 (2006), 213; Wilson, 'How Nelson Became a Hero', p. 6; Fulford, 'Romanticizing the Empire', 7, 9; Hill, 'National Bodies', 418. Such heroism based on active service applied not only to officers but extended down the command structure to ordinary seamen by the late eighteenth century. Land, *War, Nationalism*, pp. 91, 103.

25 N. A. M. Rodger, *The Wooden World: An Anatomy of the Georgian Navy* (London: Fontana Press, 1988), p. 11. This is not to imply that bureaucratic reform was even, always effective, or without lapses, as discussed in Wilkinson, *The British Navy and the State*.

26 'Instructions to Commodore Anson, 1740' in Glyndwr Williams (ed.), *Documents Relating to Anson's Voyage Round the World 1740–1744* (London: Navy Record Society, 1967), document 9.

27 Glyndwr Williams, 'George Anson's *Voyage Round the World:* the Making of a Best-Seller', *Princeton University Library Chronicle*, 64:2 (2003), 289.

28 Glyndwr Williams, *The Great South Sea: English Voyages and Encounters 1570–1750* (New Haven, CT: Yale University Press, 1997), p. 241.

29 Williams (ed.), *Documents*, p. 185.

30 Although Anson might not have written the manuscript he was closely involved with the shaping of the narrative. It is his voice that comes through the account. Translations quickly appeared with French, Dutch and German editions in 1749, a Russian edition in 1751 and an Italian in 1756. Thanks to Colin Paul for access to information on the Russian edition. Glyndwr Williams, 'Making of a Best-Seller', 302–6; Philip Edwards, *The Story of the Voyage* (Cambridge: Cambridge University Press, 1994), p. 56; Marta Torres Santo Domingo, 'Un bestseller del siglo XVIII: el viaje de George Anson alrededor del mundo', *Biblio 3W, Revista Bibliográfica de Geografía y Ciencias Sociales*, IX:531 (2004), 1–27.

31 'Art. V', 126, 136, 151; Barrow, *Life*, pp. vi–x; Laughton, *From Howard to Nelson*, pp. 161–2, 167–79; Anson, *The Life*, p. vii; James Macaulay, *From Middy to Admiral of the Fleet: the Story of Commodore Anson Re-told to Boys* (London: Hutchinson, 1891), pp. vii–viii. For a more recent assessment of readership and printing, see Glyndwr Williams, *The Prize of All Oceans: Commodore Anson's Daring Voyage and Triumphant Capture of the Spanish Treasure Galleon* (New York: Viking, 2000), chapter 9.

32 For a small sampling from the National Maritime Museum (NMM) collections: paintings BHC0360 and BHC0358; pocket and miniature globes GLB0034, GLB0052, GLB0014, GLB0029; ceramic tile AAA4501.

33 This objective reality is of course a myth. Jen Hill examines how the Arctic is often portrayed as a blank landscape, despite journals that describe it to the contrary. Hill, 'National Bodies,' 422, 437, 439.

34 For an excellent study of the cultural reception and transformation of Cook into a distinctly English hero, see Kathleen Wilson, *The Island Race: Englishness, Empire, and Gender in the Eighteenth Century* (London: Routledge, 2003), chapter 2.

35 Stephen Hornsby, *Surveyors of Empire: Samuel Holland, J. W.F. Des Barres, and the Making of the Atlantic Neptune* (Montreal and Kingston: McGill-Queen's University Press, 2011), p. 3. See also, Paul W. Mapp, *The Elusive West and the Contest for Empire, 1713–1763* (Chapel Hill, NC: University of North Carolina Press, 2011); Matthew H. Edney, *Mapping an Empire: The Geographical Construction of British India, 1765–1843* (Chicago: University of Chicago Press, 1997).

36 All biographical information taken from *ODNB* articles (accessed 10 June 2017).

37 An additional example is the Honourable John Byron, another midshipman on the Anson expedition. Byron commanded a voyage of discovery to the Pacific in 1764. He received the command based partially on his previous experience in the region, a rare commodity. One could do the same biographical compilation of promotion resulting from the Cook expeditions, which included George Vancouver and William Bligh, who would both command their own expeditions to the Pacific. Nelson's Arctic service comes to mind as well. Exploration was clearly an integrated part of the naval promotion ladder.

38 Lambert, *Admirals*, 131. The nineteenth-century biographies are adamant in listing among Anson's greatest achievements his loyalty to his gifted followers, a lesson that they wished nineteenth- and early twentieth-century officers would follow. 'Art. V', p. 134; Barrow, *Life*, p. v; Macaulay, *From Middy to Admiral*, p. viii; Anson, *The Life*, pp. viii–iv.

39 The definition of heroism, like masculinity and so much else in the eighteenth century, is open to negotiation. For more on the heroism of admirals, we await Kathleen Wilson, *Admirals as Heroes: Naval and Military Adventuring and British Masculinity* (forthcoming). For more on the intersections of maritime and gender histories, see Quintin Colville, Elin Jones and Katherine Parker (eds), 'Gendering the Maritime World', a special section of *Journal of Maritime Research*, 17:2 (2015).

40 Eimer, *An Introduction*, p. 2.

The apotheosis of Nelson in the National Gallery of Naval Art

Cicely Robinson

Situated within the Painted Hall at Greenwich Hospital from 1824 until 1936, the National Gallery of Naval Art was a major cultural and commemorative response to British victory in the French Revolutionary and Napoleonic Wars. The first suggestion to convert the Painted Hall into a gallery was made by Nelson's former commanding officer, Captain William Locker, in 1795. In the midst of war with revolutionary France, as the lieutenant-governor at Greenwich Hospital, he proposed that a gallery of marine pictures and Admiralty portraits would 'perpetuate the memory of gallant actions and the names of the brave officers, who have contributed ... to the defence and aggrandisement of their Country'.[1] For reasons that remained unrecorded, this ambitious plan was 'postponed' and never returned to during William Locker's lifetime.[2] Nearly thirty years later, in 1823, a successful adaptation of this scheme was finally brought to fruition by William Locker's son, Edward Hawke Locker, the secretary at Greenwich Hospital. By this time, the country was victorious, and Locker's revised proposal to create a 'national Gallery of Pictures and Sculptures, to commemorate the splendid Services of the Royal Navy of England' was successful.[3] Opening in the spring of 1824, the National Gallery of Naval Art was one of the first 'national' collections of art to open in Britain, preceding the foundation of the National Gallery by a matter of months.[4]

The Naval Gallery, as it became better known, was primarily a commemorative enterprise. From the outset Locker proposed that 'A series of Portraits of the most distinguished Commanders, and representations of their Achievements, would be worthy of the place'.[5] When browsing through the various editions of the gallery catalogue, it is evident that the name of one commanding officer recurs more than any other.[6] Within the Naval Gallery, Nelson was commemorated in a multitude of media from paint and sculpture to an ever-increasing collection of memorabilia which included his famous coat from Trafalgar. Prior to the foundation of the gallery, the Painted Hall was already inextricably linked to the public memorialisation of Nelson. In 1806, the upper hall provided the location for Nelson's body to be laid in state. Through an examination of the many ways in which Nelson was represented and commemorated within the Painted Hall, it is possible to explore how the Naval Gallery actively engaged with this previous history, playing an active part in the formation and continued development of a national Nelsonian mythology.

Between 5 and 7 January 1806, the Painted Hall was used as part of Nelson's funeral proceedings.[7] The upper hall was transformed into an elaborate site for national mourning. As the *Naval Chronicle* recorded, 'the painted chamber had been fitted up for this melancholy spectacle with peculiar taste and elegance'.[8] The walls were draped with black cloth, concealing Thornhill's decorative scheme that gave the Painted Hall its name.[9] Rather than natural light, the windows were concealed and several hundred candles were used to illuminate the spectacle. Nelson's coffin was positioned in the centre of the room beneath a black canopy.[10] Made from fragments of the exploded *L'Orient*, the coffin was placed inside additional caskets made of lead and wood.[11] The exterior was covered in black velvet decorated with an elaborate and patriotic design.

The upper hall of the Painted Hall occupied a central role in the public's experience of Nelson's funereal spectacle. *The Times* reported that on the first day, when 'the gate was thrown open, above ten thousand persons pressed forward for admittance'. It was reportedly so crowded that spectators found themselves 'pushed onward with such rapidity, as to afford none of them the opportunity of having more than a short transient glance of the solemn object of curiosity'.[12] Timothy Jenks observes that the overwhelming popularity of this naval spectacle 'mitigated its intended ritual effect'.[13] The chaotic overcrowding and disorder continued on the second day, with people still being crushed by the 'rushing torrent of the multitude'.[14] It was not until the third day that order was restored, when the king's Life Guards were called out to gain control of the crowds. Instead of rapidly moving past the coffin, visitors were now able to experience a designated moment of mourning. As *The Times* remarked, this made the encounter 'much more solemn and impressive'.[15] The upper hall was where the physical reality of Nelson's death was first experienced on a national scale. It was here that the transition from heroic subject to material object took place.

Immediately after Nelson's funeral, the upper hall continued to engage with the public experience of Nelsonian mourning. While the body was now absent, the elaborately carved carriage which had transferred Nelson's coffin through the streets of London to its final resting place in St Paul's now stood in its place. Designed by the Reverend Mr M'Quin as an imitation of the *Victory*, visitors were able to view the carriage in all its detail. They could inspect the representations of the bow and stern and read Nelson's personal motto, '*Palmam qui meruit ferat*' ('Let he who has earned it bear the palm'), which was engraved along the top of the carriage.[16] Alongside the expected funeral trappings, such as the black ostrich feathers and decorative fringe, a Union flag was hung at half-mast from the stern. The coffin had symbolically been placed upon the quarter-deck of this representation of the *Victory*, recalling the site where Nelson had fallen at Trafalgar. The relocation of the funeral carriage to the upper hall of the Painted Hall continued to engage with the commemorative history of the space, recalling the now absent body of the admiral. The carriage remained on display until 1823, when it was removed in order to make space for the proposed gallery.[17]

With the installation of the Naval Gallery in 1824, the way in which Nelson was represented actively responded to this previous history, rekindling the memory of the event. In 1936, the Naval Gallery was dismantled and the collection was passed on long-term loan to the newly founded National Maritime Museum (NMM).[18] While the gallery no longer exists *in situ*, the majority of the works have remained together in the NMM's collection. There is also an extensive amount of primary material available to document the acquisition and display history of this collection. Greenwich Hospital maintained extensive records of its board meetings which document the development of the gallery in great detail.[19] Numerous gallery catalogues were produced throughout the century recording the location and basic details of every work on display. In addition, the Naval Gallery was included in tour guides of London and the surrounding area and was reported on in the contemporary press. Finally, a bound volume of correspondence belonging to the founder and de facto curator, Edward Hawke Locker, resides in the National Archives.[20] Containing over 300 letters and numerous plans for the arrangement of the display, this resource provides an invaluable record of the gallery's development up until Locker's retirement in 1844.

The existence of such an extensive body of primary material makes it possible to restore some of the spatial context that has been lost following the dismantling of the gallery in the 1930s. It is possible to identify precisely which works were on display. In many cases it is also possible to examine how these works were exhibited both within the space and in relation to each other. Through a close reading of the numerous ways in which Nelson was presented within the gallery space, it is possible to examine how the Naval Gallery contributed toward the construction and continued development of the 'Nelson Legend'.[21]

On entering the vestibule, the first of three spaces that make up the Painted Hall complex, visitors were greeted by a colossal, larger-than-life-sized statue of Nelson. Positioned in the right-hand corner of the space, this statue was a plaster-cast copy of John Flaxman's commemorative *Monument of Nelson* from St Paul's Cathedral. It was one of four casts to be made for the Naval Gallery from the Admiralty monuments in St Paul's. As William Sholberl recorded in *A Summer's Day at Greenwich*, these casts were positioned in the four corners of the vestibule: 'in the right hand angles stand colossal statues of England's great naval heroes, Nelson and Duncan, and in the left those of Howe and St Vincent'.[22] The original monuments were commissioned as part of a government-funded project, which had been developing since 1791, to create a memorial pantheon within St Paul's dedicated to the commemoration of British military heroes.[23] The casts are now thought to be lost or destroyed following the closure of the Naval Gallery in the 1930s. An engraved illustration published in *A Summer's Day at Greenwich* provides us with a record of the copy of Flaxman's statue of Nelson

In line with Flaxman's original statue, Nelson is depicted dressed in naval uniform, with the pelisse that he had received from the Turkish sultan following the Battle of the Nile draped over his shoulder. In the original monument, the dimensions of the statue are slightly larger than life. In enhancing the physical proportions of the man, Flaxman was able to align Nelson with the valiant ideals of a national hero. While the engraving provides no indication of scale, the copy of Flaxman's *Nelson* is also depicted in an oil painting of the interior of the Naval Gallery, painted by John Scarlett Davis in 1831.Situated within the broader context of the vestibule interior, the painting confirms that the Naval Gallery's cast was of equally monumental proportions.[24]

From the outset, Locker aspired to obtain copies of the St Paul's monuments for the Naval Gallery. In the 1823 proposal, he recommended that copies of the colossal figures of the most celebrated Admirals [in St Paul's Cathedral] would find a very appropriate place on the floor of the Painted Hall, and Casts of those executed by our best Sculptors are to be obtained at a trifling expense which hereafter may be superseded by Marble Statues.[25]

While marble versions were never created, the instruction to commission casts was made as soon as the proposal for the gallery was approved.[26] The inclusion of these grand memorial monuments would have made it immediately clear to visitors on entering the Naval Gallery that this was a site for the celebration and commemoration of recent naval victory. As Holger Hoock has argued, with the formation of this sculptural pantheon in St Paul's, dedicated to recent war heroes, 'the hope was that public sculpture commemorating military achievements and highlighting patriotic values such as national service and sacrifice would inspire patriotism'.[27] Locker inevitably wanted to foster a similar patriotic tone within the Naval Gallery. From the outset, he stated his ambition that the gallery would serve a multitude of functions, being 'interesting to the visitor, honourable to our gallant countrymen, and encouraging to those who are entering the profession'.[28]

The acquisition of the St Paul's casts was a deliberate attempt to align the Naval Gallery with this well-established commemorative project. However, rather than replicate Flaxman's commemorative monument as a whole, it is evident from the engraving that the copy was significantly transformed for exhibition in the Naval Gallery. Within St Paul's, Flaxman positioned the statue of Nelson upon a grand and elaborate allegorical pedestal where Britannia directs the gaze of two young sea cadets up toward Nelson as their hero and role model. Allegorical figures represent the North Sea, the Nile and the Mediterranean, while Nelson's greatest victories at Copenhagen, the Nile and Trafalgar are inscribed on the pedestal's cornice.[29] Within the Naval Gallery, it is evident from the engraving that this ornate pedestal was removed. In its place, the statue of Nelson stood upon a small square plinth simply engraved with the hero's surname. The written records that relate to the commission of the cast provide no explanation for this creative intervention. The removal of the pedestal may just have been a means to reduce the expense. We should remember that the casts were originally intended as a short-term solution until marble versions could be produced, so perhaps the exclusion of the pedestal was merely a temporary measure.

The vestibule of the Painted Hall is also considerably smaller than the nave of St Paul's. The exclusion of the pedestal allowed the footprint

NELSON.

STATUE IN GREENWICH HOSPITAL

Figure 9 *Statue in Greenwich Hospital* from William Sholberl, *A Summer's Day in Greenwich*, London, 1840.

of the monument to be significantly reduced without scaling down the proportions of the main figure. It may also have been an attempt to create greater uniformity across the four sculptures: the statues of Duncan and St Vincent, produced toward the end of the St Paul's project, were only ever created with simple square bases.[30] The artistic decision to transform Flaxman's monument within the Naval Gallery arguably reflects changing attitudes towards the use of allegory in commemorative sculpture. As J. H. Markland commented in 1843, 'a monument ought to be a book, open for the multitude … In walking through St Paul's and Westminster Abbey, how forcibly are we reminded that his self-evident principle has been unheeded'.[31] The removal of the enormous allegorical pedestal placed greater emphasis upon the naturalistic representation of the man himself. Positioned in the corner of the vestibule, the statue of Nelson was placed beside J. M. W. Turner's famous depiction of the *Battle of Trafalgar*, which was presented to the Naval Gallery by George IV in 1829.[32] In this monumental depiction of the unfolding action, the code flags flying from the main mast of *Victory* spell 'd-u-t-y', recalling the last word of Nelson's signal to the British fleet, 'England expects that every man will do his duty'.[33] While the copy of Flaxman's monument restored the post-humous body of the hero, confirming the physical monumentality of the man, Turner's painting preserved Nelson's famous command as a lasting message of patriotic instruction for the nation.

From the vestibule, visitors climbed the steps into the main hall. It was here that the majority of the picture collection was placed on display. Under Locker's curatorship, a three-tiered arrangement compiled of Admiralty portraits and naval battlescapes lined the entirety of the room. This broadly chronological scheme presented a pictorial history of the British Navy, beginning with the defeat of the Spanish Armada and culminating with naval triumph in the French Revolutionary and Napoleonic Wars.[34] As the subject of numerous paintings in this picto-rial chronology, Nelson was a dominant presence within this triumphant national narrative. Collectively, these works plotted the progression of Nelson's naval career, exposing visitors to his rapid progression through the British naval system. Simultaneously, this chronological projection of Nelson's life unavoidably mapped his increasing physical injuries, arm amputation and eventual fatality.

This pictorial biography was initiated by a depiction of Nelson board-ing the *San Josef* at the Battle of Cape St Vincent, 14 February 1797. This was one of four works commissioned for the Naval Gallery in col-laboration with the British Institution during the 1820s.[35] Painted by

Figure 10 George Jones, *Nelson Boarding the* San Josef *at the Battle of Cape St Vincent, 14 February 1797*, 1827–9

George Jones, it celebrates a significant event from Nelson's early naval career. As a young commodore in command of the *Captain*, Nelson led a boarding party onto the Spanish *San Nicolas*. After successfully taking this ship, Nelson and his men turned their attention to another Spanish ship, the *San Josef*, which had run alongside.[36] Jones depicts the climax of this event as Nelson and his boarding party reach the quarterdeck of the *San Josef*. Nelson leaps upon the deck, leading his men into direct combat, lunging forward with his sword drawn toward the enemy. The Spanish commanding officer holds out his sword hilt-first, in surrender. To take not one but two Spanish prizes was a spectacular display of naval heroism. Locker remarked that 'it was on this occasion the gallantry of Nelson became so conspicuous'.[37] As soon as the battle was over, Nelson was promoted to rear-admiral and made a Knight of the Bath.[38] When this work was first hung on the walls of the Painted Hall, the *Examiner* criticised Jones's painting as a 'commonplace representation of a cut-and-thrust naval combat'.[39] It is precisely the depiction of Nelson's involvement in 'cut-and-thrust' action that makes this work such

Figure 11 Matthew Shepperson after John Hoppner, *Rear-Admiral Sir Horatio Nelson, 1st Viscount Nelson*, 1823–4

a significant contribution to the Naval Gallery's pictorial biography. This subject offered the rare opportunity to display Nelson in direct combat. It was only several months later, in July 1797, that Nelson lost his right arm in the Battle of Santa Cruz.

Following Jones's depiction of Nelson boarding the *San Josef*, visitors would look upon a copy of John Hoppner's full-length state portrait of Nelson as rear-admiral. In Locker's 1839 plan for the gallery, this was located further along the north wall.[40] The original portrait (painted in 1800–1) was commissioned by the Prince of Wales, later George IV, as the official state portrait of Nelson. As part of George IV's substantial royal gift to the Naval Gallery during the 1820s, Matthew Shepperson was commissioned to paint this copy.[41] Nelson is depicted victorious after the Battle of the Nile: the ribands of the Bath and St Ferdinand are worn across his chest; the stars of the Bath, St Ferdinand and the Ottoman crescent are upon his left breast; the badge of St Ferdinand is beside his sword hilt; and the two naval flag officer's gold medals, awarded for St Vincent and the Nile, hang around his neck. Within the Naval Gallery, the introduction of these emblems of rank and status illustrated Nelson's rapid professional ascent.

Crucially, the right sleeve of Nelson's jacket was now pinned up. This formal portrait not only commemorates Nelson's newly acquired status, but directly associates this with an act of heroism evidenced by physical injury. In reality, the action at Santa Cruz where Nelson incurred this injury in 1797 was a demoralising defeat.[42] However, through the exclusion of this battle from the walls of the gallery, Nelson's physical injury could be realigned with a broader narrative of national triumph. Following the amputation of his right arm, the pinned-up sleeve provided an effective means to identify Nelson, pictorially differentiating him from the general mass of officers whose portraits lined the walls of the gallery. Nelson's famed 'fin' is presented as an essential heroic attribute.[43] For visitors following the chronological narrative along the walls of the main hall, the introduction of the empty sleeve pictorially materialised the absent arm. This would have provided the first example of Nelson's personal experience of injury and actual bodily loss.

The pictorial biography of Nelson's life culminated with Arthur William Devis's *The Death of Nelson*, which was donated to the Naval Gallery by Lord Bexley in 1825.[44] Devis depicts the fatally wounded Nelson in the location where his death actually took place, below deck in the cockpit of the *Victory*. Devis adopted a quasi-religious iconography in order to elevate the moment of Nelson's death. Wrapped in a shroud of white

Figure 12 Arthur William Devis, *The Death of Nelson, 21 October 1805* (detail) 1807

fabric, Nelson is almost Christ-like. Lying in the darkness of the *Victory*, surrounded by grief-stricken onlookers, this composition is strongly reminiscent of the deposition from the cross. Light from the lantern casts a divine focus upon Nelson's wounded body. His deathly green pallor suggests that he rests at the very edge of expiration. The light upon his head forms a halo, and below the crossed crucifix-shaped beams of the ship's hull, Nelson is commemorated as a naval martyr. To either side, members of the crew convey a variety of emotions, some with little reserve disguising an overwhelming sense of loss. The display of masculine sentiment was central to the way in which Nelson's death was received and reported on. As Robert Southey recalled, '[it] was felt in England as something more than a public calamity: men started at the intelligence and turned pale, as if they had heard of the loss of a dear friend'.[45] When a select number of the crew from the *Victory* visited Nelson's body when laid in state, *The Times* reported that these sailors 'eyed the coffin with melancholy admiration and respect, while the manly tears glistened in their eyes, and stole reluctant down their weather-beaten cheeks'.[46] Devis's *Death of Nelson* directly engages with this narrative of national grief. In the far right a Royal Marine has collapsed, overwhelmed with emotion. With his head in his hands, the identity of this figure is deliberately concealed; an anonymous example of the grief experienced by both Nelson's crew, and the general population at large, in the wake of this tragic victory.[47]

It is in this work that visitors to the Naval Gallery would begin to witness the apotheosis of the hero. Nelson's uniform has been thrown toward the edge of the picture plane. His cloth orders remain directly on display, as lasting confirmation of Nelson's identity, as well as a continued mark of his earthly achievements. On Nelson's cloth undergarments, also stripped from his body and thrown out toward the viewer, deep red blood stains stand out against the brightly lit white cloth. This presentation of the Trafalgar uniform is central to the visualisation of the moment of apotheosis. The body of the hero is significantly separated from his earthly ties: Nelson has abandoned the material reality of his uniform and instead embraces his total physical annihilation. The way in which Nelson's clothes are left behind as physical remnants of his mortal life is essential to the manner in which he was commemorated in the remaining portion of the Naval Gallery. While the vestibule and the main hall commemorated Nelson's life, up until his final moments aboard the *Victory*, the upper hall developed into a space that venerated the subsequent moment of his death. As the remaining portion of the chapter explores, through the preservation and exhibition of an increasingly diverse display of personal belongings, the upper hall played a central role in the material memorialisation of Nelson after his death.

Once converted into the Naval Gallery, as the 1833 catalogue outlined, the upper hall was 'reserved as a repository for various articles of public interest connected with the Royal Navy'.[48] Initially, this involved a variety of nautical objects including several ship models and an astrolabe thought to have belonged to Sir Francis Drake, all of which had been presented by the Duke of Clarence (later William IV).[49] The gift of naval artefacts helped to distinguish William's patronage from that of his elder brother, George IV, who had contributed so extensively to the gallery's picture collection.[50] The donation of naval artefacts and models helped to assert William's role not just as a prince but also as the Lord High Admiral. In 1828, William gifted an artefact to the Naval Gallery that single-handedly initiated the accumulation and exhibition of Nelson memorabilia in the upper hall. The undress vice-admiral's coat worn by Nelson at the Battle of the Nile in 1798 was presented to the gallery enclosed in a box with an engraved silver tablet which, crucially, outlined the provenance of the artefact. The inscription stated that the jacket had been acquired 'as a legacy from the late the Hon. Mrs Damer'.[51]

Anne Damer, a sculptor most likely working in Naples in 1798, is thought to have persuaded Nelson to sit for a portrait bust on his return from the Battle of the Nile. Damer produced a bust depicting Nelson wearing the uniform from the battle which was sent to the City of London, and now resides in the Guildhall Art Gallery. Richard Walker observes that, while there is no definite evidence of this encounter occurring at that time in Naples, it is certain that Nelson personally gave Damer the Nile coat at some point before his death.[52] The first catalogue located the Nile coat in the upper hall, and it is most likely that it was exhibited in this location from the moment it entered the collection.[53] William's gift was fundamental in shaping the development of the upper hall. Like the funeral carriage before it, the Nile uniform provided a material means through which to re-engage with the previous history of the space, recalling the memory of Nelson's now-absent body.

This material memorial was significantly advanced in 1845 when Prince Albert presented the Naval Gallery with the jacket and waistcoat worn by Nelson at the Battle of Trafalgar. Following Nelson's instruction, the uniform had originally been given to Emma Hamilton by Thomas Hardy.[54] For several decades the whereabouts of the uniform was reportedly unknown until the writer Nicholas Harris Nicolas located it while researching his publication of *The Dispatches and Letters of Vice-Admiral Lord Viscount Nelson* (1844–6). This apparent rediscovery of the Trafalgar uniform was widely reported. *The Spectator* noted that having been given to Hamilton's neighbour, Alderman Joshua Smith, in order to settle a debt, Nicolas discovered that the uniform was available to purchase from Smith's widow for £150. In order to raise the required funds, Nicolas suggested the formation of a subscription in order to acquire the clothes for the nation, reportedly with the intention that they 'might be deposited, like the coat which Nelson wore at the battle of the Nile, in Greenwich Hospital'.[55] Before this could be carried out, Prince Albert learnt of the discovery and, as *The Spectator* reported, 'immediately desired that the purchase might be made for himself, as he should feel "pride and pleasure" in presenting the precious memorials to Greenwich Hospital'.[56] In donating the Trafalgar uniform to the Naval Gallery, Albert was following the

RELICS OF NELSON.

Figure 13 M. Jackson, *Relics of Nelson*, wood engraving, 1865

examples of both George IV and William IV, successfully aligning himself with the patriotic patronage of the British monarchy. As *The Spectator* remarked, 'there is a kind and generous wisdom in this act; for nothing could so help to identify the Queen's husband with the British people as such little tributes to the maritime pride'.[57] The Trafalgar uniform was placed on immediate display alongside the Nile uniform in the upper hall of the Naval Gallery.

From this point onwards, the acquisition of artefacts relating to Nelson continued at a pace. By the end of the century, an extensive and diverse array of Nelsonian memorabilia had been accumulated. Clothing, personal possessions, letters, medals and weapons were all placed on display in the upper hall.[58] From 1881, this included Nelson's pigtail which had been cut off posthumously after the Battle of Trafalgar, before his body was placed in the cask of alcohol.[59] The Naval Gallery's 1887 guidebook appears to be the first clearly to catalogue these objects as 'Nelson Relics in the Upper Hall'.[60] Through the acquisition of artefacts and memorabilia, the Naval Gallery was engaging with a widespread material culture that had begun to develop soon after Nelson's death. Even during the funeral proceedings, sailors from the *Victory* famously broke from official proceedings and tore off a section of the *Victory*'s standard before laying it on the coffin. This was divided up between them and kept as personal mementos.[61]

This act of rebellion set an early example of the posthumous acquisition and veneration of objects relating to Nelson. This type of material memorialisation continued to thrive in nineteenth-century Britain. As W. and R. Chambers remarked in 1833, 'one of the most observable characteristics of English society at the present day, and perhaps of society in general, is the desire of obtaining some memorials of those who have achieved greatness … Lord Nelson's relics have been especially sought'.[62] As 'relics', the way in which these objects were widely collected engaged with an established death culture that thrived in Victorian Britain. As Deborah Lutz argues, 'the secularization of relic culture in Britain had been developing and deepening since the Reformation, and with the Enlightenment and Romanticism … it became pervasive'.[63] The widespread public engagement in the commemoration of Nelson embraced a multifarious ecology of media. Through the accumulation and exhibition of a diverse array of Nelson artefacts, the Naval Gallery can be seen to play a major role in the continued development of this material commemorative culture.

To some extent, these Nelson artefacts functioned as articles of celebrity. Lutz argues that,

the increase in relic love that began in the late eighteenth century was due in part to a growing cult of personality, an emphasis on the heroic individual endemic to Romanticism and carries well into the 1830s and '40s with the worship of such figures as the Duke of Wellington and Byron.[64]

Figure 14 George Arnald, *Destruction of L'Orient at the Battle of the Nile, 1 August 1798*, 1825–7

Within the Naval Gallery, objects were carefully tied to key moments in the heroic narrative. This is evident in the exhibition catalogue. Where possible, artefacts were linked to specific times and places such as 'The Velvet Stock which he wore at Trafalgar'. Informing the visitor exactly where, when and how Nelson engaged with an object helped to enrich the biography of the hero. A snuffbox owned by Nelson, which was given to the gallery in 1847, was reportedly made out of a piece of timber from the French warship *L'Orient*.[65] In providing a physical trace from the event, this fragment helped to further animate and dramatise the history of *L'Orient*'s destruction at the Nile which was depicted in the main hall of the gallery.

In providing a material link to the life of the hero, the legitimacy of the object was essential. The exhibition catalogues clearly record the provenance of each Nelson relic.[66] Due to the popularity of this Nelsonian collecting culture, there was an increased risk that commodification could potentially endanger the authenticity of the object.[67] In 1846, the Naval Gallery became embroiled in a dispute over the origins of one Nelson artefact. Lord Saye and Sele presented the gallery with what was thought to be Nelson's dress sword, 'being the identical one that was placed on his coffin whilst he lay in state'.[68] The antiquities dealer who sold Saye and Sele the sword, Thomas Evans, claimed to have purchased the object in 1845 from Mrs Smith, the widow of Alderman Smith and the owner of the Trafalgar uniform. In 1847, Evans attempted to sue *The Times* for accusing him of 'being a manufacturer of curiosities and palming off a spurious article'.[69] The case was found in favour of *The Times*, and it was concluded that the sword could not be verified. As a demonstration of the significance of authenticity within the gallery space, the Greenwich Hospital commissioners concluded that 'it was not deemed advisable to place it before the public as a genuine relic of Lord Nelson'.[70]

This collection of Nelson artefacts also served a historical function. As material fragments of the hero's life, these objects helped to validate specific narratives. As Susan Pearce observes, historical objects and relics were often 'used as material witness to the truth of historical narratives'.[71] Within the Naval Gallery, the exhibition of the Trafalgar uniform played an active part in shaping the way in which Nelson was posthumously remembered. *The Spectator* published the following description of the Trafalgar coat as it was displayed in the upper hall:

> The coat is the undress uniform of a vice admiral, lined with white silk, with lace on the cuffs, and epaulettes. Four stars – or the Orders of the Bath, St Ferdinand and Merit, the Crescent, and St Joachim – are seen in the left breast, as Nelson habitually wore them: which disproves the story, that he purposely adorned himself with his decorations on going into battle! The course of the fatal ball is shown by a hole over the left shoulder, and part of the epaulette is torn away: which agrees with Dr. Sir William Beattie's [*sic*] account of Lord Nelson's death, and with the fact, that pieces of the bullion and pad of the epaulette adhered to the ball, which is now in her Majesty's possession. The coat and waistcoat are stained in several places with the hero's blood.[72]

In placing Nelson's actual undress uniform on display, the Naval Gallery actively challenged emerging rumours that in a vain, if not suicidal, act Nelson went into battle in full regalia and was shot as a result of making himself so visible to the enemy. Public exhibition of the Trafalgar coat helped to secure Nelson's posthumous reputation, providing the necessary evidence that he had worn his undress uniform with fabric replicas of his orders sewn on the left breast. The musket ball hole in the left shoulder of the jacket provided the essential means to authenticate the object, confirming that it was, irrefutably, the jacket worn by Nelson when hit with the fatal shot. Following the autopsy, Beatty reported that 'a very considerable portion of the gold-lace, pad and lining of the epaulette, with a piece of the coat, was found attached to the ball'.[73] As *The Spectator* confirmed, the fragments of the epaulette mentioned in Beatty's account were visibly missing from *this* coat. In displaying the dishevelled reality of the Trafalgar uniform, the Naval Gallery played an essential part in protecting a specific version of events needed to perpetuate the desired narrative of Nelson's heroism.

The musket ball hole through the left shoulder of the Trafalgar coat crucially records the path of that fatal shot, and quite literally preserves the moment and means by which Nelson committed the patriotic act of physical sacrifice. Rather than reconstructing or repairing the body of the hero, like the numerous posthumous statues and effigies commissioned in the wake of Nelson's death, the exhibition of the uniform commemo-rated the moment of its destruction. *The Spectator* reported that 'the coat and waistcoat are stained in several places with the hero's blood'.[74] The significance of this physical bodily trace upon the Trafalgar coat can be explored in terms of Catholic relic culture, which was one of the deep-rooted origins of the nineteenth-century secular relic tradition. As Lutz argues, 'the materiality of this [secular] culture has a steady and broad historical connectedness to the relics of the Catholic cult of the saints'.[75] Worn by Nelson, the uniform could be referred to as a secondary, or second-class relic. It had maintained physical contact with the deceased. However, stained with the 'hero's blood', the coat was transformed into a vessel or reliquary for a primary, or first-class relic, thus providing a stronger connection to the deceased.[76]

At Greenwich Hospital, this quasi-religious form of remembrance was fundamentally enhanced by the architecture of the site. The Painted Hall, located in the King William building, is paired with the chapel, situated opposite in the Queen Mary building. In the chapel, the corre-sponding space to the upper hall is the altar.[77] Through the accumulation and display of 'relics', the upper hall could be interpreted as a secular Nelsonian shrine. As the *Illustrated London News* remarked in 1865, 'the visitor will find Nelson's coat and waistcoat, pierced with the fatal bullet at Trafalgar, laid up for reverent admiration of those who come to look at these memorials of the hero's glorious death'.[78] In relation to Catholic relic culture, Karmen Mackendrick observes that 'technically relics are not objects of worship, though they may be venerated', and continues: 'Sacrifice may be offered at the martyrs tomb … but not to them; the sacrifices are made to God worshipped alike by the martyrs and those offering sacrifice'.[79] While Catholic relics act as an intercessor between the worshipper and God, within the secular environment of the upper hall the Nelson 'relics' arguably provided the public with a unique type of patriotic intercession.

The way in which visitors may have engaged with Nelson's 'relics' can also be comprehended in relation to a more intimate type of secular relic culture. Material mementos were often shared between friends and loved ones, both in life and in death, as personal tokens of affection.[80] Re-examining the provenance of the Nelson artefacts on display in the upper hall demonstrates that many were initially given as gifts by Nelson to his family, personal friends or naval colleagues. The Nile coat was given to the sculptor Damer, reportedly in thanks for completing the portrait bust.[81] A stocking, worn by Nelson at Tenerife in 1797, had originally been presented to Nelson's steward after the conflict.[82] There are many instances of Nelson offering personal belongings as gifts. These objects engaged with a narrative of personal friendship and sentiment rather than a culture of celebrity. When placed on public display within the gallery, these private gifts were redefined in front of a wider audience, allowing the public to share in the intimacy of personal association.

The addition of Nelson's pigtail in 1881 marks the apogee of this type of material engagement, directly responding to an established hair culture which thrived in nineteenth-century Britain. It was incredibly common at this time for people to keep locks of hair, both of the living and the dead. However, to possess someone's hair was fundamentally a personal and sentimental act. As Beatty recorded, on his deathbed one of Nelson's last requests to Hardy was, 'Pray let my dear Lady HAMILTON have my hair, and all other things belonging to me'.[83] To possess a primary relic, such as a lock of hair, was to have an intimate connection with the deceased. Lutz has argued that,

> to possess a piece of the beloved might provide a link to that body lost;
> it might comfort with its talisman-like ability to contain, and prove the
> existence of, an eternity, much as sacred relics did in the past for larger
> communities of believers.[84]

Placing Nelson's hair on public display within the gallery allowed the entire nation to share in this personal connection with the absent hero.

The way in which Nelson was commemorated within the Naval Gallery can be seen to dramatically contrast with other types of public commemorative projects from the period. The majority of schemes embraced an increasingly monumental model. At St Paul's, as previously discussed, the posthumous body of the hero was restored though the permanency of sculpture in Flaxman's *Monument of Nelson*. This trajectory arguably culminated with the construction of Trafalgar Square in the 1840s.[85] At the heart of this development, a 17 foot-high statue of Nelson by Edward Hodges Baily was situated on top of a column, separated by 170ft from the people below. While the public commemoration of Nelson became increasingly colossal and remote, the Naval Gallery cultivated a uniquely personal type of material commemorative culture. The exhibition of Nelson's 'relics' in the same location that his body had previously occupied consciously responded to the history of the site, deliberately maintaining a link to the memory of national grief and Nelsonian mourning. While other commemorative projects restored and magnified the body of the hero, the Naval Gallery engaged with the moment of its destruction. Through the exhibition of the Trafalgar uniform in particular, the Naval Gallery commemorated the moment of apotheosis when Nelson transitioned from naval hero to national martyr. This reinforced an ideology of patriotic devotion that fundamentally underpinned the gallery's founding principles. As *The Penny Magazine* reported in 1838,

> The Naval Gallery is a proud monument of the glory of England ... no man can look around upon these trophies without feeling a portion of that enthusiasm which made a shout to ring through the fleet at Trafalgar, when the signal was made, that 'England expects every man to do his duty'.[86]

The gallery played a major role in the continued development of a unique type of material memorialisation. In exhibiting a diverse assortment of artefacts as 'relics' the Naval Gallery offered the public an opportunity to share in the intimacy of personal devotion and remembrance. The promotion of this unique material culture within the Naval Gallery has continued to shape how Nelson is remembered and revered. Even at the National Maritime Museum today, the Trafalgar coat and pigtail remain central to the way in which Nelson continues to be presented and mythologised as a national naval hero.

Notes

1 The National Archives, Kew (TNA) ADM 67/44, Greenwich Hospital Board Minutes, 11 February 1795, 18.

2 TNA ADM 67/44, 11 February 1795, 18.
3 TNA PRO 30/26/27, Greenwich Hospital Naval (Picture) Gallery (1717–1835). Correspondence of Edward Hawke Locker. 'Memorandum', 20 September 1823, 19.
4 Jonathan Conlin, *The Nation's Mantelpiece: A History of the National Gallery* (London: Pallas Athene, 2006).
5 TNA PRO 30/26/27, Edward Hawke Locker, Greenwich Hospital, 23 October 1823, 1.
6 Edward Hawke Locker, *Catalogue of the Portraits of Distinguished Naval Commanders and Representations of their Warlike Achievements* (London: William Clowes, 1833); *Descriptive Catalogue of the Portrait of Naval Commanders and of the Representations of Naval Actions Exhibited in the Painted Hall of Greenwich Hospital* (London: HMSO, Eyre and Spottiswoode, 1887); *Descriptive Catalogue of the Portraits of Naval Commanders, Representations of Naval Actions, Relics, &c. Exhibited in the Painted Hall of Greenwich Hospital and the Royal Naval Museum, Greenwich* (London: HMSO, Eyre and Spottiswoode, 1906).
7 For an account of Nelson's state funeral see the *Naval Chronicle*, vol. 15, January–June 1806 (London: Printed and published by Joyce Gold, Shoe Lane, 1806), pp. 45–230.
8 *Naval Chronicle*, p. 49.
9 Richard Johns, 'Sir James Thornhill and Decorative History Painting in England' (unpublished PhD thesis, University of York, 2 vols. (2004)), pp. 156–201.
10 *Morning Chronicle*, 7 January 1806.
11 William Beatty, *Authentic Narrative of the Death of Lord Nelson* ... (London: T. Davison, 1807), p. 74.
12 *The Times*, 6 January 1806.
13 Timothy Jenks, 'Contesting the Hero: The Funeral of Admiral Lord Nelson', *Journal of British Studies*, 39:4 (October 2000), 434.
14 *The Times*, 7 January 1806.
15 *The Times*, 8 January 1806.
16 Jenks, 'Contesting the Hero', 438.
17 TNA PRO 30/26/27, 22 November 1823, 29.
18 TNA ADM 169/704.
19 TNA ADM 67/44–104, Greenwich Hospital Board Minutes, 1795–1853.
20 TNA PRO 30/26/27.
21 Now a well-known phrase, the 'Nelson Legend' was first used in Colin White (ed.), *The Nelson Companion* (Stroud: Sutton Publishing, 2005).
22 William Shoberl, *A Summer's Day at Greenwich* ... (London: Henry Colburn, 1840), p. 56.
23 Holger Hoock, 'The British Military Pantheon in St Paul's Cathedral: the State, Cultural Patriotism, and the Politics of National Monuments, c. 1790–1820' in

Richard Wrigley and Matthew Craske (eds), *Pantheons: Transformations of a Monumental Idea* (Aldershot: Ashgate, 2004), pp. 81–106; Alison Yarrington, *The Commemoration of the Hero 1800–1864. Monuments to the British Victors of the Napoleonic Wars* (New York and London: Garland, 1988), pp. 79–92.

24 John Scarlett Davis, *Interior of the Painted Hall, Greenwich Hospital* (1830), oil on canvas. 37.761, Walters Art Museum, Baltimore. See also Catherine Roach, 'John Scarlett Davis, Interior of the Painted Hall, Greenwich Hospital', catalogue entry 140 in Eleanor Hughes (ed.), *Spreading Canvas: Eighteenth-Century British Marine Painting* (New Haven, CT, and London: Yale University Press, 2016), pp. 279–81.

25 TNA PRO30/26/27, 23 October 1823, 2.

26 TNA ADM 67/72, 1 November 1823, 247–8.

27 Holger Hoock, *The King's Artists: The Royal Academy of Arts and the Politics of British Culture, 1760–1840* (Oxford: Clarendon Press, 2003), p. 258.

28 TNA PRO30/26/27, 20 September 1823, 20.

29 Thomas Allen, *The History and Antiquities of London, Westminster, Southwark and Parts Adjacent*, 4 vols. (London: G. Virtue, 1827–37), III, p. 329.

30 Yarrington, *Commemoration of the Hero*, p. 66.

31 J. H. Markland, *Remarks on English Churches & on the Expediency of Rendering Sepulchral Memorials Subservient to Pious & Christian Uses* (London: G. Bell, 4th edn, 1847), p. 80.

32 TNA ADM 67/80, 8 August 1829. J. M. W Turner, *The Battle of Trafalgar, 21 October 1805*, 1822–4, oil on canvas. BHC0565, Greenwich Hospital Collection, NMM, Greenwich.

33 Cicely Robinson, 'Turner's Battle of Trafalgar at the National Gallery of Naval Art' in Christine Riding and Richard Johns (eds), *Turner and the Sea* (London: Thames and Hudson, 2013), pp. 124–9.

34 PRO 30/26/27, Naval Gallery plan, folded and unbound, dated 1839.

35 TNA PRO 30/26/27, 18 May 1827, 148; NAL MSL/1941/677–683, BI Minutes, V, 11 June 1827, 67–8.

36 Nicholas Harris Nicolas, *The Dispatches and Letters of Vice-Admiral Lord Viscount Nelson*, 7 vols. (London: Henry Colburn, 1845), II, pp. 335–40.

37 Charles Knight and Edward Hawke Locker (eds), *The Englishman's Library, A Series of Historical, Biographical and National Information [...]* (London: Charles Knight, 1824), p. 152.

38 N. A. M. Rodger, 'Nelson and the British Navy: Seamanship, Leadership, Originality' in David Cannadine (ed.), *Admiral Lord Nelson: Context and Legacy* (Basingstoke: Palgrave Macmillan, 2005), pp. 12–15.

39 *Examiner*, 8 February 1829.

40 PRO 30/26/27, Naval Gallery plan, 1839.

41 TNA ADM 67/74, 30 April 1825, 74; TNA PRO 30/26/27, Letters from Charles Long to Edward Hawke Locker, 25 October 1824, 114; 1 November 1825, 140.

42 Nicolas, *Dispatches and Letters*, II, pp. 423–8.

43 Nelson regularly referred to his amputated right arm as his 'fin': Colin White, 'Nelson Apotheosised: The Creation of the Nelson Legend' in David Cannadine (ed.), *Admiral Lord Nelson: Context and Legacy* (London: Palgrave Macmillan, 2005), p. 95.

44 National Art Library (NAL), MSL/1941/677–683, British Institution Minutes, V, 6 July 1825, 40. TNA PRO 30/26/27, Naval Gallery plan, 1839.

45 Robert Southey, *Life of Nelson* (London: John Murray, 1813), p. 170.

46 *The Times*, 8 January 1806; *Morning Chronicle*, 10 January 1806; *Star*, 9 December 1805.

47 William Bromley, *Key to the Engraving of A. W. Devis's Death of Nelson*, 1812, NMM, PAI7637.

48 Locker, *Catalogue* (1833), 3.

49 TNA ADM 67/82, 7 May 1831, 207. The so-called 'Drake's Dial' (NMM AST0172) is in fact an astronomical compendium of 1565 by Humfrey Cole. See Hester Higton, *Sundials at Greenwich. A Catalogue of the Sundials, Nocturnals and Horary Quadrants in the National Maritime Museum, Greenwich* (Oxford: Oxford University Press and the National Maritime Museum, 2002), pp. 301–5.

50 TNA PRO 30/26/27, 'Pictures in Greenwich Hospital', undated, 41.

51 Nicolas, *Dispatches and Letters*, VII, pp. 347–8, note 8.

52 Richard Walker, *The Nelson Portraits* (Portsmouth: Royal Naval Museum, 1998), p. 73.

53 Locker, *Catalogue* (1833), 3–4.

54 Beatty, *Death of Nelson*, p. 42

55 *The Spectator*, 5 July 1845, p. 9.

56 *Ibid.*

57 *Ibid.*

58 *Descriptive Catalogue* (1906), pp. 51–4.

59 Beatty, *Death of Nelson*, pp. 61–2; *Descriptive Catalogue* (1887), p. 52.

60 *Descriptive Catalogue* (1887), p. 51.

61 *The Times*, 10 January 1806. David Howarth and Stephen Howarth, *Nelson: The Immortal Memory* (New York: Viking, 1989), p. 360; Gillian Russell, *Theatres of War: Performance, Politics and Society, 1793–1815* (Oxford: Clarendon Press, 1995), p. 87.

62 W. and R. Chambers, *The Book of Days: A Miscellany of Popular Antiquities*, 2 vols. (London: W. and R. Chambers, 1833), p. 479.

63 Deborah Lutz, *Relics of Death in Victorian Literature and Culture* (Cambridge: Cambridge University Press, 2015), pp. 156–7.

64 *Ibid.*, p. 25. See also Stuart Semmel, 'Reading the Tangible Past: British Tourism, Collecting and Memory after Waterloo', *Representations*, 69, Special Issue: Grounds for Remembering (winter, 2000), 9–37.

65 'Illustrations of Greenwich Hospital', *Illustrated London News*, 22 April 1865, p. 375.

66 *Descriptive Catalogue* (1887), p. 52.
67 Lutz, *Relics of Death*, p. 9.
68 TNA ADM 67/100, 3 May 1849, 153–4.
69 *The Times*, 30 June 1847. See also Mark Westgarth, *A Biographical Dictionary of Nineteenth-Century Antique and Curiosity Dealers*, Regional Furniture, XXIII (Glasgow: Regional Furniture Society, 2009), p. 96.
70 TNA ADM 67/100, 3 May 1849, 152–5.
71 Susan Pearce, *On Collecting: An Investigation into Collecting in the European Tradition* (London: Routledge, 1999), p. 116.
72 *The Spectator*, 5 July 1845, p. 9.
73 Beatty, *Death of Nelson*, p. 68.
74 *Ibid.*, p. 34.
75 Lutz, *Relics of Death*, p. 4.
76 Karmen Mackendrick, *Fragmentation and Memory: Meditations on Christian Doctrine* (New York: Fordham University Press, 2008), pp. 109–10.
77 John Bold, *Greenwich: An Architectural History of the Royal Hospital for Seamen and the Queen's House* (London and New Haven, CT: Yale University Press, 2000), pp. 140–1.
78 *Illustrated London News*, 22 April 1865, p. 375.
79 Mackendrick, *Fragmentation and Memory*, p. 110.
80 Pamela A. Miller, 'Hair Jewellery as Fetish' in Ray B. Browne (ed.), *Objects of Special Devotion: Fetishism in Popular Culture* (Bowling Green, OH: Bowling Green University Popular Press, 1982), pp. 89–106.
81 Walker, *The Nelson Portraits*, p. 73.
82 *Descriptive Catalogue* (1887), p. 61.
83 Beatty, *Death of Nelson*, p. 42.
84 Deborah Lutz, 'The Dead Still Among Us: Victorian Secular Relics, Hair Jewellery and Death Culture', *Victorian Literature and Culture*, 39 (2011), 130.
85 Yarrington, *Commemoration of the Hero*, p. 310.
86 *Penny Magazine*, 6 January 1838, pp. 1–3.

Naval heroism in the mid-Victorian family magazine

Barbara Korte

If the history of Britain can be seen through the prism of its navy, the history of the Royal Navy can be viewed through the prism of the heroic. Such a view is particularly informative regarding relations between the navy and the nation because heroes and heroisms are constructs through which communities negotiate their identities and their defining ideals and values. Heroes are, as Geoffrey Cubitt notes, 'endowed by others … with a special allocation of imputed meaning and symbolic significance', which makes them 'the object of some kind of collective emotional investment' and explains why heroes are figures through which individuals 'establish their participation in larger social or cultural identities'.[1] Of course, there are many perspectives under which the relationship between navy and nation can be scrutinised, and not all of them have the glamour of heroic reputation. However, the Royal Navy, which 'remains to a greater extent than people realise a fundamental element of the British national identity',[2] has produced heroes galore and preserved their memory for itself and civil society: from famous admirals and explorers to common seamen and even ships.[3] A promotional leaflet for Portsmouth Historic Dockyard available in 2014 featured images of Nelson and HMS *Victory* with the caption, 'A hero lost, a battle won'.

The navy as an institution has also been heroised itself: for waging the nation's wars, protecting its trade, expanding its empire and increasing its knowledge about the world.[4] For a country that has defined itself as an 'island nation' since Elizabethan times, and in which the navy has had significant impact on public life, such heroisation seems almost natural: 'British island nationalism nourished itself on the myths and symbols of sea power: Trafalgar, Nelson, Britannia, Jack Tar. Central to this imaginary was the Royal Navy.[5] In fact, however, it is the result of the continued construction and reconstruction of heroic images. Such images have been produced through performance (Nelson's funeral, naval reviews, battle re-enactments) as well as commemorative objects and exhibitions (such as the Naval Gallery at Greenwich), but also through re-presentation in a wide range of popular media: paintings, caricatures, poems, songs (notably those of Charles Dibdin in the eighteenth century), nautical melodrama and last but not least fiction, such as the novels of Captain Frederick Marryat. As Fulford notes:

> In the years between Trafalgar and the accession of Queen Victoria romantic portraits of the navy provided moral exemplars for the domestic and imperial spheres. They promoted the chivalry of the ocean when the chivalry of the land was in doubt.[6]

This chapter takes a cultural approach and investigates how heroic images of the navy and its relationship to the nation were represented and negotiated in a powerful medium of the Victorian period that aimed to entertain and inform a wide audience: the general interest magazine, whose contribution to the discourse about naval heroics remains largely unstudied. In a print market that expanded rapidly in the course of the nineteenth century, great numbers of such magazines presented their intended readerships with fictional and factual material that reflected their interests and desires, negotiated opinions on all matters of life present and past, provided orientation and a sense of order in a changing world and so contributed to shaping their readers' identities. As Richard Altick notes in his landmark study of the English common reader, periodicals 'are best adapted for the needs of a mass audience', appealing 'to the millions of men and women who consider the reading of a whole book too formidable a task even to be attempted'.[7] By 1859, magazines were perceived as a distinctly popular medium, as the critic E. S. Dallas pronounced in *Blackwood's (Edinburgh) Magazine*:

> The rise of the periodical press is the great event of modern history … It is necessary … to the success of a periodical, that it should attain an instant popularity – in other words, that it should be calculated for the appreciation, not of a few, but of the many. Periodical literature is essentially a popular literature.[8]

Throughout Queen Victoria's reign, this branch of 'popular literature' reminded its various readers of the navy's importance for their country. In 1834, the *Saturday Magazine* voiced the argument that,

Every thing that can tend to illustrate the history of the Royal Navy, must always be regarded with feelings of the highest interest by Britons. Associated with the most brilliant passages of our annals, the essential protection of our mercantile enterprise and national prosperity, and rendered illustrious by the names and deathless examples of a Nelson, a Collingwood, or a Blake, it is difficult to reflect on the 'wooden walls' of our country, without a glow of enthusiasm, or burst of patriotic feeling.[9]

Historical sketches of the navy were a staple across the magazine market, and six decades later, readers of *All the Year Round* were still informed that: 'As a maritime nation we naturally take most pride and delight in our Naval Heroes. And what a cluster of them do we not owe to Bonaparte!'[10] The discourse about the navy in Victorian magazines was not simply laudatory, however. It also reflected the fact that at a time when Britain was still the only world power, its navy appeared to have entered an unspectacular and post-heroic phase in its history that seems to be epitomised in Turner's famous painting of the *Temeraire* (1839). The writer on 'The Social History of the Navy' in *Cornhill Magazine* in September 1865 even conceded that the navy might not be sufficiently known to the British public:

Nothing could be more unfair than to charge the British public with anything like a want of appreciation of the British Navy. But owing, we suppose, to the nature of the case, to the fact that naval life is, from its necessary conditions, isolated from that of the rest of the country, very little is known about the history and organisation of the Navy; and it is seldom heard of, except when it is engaged in fighting, or on such rare occasions of holiday and display as this autumn has witnessed.[11]

An elegiac view of the navy and its past exploits was also adopted in the periodical press. An 1833 *Blackwood's Magazine* article about Vice-Admiral Blackwood states that:

This Island has mainly owed her greatness to her Navy; nor in all the revolutions among kingdoms and empires, that may be destined to take place in time, can we imagine a condition of the world in which her greatness will not still have to be guarded by the same power. It represents the national character in its most formidable attributes, and embodies the national might in the most magnificent impersonation ... The glories even of Hawke and Rodney were eclipsed by those of Jervis and Nelson – and the dominion of the seas settled at Aboukir and Trafalgar ... We are not among the number of those who fear for the decay of our navy. Within these few years, indeed, many of our most illustrious naval heroes have died; and the rising race of officers and seamen have chiefly fought but at Algiers and Navarino, against the moored ships or the batteries of barbarians, which were, of course, demolished, under Exmouth and Codrington, and in a way worthy [of] their former fame. But as long as the spirit survives, there will be no want of officers and men for our ships; let that languish, and the navy of England, going to rot in harbour, need never more put to sea.[12]

An article from an 1878 issue of *All the Year Round* asserts almost stubbornly that, 'Swelling sails may have disappeared ... but the solid residuum of true manhood is yet with us, and while that remains the halo of heroism will never fail to surround the British tar'.[13]

By the 1870s and 1880s, the maritime glories of the Napoleonic Wars were fading from living memory.[14] The navy was important as a world-wide peacekeeping force but had comparatively few opportunities to prove its mettle in combat and so to refresh its heroic reputation with the general public. Arctic exploration had to substitute for naval battles. For instance, an 1877 *Chambers's* article entitled 'The British Navy, As It Was' claimed initially that, 'The return of the Arctic Expedition to this country after many months' sojourn amid the ice-floes of the mysterious Polar Sea, has once more directed public attention to that gallant service which has been the glory and safeguard of these islands'.[15] Descriptions of military action, such as the following, of a heroic ship and its brave crew during the bombardment of Sebastopol, are a rarity in Victorian magazines:

> The men, I mean the men before the mast, showed such true English pluck and spirit, that when a shell exploded and wounded one slightly, striking an officer near him sharply on the leg, though without making a wound, the tar merely hitched up his trousers, and said quaintly to his officer, 'That was a near shave, sir'. Even a British canary refused to show the white feather when the cabin, in which its cage was hung, caught fire from the explosion of a shell, and it sang merrily during the whole action. It was touching to hear, in such simple language, how those brave men, in the heat of battle, had cared for the little bird and rescued it.[16]

Apart from its involvement in the Crimean War (1854–6) with Napier's Baltic Fleet, and the bombardment of Alexandria in 1882, the mid-Victorian navy's role was primarily one of global peacekeeping. The public scare regarding Britain's loss of sea power and the succeeding new navalism that dramatically intensified the attention paid to the navy was not unleashed until the mid-1880s.[17] And yet, the navy's role for the nation concerned the mid-Victorian public. As an article in *Chambers's* stated in 1859, 'what John Bull most wants is a correct statement of the actual condition of affairs,' and such statements were given not only in newspapers, but in popular magazines for 'leisure hour' reading.[18]

The following cross-title analysis of some widely read family magazines published between 1850 and roughly 1880 traces the entangled discourses of navy, nation and the heroic with respect to some key cultural themes. The periodicals investigated are *Chambers's Journal* (from 1834), *The Leisure Hour: A Family Journal of Instruction and Recreation* (from 1852) and Charles Dickens's *Household Words* (1850–9), which he continued with *All the Year Round*.[19] While these magazines often portrayed famous naval men and their exploits, the focus of the pages that follow will be on articles dedicated to naval heroics more generally or that see the navy as an institution through the lens of the heroic.

Family magazines targeted a cross-age and cross-gender readership, and served mainly middle-class readers and educated lower-class readers who perused the periodical press without a specialist interest but with a desire to keep in touch with the major concerns of their time, and in an accessible mode of presentation. Even if family magazines reflect a focus on social cohesion and stability rather than social conflict, they reveal the *multiple* facets with which Victorian 'common' readers perceived one of their defining national institutions and its members.[20] Depending on the magazines' editorial policies and ideological orientation, their interests in and attitudes towards the navy and its heroes tend to vary. *The Leisure Hour*, for instance, a publication of the Religious Tract Society, tended to emphasise moral issues and presented the navy as a professional option, while *Chambers's*, as a journal with a special focus on science, showed a strong interest in the navy's technological innovations, and Dickens's magazines took a particular interest in the situation of common seamen. Further variation was introduced by the wide range of forms and styles in which the navy and naval heroes could be depicted: in factual articles, essays, anecdotes, biographies and obituaries, as well as in fiction and poetry. The magazines overlap, however, in terms of dominant concerns and provide an excellent source for the study of discursive formations around the mid-Victorian navy, and it is of particular value that they permit us to see the contemporary naval-heroic discourse and its various inflections within a wider social and cultural context. This context involved issues of masculinity, class, a new professionalism, techno-logical advancement and last but not least the period's qualified attitude towards heroes and their admirable traits. The days of Carlylean hero worship were over, and heroes of superhuman stature were considered with suspicion; as *Chambers's Journal* noted in an article about Sir Walter Ralegh, 'The increase of civilisation is continually rendering the attainment of individual greatness more and more difficult'.[21] Nevertheless, the Victorians still esteemed heroes when they could be perceived as models of exemplary behaviour, not only in terms of physical courage but especially in terms of moral principles and humanitarianism, for example as representatives of a hero type which Samuel Smiles propagated in his influential 1859 publication, *Self-Help: With Illustrations of Character, Conduct, and Perseverance.*

Many articles about the navy in mid-Victorian magazines assert that it remained an important national institution, and since navy and nation were to be thought of in conjunction, its superiority had to be carefully maintained.[22] An entertaining form with which to remind and reassure readers of the navy's continued importance were travel and topographical articles, which were generally a staple of the Victorian periodical press. *The Leisure Hour* described a 'Visit to the Birth-Place of Sir Francis Drake', which its readers might also undertake,[23] and Portsmouth was presented as the place where the state of the modern navy could be inspected in immediate neighbourhood with its glorious past, notably with Nelson's *Victory* as a material reminder of the navy's most recent heroic past to which 'two generations of pilgrims have flocked as towards a shrine of patriotism and valour'.[24] In an 1855 article in *Household Words*, the narrator-reporter feels reinvigorated by a visit to Portsmouth after having been,

> very much depressed in spirits last week, after reading some German pamphlets which proved that England was ruined, and several Irish and American newspapers which positively asserted that the sun of tyrannical Albion had sunk forever.[25]

Like the old ships still to be admired at Portsmouth, hero figures helped to keep the spirit of navy and nation alive. The great heroes of the Napoleonic Wars took first rank in this gallery of heroes, but their predecessors – such as Drake and Benbow – were also invoked. An article in *Household Words* had to admit, however, that not all old heroes had survived in modern memory. Its 1852 article on 'bold' Admiral Robert Blake (1599–1657), the man behind England's rise to naval supremacy, identified two obstacles to Blake's continued commemoration:

> One of these is the glory of our latest batch of heroes – the Nelsons and Collingwoods – which is too brilliant for it to be easy to see back through

it. The other obstacle is, that the times are so very different. Benbow (who represents the period between Blake and Nelson) is as dead as the Dodo, and now enjoys a semi-facetious reputation, something like that of his pig-tail. And still more is it difficult to picture to one's self the old Puritan officers and the old sailors of the Civil War times.[26]

The article here demonstrates a meta-heroic awareness that heroic reputation is never a constant but depends on context and encounters of circumstances, that it has trends and counter-trends, peaks and lows in the sense that Fernand Braudel understands his concept of conjuncture.[27] The survival of heroes in cultural memory after a peak of heroic reputation depends on their continued relevance or reinscription into active memory (to which the article on Benbow was itself contributing).

It is characteristic of the Victorians' reserved attitude towards the heroic, and their special esteem for moral heroism, that the famous individuals they designated as heroes were praised with qualifications. They were honoured for their great and courageous deeds and their patriotism, but their human weaknesses were also noted. Nelson is a case in point, since his relationship to Lady Hamilton was unacceptable by Victorian moral standards.[28] He could be redeemed, however, by his sense of duty, quite in the spirit of his famous last signal, which is accordingly emphasised in an article about Trafalgar in *All the Year Round* from 1867. It draws Nelson as a man who knows his duty to his country even though he is physically unfit for heroic action:

Fragile, thin, and sickly, weakened by ague in childhood, beaten down by fever in the East Indies, almost killed by dysentery at Honduras, always sick at sea, an eye lost at Corsica, an arm at Cadiz, cut about the head at the battle of the Nile, struck in the side in another engagement, his cough dangerous, he scarcely hoped to fight more than one more battle. Yet his heart was sound as ever, and the unquenchable lion spirit glowed within him, in spite of all vexatious disappointments, the French reluctance to a fair open sea-fight, and all the mean Admiralty intrigues, shuffles, and ingratitudes.[29]

Given his fragility, Nelson's last great effort was all the more heroic, and almost an act of martyrdom for his native land.[30]

Like Nelson, Elizabethan seadogs such as Sir Francis Drake also needed to have their image polished, since it was tainted by the piratical nature of some of their activities.[31] This made them precarious as antecedents of a navy that, in mid-Victorian times, was important as a guardian of trade. In Drake's case, however, the defeat of the Spanish Armada helped to redeem him as a heroic figure for the nation. An article in the *Leisure Hour* from 1882 emphasised his continued national significance at a time when the idea of a Channel tunnel raised anxieties of invasion:

> The history of the great seaman, who was not only the first Englishman to circumnavigate the world, but one of the first, if not *the* first, to lay the foundation of England's supremacy at sea, cannot fail, at all times, to be interesting to a maritime people. Especially is it full of interest at the present moment, when the public mind is engaged with the question of the proposed tunnel to connect England with France.[32]

What also tainted the image of some of the older naval heroes was the fact that their behaviour was often too rough by Victorian standards. Admiral John Benbow's (1653–1702) reputation with readers of *The Leisure Hour* could be saved, however, by the fact that he could be styled as a patriot and as a 'self-made man' who had risen 'from humble life to a position of high rank in the service of his country'.[33] Benbow was here reconstructed as a mid-Victorian role model. The article ends with a depiction of Benbow's grave in Jamaica (thus also identifying him as a builder of the empire) that gives a final verdict on his heroism and its continuing significance:

> In concluding this slight sketch, we may express our hope and belief that our navy, although its officers are no longer distinguished for the blunt vulgarity of olden times, can yet produce, when the necessity for them arises, spirits as loyal, brave, and patriotic as the lion-hearted Benbow.[34]

Despite their tributes to the navy's great admirals and captains, mid-Victorian family magazines also pointed out that the famous men were not the only heroes of the battles they fought. The magazines contributed to the democratisation of the heroic by emphasising the fact that the named heroes needed the unnamed ones in order to succeed.[35] *All the Year Round*'s article about Trafalgar may focus on Nelson and his heroic death, but it also mentioned that, during the 'climax of the battle', '[o]ur brawny sailors, stripped to the waist, their huge cable pigtails dangling at their backs, their skins black with powder or smeared with blood, were running out the guns, loading savagely, and firing fast as the wadded shot could be driven in'.[36] An *All the Year Round* article from 1864 is entitled 'The Spirit of Nelson' but depicts 'the heroic spirit of one "little midshipman"' during an accident that befell HMS *Orlando*. The boy stayed at his post, doing his duty, while older seamen saved their own lives by swimming away.[37] The navy as a heroic institution depended on the collective heroism of all ranks, such articles suggest, and they thus mirror other articles in which the magazines presented the navy as a respectable career and work opportunity, especially since the navy had reformed its manners (bringing military and moral virtues into alignment). The *Leisure Hour*, for example, gratefully noted the 'contrast between Jack as we see him now … and Jack in the days of the mutiny at the Nore!':

> Men and officers are quite different from what they were in the 'good old times', when pigtails and drunkenness, the rope's end and impiety, were alike characteristic of the race. Courage and daring the British sailor always had, but recent times have shown that these virtues may flourish without the vices which formerly too often shadowed them. The majority of our sea captains used to be of the Benbow type; and while there were always honourable exceptions, too many were conspicuous for coarseness both of morals and manners. Many of those who are now the boast of the British navy are Christian gentlemen as well as gallant officers, and their fearing God makes them the more fearless of man, and the more ready to face any peril.[38]

Family magazines also appreciated the navy's new methods of recruiting, training and treating its men.[39] Discipline and cleanliness on ships and welfare for sick and aged seamen were now a standard of the modern navy.[40] Articles relating a reporter's visit to a modern ship, and especially a new training ship, presented the navy as a hard but rewarding work environment that had been successfully adapted to the civilian standards of Victorian society.[41] An 1881 *Leisure Hour* article about a day spent on board of one of the navy's most modern ships explicitly recommended the navy as a profession in which people from humble origins could rise through hard work:

> The life of the British sailor is by no means an easy one, and certainly has its discomforts, but the navy has often been the making of some poor wandering boy without parents or home who has gone to sea, and, instead of remaining a miserable wretched outcast, has found in the service a home, a good education, and a profession in life of which Englishmen are proud.[42]

Such articles were also written against the popular stereotype of Jack Tar as an incarnation of the 'free-born Englishman' that had existed since the eighteenth century and was still supported by Victorian cultural production, for instance on the music-hall stage and in popular song.[43] Articles in family magazines pointed out, however, that romanticised naval heroism could be misleading and nourish false expectations, especially in the lower classes. A *Chambers's* article from 1851 emphasised how, for most of the time, life at sea was prosaic hard work and admonished young readers and their parents to be realistic:

> There seems to be an inherent witchery in the very idea of the 'glad waters of the dark-blue sea;' but this has been stimulated a thousandfold by the popular songs of Dibdin and others, portraying sailors in such colours that they cannot recognize themselves, and also by certain modern fictions, which, however admirable as works of art, convey anything but a correct notion of the real work-a-day life of the gallant but plain, honest fellows who man England's wooden-walls.[44]

The Victorian seaman, such sobering articles suggest, needs to be able to prove himself a hero and perform extraordinary deeds when necessary; but his life is determined, first of all, by the performance of everyday duties. Heroism in the navy is tempered with the Victorian work ethos.

The translation of romantic adventure into professional work is only one aspect in which the Victorian navy departed from the heroic myth of the Trafalgar fleet. A post-romantic, post-Trafalgar mood also emerges in Victorian family magazines when the modern navy is presented as one impregnated by technological and scientific innovations. Evocations of naval heroism are here entangled with a general cultural awareness of technological progress, so that the navy becomes a *pars pro toto* for what the whole nation was experiencing in many areas of mid-Victorian life. As has been extensively shown, the modernisation of the navy in mid-Victorian times involved equipping ships with steam, screw propellers and iron-clad or fully iron hulls, partly due to competition with the French Navy, and this innovation was also a subject in the family magazines.[45] As a result, visitors to places like Portsmouth were struck by the juxtaposition of old sailing ships with their modern successors. The family magazines frequently take up these contrasts, and they significantly ascribe heroic features to the old and not the new ships, thus following a naval tradition that had heroised ships as well as men, and especially the old ships of the line that had fought at Trafalgar. It is hardly surprising that Turner's painting of the *Temeraire* was referenced in the second part of a series which *All the Year Round* dedicated in 1874 to the 'Old Fighting Ships' that had fought against Napoleon. The article emphasised how Turner idealised the old ship that was towed away to be finally dismantled. The fourth and last part of the series voiced the hope that the navy's traditional heroic aura would translate into modern times: 'Such were the deeds of our old sailors; nor will their descendants be slow to match them if

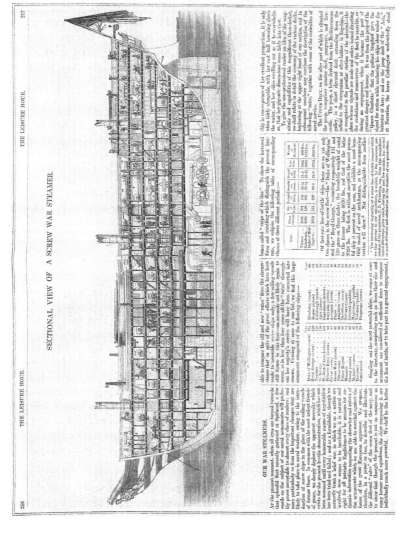

Figure 15 Image from 'Our War Steamers,' *The Leisure Hour*, 6 April 1854

occasion requires – though oak has now turned to iron, and iron has forgotten how to sink'.[46]

Inevitably, however, the transformation from oak to iron also raised the question of whether technological progress would lead to a de-heroisation of the British Navy. At the end of the nineteenth century, it was possible to envisage a new technological heroism,[47] but it took time for such a view to take hold. An article published in an 1861 issue of *All the Year Round* on the new type of 'Iron War-Ship' exemplified by HMS *Warrior* states explicitly that the old heroes would not recognise the modern fleet:

> How old Benbow, in his grand laced cocked-hat, deep-flapped white satin waistcoat, blue coat, gold epaulettes, knee-breeches and silver buckles, would be astonished, could he rise from the dead during a modern sea-battle, and go on board such a vessel as the Warrior as it moved into action.[48]

The article flashes back from the present to the heroic time of Trafalgar, and then returns to the present with another comparison of the old and the modern navy:

> But the new Warrior in action will appear far different to the old Victory. She will not float into battle with puffing sails and defiant flags. When the men are above at their guns, the helmsman is behind his iron shield, and the riflemen are immured in their iron tower, there will be below a busy world of firemen and engineers also at their several posts, standing in the orange blaze at furnace doors, like mute spirits, ready to urge the vessel to her gigantic rush upon the enemy, what time the tremendous two hundred pounders are loading with the solid essence of death and ruin ... The vast vessel grinds down on the foe, like a mad elephant upon a gang of beaters. It severs beams, and crushes masts – men are but flies before its relentless fury, its Cyclopean power ... Our ships are changed things; they are now great machines – no longer the slow things of Nelson's time. They require new fittings, new manoeuvres, new handling. Admirals and captains will no longer be the men they once were. Mere dogged bravery and reckless bull-dog courage will not do now; we shall want science, and more comprehensive schemes of combination.[49]

It is implied here that the heroism of men is subordinated to the machine they operate, yet can a machine be heroic? It seems significant that *Warrior* is compared to the brute Cyclops and not a Homeric hero. *The Leisure Hour* in 1881 found a more reassuring metaphor for the relationship between mechanised ships and heroic men when it stated: 'Every vessel is now a complex machine, a marvel of resource, in which, however, the capacity and courage of our seamen are still as the heart to the body'.[50] Here the idea that technological progress might prove destructive to the heroic nature of the navy is denied the very moment it is raised. The navy may be modern, but its spirit is rooted in the tradition of naval heroism which the family magazines helped to keep alive.

As this exploratory investigation of mid-Victorian family magazines has shown, one of the ways in which this medium for the general public engaged with the navy and its significance for the nation was through templates of the heroic. It should be emphasised here that this was not the only way in which the navy was envisaged. The Victorian family readership of the middle and educated lower classes was also familiarised with distinctly unheroic aspects of the navy and the life of its men: the financial problems of officers on half-pay, the situation of pensioners, the poverty and ill-health in which some sailors lived and alcoholism within the navy. The magazines involving Charles Dickens, a writer and editor with a keen sense of social inequality and injustice, were particularly sensitive to such issues.[51] It was also noted that the administration of the navy as a national institution was deficient. But a discourse about naval heroism was present throughout the period, and it was interwoven with other cultural themes that concerned British common readers during the mid-Victorian years: Britain's status as a civilised country with high moral standards, and its standing at the head of technological progress.

As to the heroic itself, it is obvious that the discussion of naval heroism was subjected to the same restraint that characterised the mid-Victorian attitude towards the heroic in general: great national heroes of exceptional stature such as Nelson were honoured, but even their presentation was tempered by a prevalent view that heroes should be examples that could be emulated and so should be exemplary rather than exceptional. This goes hand in hand with a democratisation of the heroic that is apparent in the presentation of common seamen's heroism alongside the heroism of their famous commanders. At the same time, there was tangible regret that the great romantic phase of the navy, embodied by Nelson and his Trafalgar fleet, belonged to a past that was irretrievable, not least because of the navy's technological modernisation. Nevertheless, the importance of the navy for the nation, as a heroic institution, was still present, and its memory was kept alive. The navalism that emerged in the final decade of Queen Victoria's reign could thus easily reactivate residual templates of the heroic, especially the Nelson figure and the narrative that was attached to it. The family magazines of the Victorian period contributed to all these processes of heroisation and the reflection of naval heroics. They were a leading popular medium of the Victorian period, and have great potential for further research on the public perception of the British navy in the nineteenth century and its heroic and post-heroic dimensions. However, as unspecialised reading suitable for a family audience that included women and children, the view offered by mid-Victorian family magazines is also limited. It does not comment on the more sordid aspects associated with sailors' lives, noting improvements in these respects rather than explicitly stating what had to be improved, and it is also of limited interest to the military historian concerned with technical and strategic detail or naval policy. However, digitisation has made a wide range of Victorian periodicals available for study, and the analysis of other publications will reveal further facets to the Victorian image of the navy and its mid-Victorian perception.

Notes

1 Geoffrey Cubitt, 'Introduction' in Geoffrey Cubitt and Allen Warren (eds), *Heroic Reputations and Exemplary Lives* (Manchester: Manchester University Press, 2000), p. 3.

2 N. A. M. Rodger, 'Introduction' in Quintin Colville and James Davey (eds), *Nelson, Navy and Nation: The Royal Navy and the British People, 1688–1815* (London: Conway, 2013), p. 8.

3 As yet, this heroisation has only received scarce scholarly attention. See, for example, C. I. Hamilton, 'Naval Hagiography and the Victorian Hero', *The Historical Journal*, 23:2 (1980), 381–98; and Cynthia Fansler Behrman, *Victorian Myths of the Sea* (Athens, OH: Ohio University Press, 1977), especially the chapter on Nelson.

4 For a recent celebratory approach see Arthur Herman, *To Rule the Waves: How the British Navy Shaped the Modern World* (London: Hodder and Stoughton, 2005).

5 Alex Law, 'Of Navies and Navels: Britain as a Mental Island', *Geografiska Annaler*, 87:B(4) (2005), 270.

6 See Tim Fulford, 'Romanticizing the Empire: The Naval Heroes of Southey, Coleridge, Austen, and Marryat', *Modern Language Quarterly*, 60:2 (1999), 162. See also Margarette Lincoln, *Representing the Royal Navy: British Sea Power, 1750–1815* (Aldershot: Ashgate, 2002), especially p. 6.

7 Richard Altick, *The English Common Reader: A Social History of the Mass Reading Public, 1800–1900* (Columbus, OH: Ohio State University Press, 1998), p. 318.

8 'Popular Literature – the Periodical Press', *Blackwood's Edinburgh Magazine*, January 1859, pp. 100–1.

9 'Some Account of the Royal Navy of Great Britain', *Saturday Magazine*, 22 February 1834, pp. 73–80.

10 'A Chapter in Naval History', *All the Year Round*, 20 January 1894, pp. 55–60. The article, which sketches the life of a forgotten naval hero, Admiral John Markham, is remarkable for its meta-heroic awareness of the making and unmaking, remembering and forgetting of heroes.

11 'The Social History of the Navy', *Cornhill Magazine*, September 1865, pp. 374–84.

12 'Memoir of Vice-Admiral the Honourable Sir Henry Blackwood ...', *Blackwood's Edinburgh Magazine*, July 1833, pp. 1–2.

13 'Songs and Sailors', *All the Year Round*, 5 April 1878, pp. 485–8.

14 See Eric J. Grove, *The Royal Navy Since 1815: A New Short History* (Basingstoke: Palgrave Macmillan, 2005); J. R. Hill (ed.), *The Oxford Illustrated History of the Royal Navy* (Oxford: Oxford University Press, 1995).

15 *Chambers's Journal*, 17 March 1877, pp. 161–4.

16 'The Saucy Arethusa', *Household Words*, 9 December 1854, pp. 396–7.

17 See W. T. Stead's series of articles on the topic in the *Pall Mall Gazette*, starting with 'What is the Truth about the Navy?', 15 September 1884, p. 1. See also Andrew Lambert, 'The Shield of Empire, 1815–1895' in J. R. Hill (ed.), *Oxford Illustrated History of the Royal Navy* (Oxford: Oxford University Press, 2002), p. 195.

18 'Our Screw Navy', *Chambers's Journal*, 9 April 1859, pp. 229–32.

19 For characterisations of these publications see the entries in Laurel Brake and Marysa Demoor (eds), *Dictionary of Nineteenth-Century Journalism* (Ghent: Academia Press, 2009).

20 The navy was also a frequent subject of Victorian boys' magazines, where its image was, on average, more glorious and adventurous than in the family magazines. See, for example, 'The Boys at the Big Guns', *The Boy's Own Magazine*, January 1863, pp. 63–6; or 'Adventures of Sir Francis Drake', *Boy's Own Magazine*, 17 May 1879, p. 283. A far more critical debate about the navy and its heroisations marks articles from early Victorian radical periodicals. See, for example, the Chartist *Northern Star's* article about Greenwich Pensioners who were obliged to beg under the new Nelson's Column, 4 November 1843, p. 4.

21 'Sir Walter Raleigh', *Chambers's Journal*, 16 May 1868, pp. 308–11.

22 See, for example, 'Fleets and Navies – England', *Blackwood's Edinburgh Magazine*, September 1859, pp. 324–39.

23 *The Leisure Hour*, 1 September 1859, pp. 548–50; see also 'Sir Walter Raleigh's Birthplace', *Chambers's Journal*, 26 September 1891, pp. 609–12.

24 'Portsmouth with a War Face', *Leisure Hour*, 23 March 1854, p. 190. See also, 'Portsmouth', *All the Year Round*, 24 September 1859, pp. 517–23;

'Portsmouth: Now, and in the Olden Time', *Leisure Hour*, 5 June 1875, pp. 359–64. Magazines often printed articles about famous old ships and their later fate; see, for example, 'The Career of a Line-of-Battle Ship', *Chambers's Journal*, 21 October 1854, pp. 270–2.

25 'A Yarn About Young Lions', *Household Words*, 17 March 1855, p. 145.

26 'Bold Admiral Blake', *Household Words*, 19 June 1852, p. 326.

27 See, for instance, Braudel's 1958 article 'History and the Social Sciences: The *Longue Durée*' in Fernand Braudel, trans. Sarah Matthews, *On History* (Chicago: University of Chicago Press, 1982), pp. 25–54.

28 See Marianne Czisnik, *Horatio Nelson: A Controversial Hero* (London: Hodder Education, 2005).

29 'Old Stories Re-Told: Trafalgar', *All the Year Round*, 27 July 1867, p. 108.

30 This emphasis on physical sacrifice is in accordance with famous paintings of the dying Nelson. Czisnik notes that, as Nelson 'was regarded as a martyr for his nation, his dead body prompted similar veneration to that given to a martyred saint', Czisnik, *Horatio Nelson*, p. 4. *Leisure Hour* looked back to 'The Funeral of Lord Nelson' on 25 November 1852, pp. 753–7.

31 See, for example, 'Sir Francis Drake', *All the Year Round*, 17 November 1888, pp. 464–8; or 'Sir Walter Raleigh', *Leisure Hour*, 13 March 1869, pp. 168–71. In its series on 'Remarkable Adventurers', *All the Year Round* was careful to draw a line between heroic behaviour and piracy and commended only two of the buccaneers of the late seventeenth century, William Dampier (1 January 1876, pp. 327–33) and Sir Henry Morgan (4 March 1876, pp. 534–9).

32 'Sir Francis Drake', *Leisure Hour*, July 1882, pp. 436–9, and August 1882, p. 454.

33 'Something about Benbow', *Leisure Hour*, 17 January 1863, p. 44.

34 *Ibid.*, p. 46.

35 For the wider context of this democratisation see John Price, *Everyday Heroism: Victorian Constructions of the Heroic Civilian* (London: Bloomsbury Academic, 2014), and Melvin Charles Smith, *Awarded for Valour: A History of the Victoria Cross and the Evolution of British Heroism* (Basingstoke: Palgrave Macmillan, 2008). An article in *All the Year Round*, 6 August 1859, pp. 350–5, tells 'How the Victoria Cross Was Won' by naval servicemen.

36 'Old Stories Re-Told', p. 113; see also 'The Story of a Sailor's Life', published in *Household Words* in five instalments from 24 May to 21 June 1851.

37 'The Spirit of Nelson', *All the Year Round*, 24 December 1864, pp. 468–9. See also the poem 'Nelson: An Old Man-o'-War's-Man's Yarn', whose speaker is a common seaman to whom Nelson with his special 'touch' was an inspiration, *All the Year Round*, 16 June 1860, pp. 228–30.

38 'Captain Thornton Bate, R.N.', 10 March 1859, p. 158.

39 See, for example, 'The Learned Sailor', *Household Words*, 1 July 1854, pp. 458–62; 'Training Ships for Boys in the Royal Navy', *The Leisure Hour*, 11 June 1864, pp. 373–5. Articles also regularly noted that impressment belonged to

the past. See, for example, 'Portsmouth with a War Face', *The Leisure Hour*, 23 March 1854, pp. 190–2; 'Jack and the Union Jack', *Household Words*, 25 February 1854, pp. 32–3; 'Press-Gangs of the Last War', *Chambers's Journal*, 18 March 1854, pp. 165–7.

40 As *Household Words* reported on 23 August 1851, pp. 516–19: *Dreadnought*, an old warship engaged in the Battle of Trafalgar, had been transformed into a Seamen's Hospital, and was thus still used for a noble purpose.

41 'Aboard the Training Ship', *All the Year Round*, 8 October 1859, pp. 557–62.

42 'A Day on Board H.M.S. "Minotaur"', *Leisure Hour*, October 1881, p. 602.

43 See Raphael Samuel, 'Introduction: The Figures of National Myth' in Raphael Samuel (ed.), *Patriotism: The Making and Unmaking of British National Identity*, vol. 3 (London: Routledge, 1989), p. xxxi. See also Lincoln, *Representing the Royal Navy*, p. 3: 'Over the years, the ordinary seaman, so often a problematic, potentially disruptive figure, was made safe and acceptable as "Jack Tar", a caricature that glossed over his moral laxity and capacity for violence. It was this figure that was repeatedly celebrated in popular song, theatre and prints'.

44 'The "Romance" of Sea-Life', *Chambers's Journal*, 6 December 1851, p. 366. In exactly the same spirit, see 'The Ideal and the Real, Afloat and Ashore', *Chambers's Journal*, 18 February 1854, pp. 103–5; 'Jack and the Union Jack', *Household Words*, 25 February 1854, pp. 32–3.

45 See Lambert, 'The Shield of Empire', p. 188. For magazine articles on the issue see, for example, 'Our War Steamers', *The Leisure Hour*, 6 April 1854, pp. 216–19 (an article with large illustrations); 'Our Iron-Clad Navy', *Chambers's Journal*, 6 November 1869, pp. 709–12, and 13 November 1869, pp. 729–31; and 'Tactics of Steam Fleets', *The Leisure Hour*, 25 August 1859, pp. 532–4.

46 *All the Year Round* series appearing on 10 January 1874, pp. 246–50; 24 January, pp. 300–6; 7 February, pp. 347–52; and 21 February, p. 395.

47 See Jan Rüger, 'Nation, Empire and Navy: Identity Politics in the United Kingdom, 1887–1914', *Past and Present*, 185 (2004), 159–87: 'The navy was the Empire's safeguard and global link, and it was clad in a striking imagery of heroism, steel and guns, combined with the fascination of modern technology', p. 178.

48 'The Iron Warship', *All the Year Round*, 26 October 1861, p. 106.

49 *Ibid*., p. 107. See also, 'A Chat About Ironclads', *Chambers's Journal*, 21 November 1885, pp. 743–5, which states that, 'If the immortal Nelson could rise from his tomb in St Paul's Cathedral and go on board Her Majesty's ship *Inflexible*, he might reasonably be excused for thinking he was in a different world from that which he left some eighty years ago. Probably the only familiar sights to him would be an anchor or a stray coil of rope', p. 743.

50 'A Day on Board H.M.S. "Minotaur"', *Leisure Hour*, October 1881, p. 599.

51 See 'Jack Alive in London', *Household Words*, 6 December 1851, pp. 254–60;

'Physiology of Intemperance', *Household Words*, 25 January 1851, pp. 413–17; 'Soldiers and Sailors', *All the Year Round*, 2 March 1861, pp. 486–91; 'Committed to the Deep', *All the Year Round*, 3 May 1862, pp. 178–82; 'Old Blues Adrift', *All the Year Round*, 17 June 1865, pp. 494–7.

9

'What is the British Navy doing?'
The Royal Navy's image problem in
War Illustrated magazine

Jonathan Rayner

This chapter examines the representation of the Royal Navy in the popular British publication *War Illustrated*, a weekly magazine published throughout the First World War. The magazine was in its own words 'a weekly picture-record of events by land, sea and air', incorporating maps, photographs and illustrations and the work of war artists alongside weekly reporting, editorials and informed commentary on the events and conduct of the conflict. In the analysis of the war, its articles included contributions and regular columns from such notable contemporary figures as Sidney Low, H. G. Wells, Jerome K. Jerome and Fred T. Jane. *War Illustrated* was published in London by William Berry, the owner of the *Daily Telegraph*. It first appeared on 22 August 1914, a little over a fortnight after the declaration of hostilities, and remained in print until February 1919. By the end of the First World War, its weekly circulation had reached three-quarters of a million copies.[1]

As a reflection of the popular appeal of and public interest in the navy in the decades leading up to the war (a period distinguished by highly competitive naval construction in Britain and Germany[2]), images of and stories about the wartime activities of the Royal Navy occurred frequently in the magazine throughout the conflict. Indeed, evidence of the importance of naval rather than military imagery was manifested in the front cover illustration of the very first edition, a portrait illustration of the dreadnought battleship HMS *King George V*.[3] This chapter concentrates specifically on the representation of the navy occurring in *War Illustrated* between the start of the war in 1914 and the Battle of Jutland in mid-1916, and also considers the lengthy retrospective coverage which Jutland and its outcome continued to receive. This timespan has been selected to allow a focused analysis of the particular changes the navy's role – and the service's public image – underwent in the first half of the conflict, and how preconceptions about that role and image persisted alongside and in spite of the evolving experience of the war. The expectation of an early and decisive fleet action (which was key to the navy's planned war role and its identity in the public imagination), was frustrated during the first two years by the German fleet's avoidance of battle, and by the multitude of other, diverse tasks which the fleet assumed.[4] However, these pertinent, inconvenient realities did nothing to lessen and in some cases served to increase public demands for a decisive naval contribution to the war.

Representing what was actually happening at sea to a public expecting an immediate twentieth-century Trafalgar constituted a media-related imaging problem for *War Illustrated* as much as a public relations image problem for the navy itself. For information and propaganda purposes, still photography was handicapped at the front lines on land and on board ships and aircraft simply by the practicalities of contemporary equipment: the same was true to an even greater extent for moving picture cameras. For example, the restraints upon the visual representation of the conflict led to a preference for the fashioning of factual rather than fictional filmmaking for propaganda purposes, and the delaying of production of any kind of official propaganda film until the end of 1915.[5] What could be shown of the activities in all theatres of the war was circumscribed technically and practically even before constraints of security and censorship were taken into consideration. Therefore, the problems for *War Illustrated* in attempting to record and report the conflict, and the navy's dilemma in broadcasting what it was doing and deflecting criticism from what it was not doing, share some of the same characteristics.

These problems can be categorised in terms of portrayal (what it is possible practically to depict), propaganda (what it may be appropriate and prudent to show) and perception (how what is shown may fit with the public's grasp of the navy's role and responsibilities, and how the representation of its actual wartime tasks could be accommodated within popular expectations of the service). It is worth noting that *War Illustrated* was not simply a propaganda organ: its reporting of failure and losses, and its criticism of the political, military and naval establishments was often as painfully cutting and candid as its imagery was fervently, simplistically patriotic. The magazine's editorial selections between visual and verbal sources, and between photography, graphics, diagrams and artwork in the accompanying illustrations, reflect linguistic, rhetorical and representational choices made in performing journalistic and propagandist functions. The interpretation of the interplay between these textual features offers insight to the magazine's accommodation of the establishment's consensual discourses and its readership's popular demands, as well as its navigation and negotiation of its own and its subjects' image problems.

The first months of war

The reporting threads associated with naval matters which dominated the first months of the war and which are represented in *War Illustrated* include: surface action in the North Sea (for example the Battles of Heligoland Bight and Dogger Bank); the worldwide pursuit and destruction of enemy commerce raiders like the SMS *Emden*; the blockade of Germany – and the Royal Navy's strict observance of international law in doing so; attacks on merchant ships by U-boats (which are frequently linked to propaganda discourses on German tactics of 'frightfulness' and 'piracy'); and operations by British submarines. Consistent features of the magazine which facilitated these discourses were the weekly articles on 'The War by Sea' (commencing in January 1915 and written by naval correspondent and MP Carlyon Bellairs), similar columns for 'The War by Land' and 'The War by Air', and longer illustrated articles in a series entitled 'The Great Episodes of the War'. The first articles in this series recorded the Battle of Mons, while a lengthy report on the Battle of Heligoland Bight constituted the third.[6] Subsequently the Battle of Dogger Bank and the sinking of the *Lusitania* were also treated as 'Great Episodes'.[7] Photographs of ships (mostly seen at anchor or in port, sometimes at sea, and occasionally pictured in training to provide an analogy to or substitute for depictions of actual action) enjoyed a privileged, documentary authenticity. However, dramatic illustrations by war artists such as Stanley Wood were frequently included (to a greater extent than in contemporary publications such as the *Illustrated War News*) to depict events for which no other visual record existed. Naval representation, then, from the war's outset to the eve of Jutland, was determined by certain abiding visual and verbal characteristics and formal continuities in *War Illustrated*'s coverage, which would continue to exert considerable influence upon its reporting until the war's end.

An early example of the magazine's handling of a naval story can be seen in an article from late August 1914, which relates the first reported encounter between a British warship and an enemy submarine. This article described the closely guarded secrets of the mechanisms of British submarines in awed tones, and noted the pre-war fears inspired by submarines ('the wonderful mechanical fish … that was expected to alter entirely the conditions of modern naval warfare') before reporting the destruction of a U-boat by HMS *Birmingham*.[8] This incident was said to have 'decided the matter', as the enemy submarine was easily sunk by gunfire.[9] The intended reassurance or even complacency evident in this dismissal of the submarine menace contradicted the mystical admiration voiced for the technological wizardry of submarines (shown in a detailed and labelled technical drawing which dwarfed the photographs of the ships involved, and revealed the vessel's intricate interior). A decidedly more wary report of the submarine danger followed a month later, when two naval losses (of HMS *Pathfinder* and HMS *Speedy*) were noted, both being described in terms of the 'unfair tactics' used by the Germans (specifically submarine torpedo attack and indiscriminate sea mining).[10] Offsetting these losses was the reported acquisition of two battleships under construction in Britain for Turkey, which were to be added to the Grand Fleet as HMS *Erin* and *Agincourt*. The photographs on the page showed HMS *Pathfinder*, *Speedy* and *Agincourt* framing a portrait of Admiral Lord Charles Beresford, commander of the Royal Marine Brigade within the newly formed Naval Division which was in training before service in France. While it decried the cowardliness of the German Navy which declined fleet action, this report nonetheless welcomed the augmentation of the untested dreadnought fleet even as it recorded losses from different and increasing significant forms of combat. Unsurprisingly perhaps, the expansion of the dreadnought fleet was emphasised more than the loss of elderly, vulnerable ships to mines and torpedoes.

No such counterbalance was available the following month, when the losses of four cruisers to submarines, including three sunk in one day by *U-9*, were dutifully reported, accompanied by a painting ('by a well-known German artist') of the submarine's triumphant return to Wilhelmshaven after its 'daring exploit'.[11] Retrospectively, the frankness with which this catastrophe was reported is noteworthy: all that could be salvaged from this disaster was the noting of the admiration *U-9*'s commander Otto Weddingen expressed for the bravery of British sailors, and distaste for the Germans' 'rejoicing' at these losses. Conversely, German gallantry was acknowledged in the recording of the destruction of SMS *Emden* (described as 'the famous raider of British commerce in Eastern Seas') in the Indian Ocean.[12] The reporting of this story (incorporating a map of *Emden*'s voyage, flamboyant illustrations and photographs of the havoc she wreaked, and a pre-war portrait of the ship), sought to distinguish the war at sea from that on land, and also differentiate the conduct of the enemy's surface ships from that of U-boats. In stark contrast to the magazine's frequent demonisation of the enemy in line with contemporary propaganda, *Emden*'s commander Captain von Müller was described in glowing terms, even while (comparably to the *U-9*'s success) the magazine admitted the very substantial financial loss that his activities had inflicted:

> The captain of the *Emden* was a foeman whose daring excited the admiration of the entire world, and his reputation is untarnished by any act of barbarity such as his countrymen have perpetrated, in their battles on land. He acted the part of a sportsman and a gentleman in his conduct of the war, and the British attitude towards him shows that, while we object to barbarism in warfare, we pay tribute to gallantry.[13]

Within weeks, any sense of civility vanished with the bombardment of the coastal towns of Scarborough, Hartlepool and Whitby by German warships. The attack on Scarborough was depicted in a two-page artist's illustration (see overleaf). These events were propagandised in terms of cowardice and 'frightfulness' (the blanket term used for alleged German atrocities in Belgium and France) and described as 'an audacious and futile raid on unprotected towns'.[14] The report recorded with disappointment that this attack was hoped to be a precursor to a major fleet engagement (and indeed the German motive for the raid was to lure the Grand Fleet into a pre-prepared mine and submarine trap), but the attackers escaped without being engaged by British ships.[15] The caption accompanying this image attempted to strike a balance between sensationalising the damage and casualties (condemning the raid as a 'senseless and childish attack') while asserting that the 'British public was startled, but not dismayed' by this bombardment.[16] However, such rhetoric in the reporting of the raid was somewhat self-defeating, since it appeared that the Royal Navy, despite possessing the most powerful battle fleet in the world, was unable to safeguard these 'defenceless' coastal towns. This event, and the questions it provoked, appeared to act as a focal point for the armchair critics of the navy's apparent ineffectuality in the war to date, and *War Illustrated* was quick to respond.

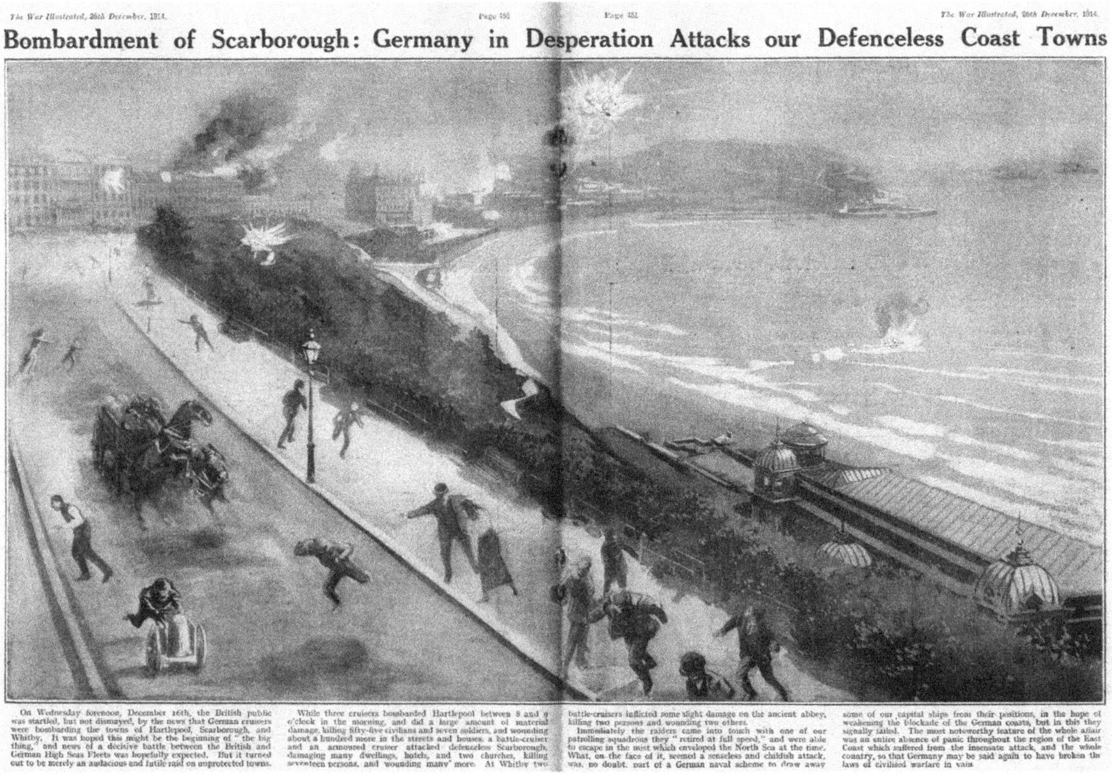
The War Illustrated, 26th December, 1914. Page 450 Page 451 The War Illustrated, 26th December, 1914.

Bombardment of Scarborough: Germany in Desperation Attacks our Defenceless Coast Towns

On Wednesday forenoon, December 16th, the British public was startled, but not dismayed, by the news that German cruisers were bombarding the towns of Hartlepool, Scarborough, and Whitby. It was hoped this might be the beginning of "the big thing," and news of a decisive battle between the British and German High Seas Fleets was hopefully expected. But it turned out to be merely an audacious and futile raid on unprotected towns.

While three cruisers bombarded Hartlepool between 8 and 9 o'clock in the morning, and did a large amount of material damage, killing fifty-five civilians and seven soldiers, and wounding about a hundred more in the streets and houses, a battle-cruiser and an armoured cruiser attacked defenceless Scarborough, damaging many dwellings, hotels, and two churches, killing seventeen persons, and wounding many more. At Whitby two battle-cruisers inflicted some slight damage on the ancient abbey, killing two persons and wounding two others.

Immediately the raiders came into touch with one of our patrolling squadrons they "retired at full speed," and were able to escape in the mist which enveloped the North Sea at the time. What, on the face of it, seemed a senseless and childish attack, was, no doubt, part of a German naval scheme to draw away some of our capital ships from their positions, in the hope of weakening the blockade of the German coasts, but in this they signally failed. The most noteworthy feature of the whole affair was an entire absence of panic throughout the region of the East Coast which suffered from the insensate attack, and the whole country, so that Germany may be said again to have broken the laws of civilised warfare in vain.

Figure 16 'Bombardment of Scarborough: Germany in Desperation Attacks our Defenceless Coast Towns', *War Illustrated*

The naval theatre

Pointedly, just a week later in an illustrated article, Fred T. Jane sought to answer the criticism levelled at the navy by a two-page explanation and justification of its crucial contribution to the conflict. This piece illustrated some of the difficulties and underlying agendas pertaining to the navy's representation. It was accompanied by a photograph of the wreck of the cruiser *Emden*, taken after the battle in which she was destroyed by 'HMS[*sic*] *Sydney*'.[17] The caption described this victory, without any apparent irony, as an excellent example of the effectiveness of the 'British' (rather than Australian) navy's gunnery.[18] Against charges of ineffectiveness against the German coastal raids, Jane offered several arguments in defence, stressing the inevitability of such attacks as much as the historical British penchant for criticism of the navy:

> It is a curious thing that we have never had a big war but that the public has profoundly mistrusted the Navy ... What is the Navy doing today? It would take far less space to answer if the public asked 'What is the Navy *not* doing?'.[19]

In offering a riposte to accusations of the navy's alleged shortcomings, the article provided an authentic photographic image from the aftermath of an unequivocal naval victory, though its 'British-ness' might be more disputable. (The inclusion of the photograph of the wreck of the *Emden* in this article stands in contrast to the highly dramatic illustrations of the destruction of the *Emden* and the presumed loss of SMS *Yorck* in an earlier issue.)[20] However, Jane also felt moved to address the more pervasive, underlying dissatisfaction felt throughout the country because of the non-occurrence of the expected, decisive fleet action:

> We have been at war for some months now and there has been no 'Trafalgar'. Of course not. Reader of this, you go to the theatre now and again. You see the limelight turned on to the hero what time he finally disposes of the villain. But you would not miss the hero if, when the limelight came on, the villain wasn't there! ... Those on our side have to wait and wait for the appearance of the villain. The audience may find it dull; but they cannot expedite matters by saying so, or by cursing for inactivity our favourite actors who are on the stage with the limelight turned off. They have to wait till 'enter the villain'. Then – well, maybe all the dull delay will be made up for.[21]

Jane's exculpation of the navy's responsibility and (in)conspicuousness to the British public in metaphorical terms of theatrical entertainment, dramatic roles and highly moral narrative expectations may appear frivolous or insensitive to the victims of the east coast raids or U-boat attacks (earlier in his article Jane had compared the east coast bombardments to a football match!). However, this chimes strikingly with conceptions of performative 'naval theatre' defining the service's public presence and self-presentation to the British populace.[22] The theatrical allusion is also redolent of the contemporary attitudes the article attempted to allay: the presumed requisites of the naval war and the expected outcome of the preordained, climactic clash of the battle fleets. However, the unfolding war at sea had so far failed to conform to the anticipated pattern. If the script could not be followed, the consequences would be rewriting and ad libbing, and different players on stage.

One answer to the challenge of showing the navy's activities in reassuring as much as truly representative ways can be seen in examples which, in the absence of photographs of action, substitute portraits of the ships and men involved in other events, and striking illustrations of unseen or unrecorded episodes. An example published in *War Illustrated* in 1914 was a photographic collage of some of the ships and officers engaged in the Battle of the Falkland Islands. The news of this victory close to the end of the first year of the war was said to have 'sent a thrill of pride through the Empire and called forth the admiration of its Allies'.[23] Both the men (identified as Rear Admiral Gough-Calthorpe, Captain Ruck-Keene and Commander Hutchings) and the ships (HMS *Cochrane*, *Achilles*, *Shannon* and *Natal*) were depicted in decorous peacetime portraits (and in Hutchings's case, even in dress uniform).[24] The only war-like imagery on this page was the centrepiece photograph showing 12-inch guns firing (presumably in training). In lieu of other more immediate resources, these images are used to maintain a narrative of British naval mastery, implied as much by the static and conservative imagery as by the captions' reassuring rhetoric.

An even more deliberate resort to conservative imagery and reference, also relating to the Battle of the Falklands Islands, was a description of the victory in Nelsonian terms on the magazine's cover. Ironically, this was for the edition in which Jane's apologia for the navy appeared. The cover illustration depicted Admiral Sturdee standing on the deck of his ship cradling a telescope, looking with satisfaction to the horizon where a German ship could be seen sinking. Enforcing the connection with a Royal Naval tradition of victory embedded by and associated with Nelson since the early nineteenth century, the caption read 'The Sturdee Touch: Sweeping the High Seas'.[25] In this example, a reassuringly straightforward

Figure 17 'The Sturdee Touch: Sweeping the High Seas', *War Illustrated*

and unequivocal British victory (albeit following the defeat of the Battle of Coronel[26]) could be elevated through Nelsonian allusion, within the same edition of the magazine in which Jane had deflected criticism of the lack of a new 'Trafalgar'. Similarly, the humane treatment of the crews of German ships sunk at the Battle of the Falklands was reported as emulating Nelson's compassion towards defeated enemies.[27] However, the conspicuous citation of Nelson within *War Illustrated*'s pages, as a stabilising, consensual and 'vital part of British national identity', was also indicative of his talismanic value as referential and reverential 'refuge in times of crisis' – which in this case meant not just the current war but the critical lack of a conclusive naval victory within it.[28] The burgeoning range of activity that the naval operations – and therefore their reporting – encompassed would prompt other searching solutions to the problematic issue of representing the naval war.

The emerging submarine

A growing area of representation and an increasingly important topic of reporting was the impact of the submarine. What might be construed as self-defeating honesty or failed propaganda was discernible in the reporting of the campaign against the U-boats. Both the front and back covers from the edition of 27 February 1915 confronted the growing danger of the U-boat blockade of Britain. The cover illustration, which appeared almost under-dramatised in comparison with many of the magazine's non-photographic images, showed 'Brave British Merchant Sailors on the look-out for German Pirates'.[29] The back cover featured a map of the British Isles marking the submarine blockade (the coastal zone in which Germany declared merchant shipping would be attacked) which came into force on 18 February 1915.[30] The rhetoric of propaganda was evident in this declaration being described as a 'desperate act', and the sinkings of British ships to date being shown along a 'line of submarine frightfulness'. Yet the full and frank admission of the blockade, its victims and effects seemed, like the reporting of the Scarborough raid, only to amplify the criticism of the navy's apparent ineffectiveness. Throughout the war, *War Illustrated*'s reporting of the submarine peril (like that of contemporary publications) would manifest an imperfect and protean blend of reassuring dismissal and alarming embellishment of the danger.

Fred Jane's defence in response to the navy's critics – that the navy's activity and therefore its success were largely invisible to the man on the street – reflected ironically upon the high profile given by *War Illustrated* to a subject that may have appeared not only invisible but 'un-English' to pre-war readers: the multiplying activities of British submarines. This narrative expanded to fill the gaps left by the apparent inactivity or inef- fectuality of the battle fleet, but equally was represented in the magazine's pages from the earliest stages of the conflict. The cover illustration from 31 October 1914 was a dramatic illustration of a Royal Navy submarine patrolling on the surface, with its alert crew having spotted a potential target. In contrast to the earlier diminution of the (German) submarine threat, the British boat is dubbed 'the deadliest thing that keeps the seas'.[31] The caption for a photograph of a British submarine surfaced in the Channel struck a similar note, identifying it as 'a unit in the submarine fleet that guards our coasts'.[32] From the first months of the war, therefore, submarines were highlighted as novel but crucially significant elements of British sea power, ironically more active and 'visible' than the dread- nought fleet.

Other full-page illustrations included in the magazine were equally redolent of the daring and adventurousness associated with the sub- marine. One of these was devoted to the miraculous mid-ocean rescue by *E4* of sailors from HMS *Defender*, adrift in a whaler after the Battle of Heligoland Bight. The cutaway illustration of the submarine's inner mechanisms recalled that of the article from the previous month and, as with that report, the submarine's aura of technological wonder was expressed in the caption: 'One incident in the naval action off Heligoland on August 28th reads more like a Jules Verne romance than cold fact'.[33] A comparably romanticised illustration adorned the cover on 9 January 1915, commemorating the rescue by submarines of naval pilots engaged in the seaplane raid on Cuxhaven on Christmas Day 1914.[34] Submariners and pilots were alike portrayed as working at the forefront of naval tech- nology, and by depicting the moment of rescue the British submarine was again cast in the role of saviour rather than offensive, deceptive weapon. These prominent images appear to mobilise or parallel the heroic ideals and imperial discourses of racial and technological superiority, identified by Michael Paris in pre-war publications fostering a martial and heroic spirit in British youth.[35] As with *War Illustrated*'s hyperbolical accounts of personal heroism and sacrifice accompanying illustrations of incidents on land, the full-page depictions of the activities of submarines and their crews emphasised individual gallantry alongside, and facilitated by, the mystical technology of the craft themselves.

Further reporting of the activities of submarines supported by photo- graphic representation persisted through later editions. An article from

Figure 18 'British Submarines turn Tables on Von Tirpitz/Hero of the Underseas Wins Fame on Terra Firma', *War Illustrated*

November 1915 described the brave exploits of submarines in the Baltic and the Sea of Marmara.[36]

A collage of captioned photographs included a picture of the German cruiser SMS *Prinz Adalbert* sunk in July 1915.[37] The accompanying caption also noted proudly that 'our submarines in the Baltic have also sorely affected German commerce'.[38] The full facing page was devoted to a dramatic illustration of the story of Lieutenant Guy D'Oyly Hughes, first officer of submarine *E11*, being rescued after blowing up a railway line and taking prisoners on the Turkish coast. Although here again the submarine was the literal vehicle for another tale of personal heroism (D'Oyly Hughes received the Distinguished Service Order for his actions), this two-page spread also likened the British submarine to the German U-boat (mimicking and repaying von Tirpitz's tactics in kind in evading countermeasures and inflicting shipping losses) where previously a determined distinction between British and German submarines had been maintained.

A two-page collection of photographs from the following February depicted more usual but highly successful submarine operations in the Baltic. British boats were shown operating in dangerously icy conditions, rescuing survivors from German ships they had sunk, and one of the most successful submarine captains, Commander Max Horton, was pictured cooperating with a Russian naval officer.[39] In these examples, the heroism of individuals, covert operations and daring rescues commemorated in large cover illustrations had been gradually displaced by more detailed photographic reportage of the British submarine's war. It can be posited that this subject was extensively represented not simply in order to distinguish British submarines' conduct of the war under cruiser rules (in other words, stopping and searching merchant ships on the surface, rather than attacking submerged and without warning) from the unrestricted warfare of the U-boats, but also as a positive manifestation of British naval power which could be broadcast in the absence of activity by the battle fleet. The popular mystique of the submarine noted earlier, and its positive propaganda value for the navy and the nation at this point in the conflict, formed the basis and justification for this comparatively extensive coverage. Notably, these prominent images of British submarines frequently portray them not submerged in an aggressive, ambushing situation but surfaced in a patrolling, protective role, uncharacteristically 'keeping the sea' in a manner more associated with surface ships. This representational choice served not only to distinguish British submarines from German U-boats to the latter's disfavour (in line with contemporary propaganda discourses), but also strove to align and equate the submarine with more familiar, conventional and honourable warship types. Although distinguished by (and celebrated for) the technical novelty and tactical innovation which facilitated and defined its stealthy, offensive capability, the British submarine was also tamed and curbed in cultural representations such as those of *War Illustrated* by its likening to surface warships.

Jutland and after

The magazine's representations of the main British fleet, and of the expectations of a decisive North Sea encounter, were juxtaposed against this narrative thread of the successes, impact and innovations of British submarines. A full year after Jane's article in the navy's defence, the service's mundane, invisible but ultimately war-winning tasks achieved recognition, with a page of captioned photographs which offered a reassuring insight into the increasing anti-submarine patrols being undertaken by destroyers and naval seaplanes. This report was noteworthy not so much for its downplaying of the threat which precipitated these elaborate measures (British destroyers are described as 'setting out to look for "fun", otherwise U-boats, in the North Sea') as for its unusually vital and realistic depiction of actual operations, using photographs identified as exclusive to *War Illustrated*.[40] By contrast, a cover illustration devoted to the 'Blockade in Action' portrayed the daily boarding and examining of ships and cargoes which, though unglamorous, were nonetheless instrumental in Germany's defeat.[41] The prominence of this relatively unexciting image appears as another riposte to the critical questioning of the navy's work.

The novelty and immediacy of photography of operations at sea also characterised a montage of images of the Grand Fleet and its commander Admiral Jellicoe aboard HMS *Iron Duke*, published in January 1915. These photographs, showing the dreadnoughts exercising during winter storms, were described as 'among the first' of their kind to be published since the outbreak of war, underlining the conspicuously low profile that the 'Empire's strongest line of defence' had actually assumed.[42] This page of pictures was inserted within the 'Great Episodes' report on the Battle of the Falklands, thereby linking the edition's key naval stories and connecting success in one engagement with preparedness for another. However, the battle fleet's continuing inactivity, and the intangibility of its role in the public eye, were emphasised by a curious cover image from the following year. Here an illustration showed the bridge of a destroyer on patrol, awaiting the appearance of the High Seas Fleet. One of the sailors on lookout has turned his angst-ridden face away from the horizon towards the reader. The caption 'The North Sea Vigil: Will They Never Come?', and the frustration and anxiety exhibited in the British sailor's expression, appeared to confirm the public's as much as the service's exasperation at the unchanging, unresolved naval equation.[43] This image, appearing after eighteen months of war, encapsulated the navy's public relations problem, which even a patriotic, propagandist publication could not solve or avoid highlighting. Given this weight of expectation, the actual reporting and representation of the Battle of Jutland was noteworthy for its ambivalence. The cover illustration from 17 June 1916 shows barefoot sailors on the decks of a doomed destroyer.[44] The caption read 'Game to the Last! British Destroyer *Shark*, Decks Awash, Defies the German Fleet'. This image appears highly reminiscent of Frank Salisbury's famous paint-ing from 1917 of Boy Cornwell VC, at his post during the battle aboard HMS *Chester*, and epitomised the equivocal contemporary coverage of the indecisive action.

That a minor naval vessel, lost in a heroic night attack against German battleships, should stand for the entirety of the engagement on the magazine's cover, again underlined the misapprehension of what the dreadnought fleet could or did achieve. The apparent inconclusiveness of the main action remained hidden and the question of victory or defeat unanswered, deflected by the visual concentration on an unambiguous image of glorious, sacrificial bravery.

The delays in reporting the details after the battle, followed by the admission of greater losses incurred than inflicted on the enemy, com-pounded the fleet's image problem before Jutland by a failure to capitalise on the battle when it did occur.[45] Given the expectation surrounding the battle, *War Illustrated*'s reporting was, remarkably, both hedged and critical. An article by Percival Hislam expanded on the known facts of the engagement: pointedly it was not treated as one of the 'Great Episodes of the War'.[46] Although it was headed 'The British Victory in the North Sea', Hislam's article acknowledged the Admiralty's faux pas in its reporting of the battle, and ended with an admonitory paragraph listing the questions which remained not only over the release of information, but over the conduct of the battle itself:

Why were Beatty's battlecruisers left so long without support … Was the disposition of our forces faulty to begin with … Was Admiral Beatty so roused by the near approach of the enemy that he felt constrained to launch his attack, even at the risk of its being premature, and so, by giving them ample notice, enabled them to slip out of a trap that might have led to a twentieth-century Trafalgar?[47]

The two-page illustration which accompanied the article was significant in its vividness and yet its complete absence of detail: as an image of the battle it was impossible to discern what was going on amid the clouds of coal- and gun-smoke, which ironically may have made it a very accurate representation of the battle from the navy's as much as from the nation's perspective. Perhaps the best indication of the ambivalence or awkwardness with which Jutland and the navy were handled was in their subsequent coverage in the magazine. Revealingly, there are no further naval cover stories or illustrations until December 1916, when Admiral Beatty is pictured on the bridge of a battleship, to mark his assumption of command of the Grand Fleet.[48] However, Jutland and the navy's problem (indeed Jutland *as* the navy's problem) persisted in *War Illustrated*'s reporting almost until the war's end.

Conclusion

Despite its entirely understandable commitments to the preservation of secrecy and morale, *War Illustrated* was not simply a propaganda mouthpiece. This was discernible in its critical stance on general aspects of the conflict, and unarguable in its perspective on certain events in particular, such as the debacle of the Dardanelles and the disappointment of Jutland. The palpable concerns within Hislam's summary of the battle remained in an article appearing nearly a year later. Under the title of 'All's Well with the Navy', Gerard Fiennes reassured readers of the navy's effectiveness in an echo of Jane's earlier defence.[49] However, Fiennes' article could not resist acknowledging the weight of expectation amassed by tradition and public perception:

> The ordinary Briton went to war with a belief in his Navy as profound as it was unthinking. 'Britannia rules the waves' and 'England expects that every man will do his duty'. Such was his simple *Credo*. He knew the story of the Armada, of Trafalgar, and (perhaps) of Quiberon Bay ... The German flag was to be swept from the sea forthwith.[50]

Countering the assumption that a decisive naval victory was possible under the circumstances of the present strategic situation (and that it could in any case affect the outcome of the entire war), Fiennes emphasised the undramatic truth of the battle's outcome: that irrespective of

Blunders of German Diplomacy   By Sidney Low

Vol. 4   Game to the Last! British Destroyer Shark, Decks Awash, Defies the German Fleet   **No. 96**

Figure 19 'Game to the Last: British Destroyer *Shark*, Decks Awash, Defies the German Fleet', *War Illustrated*

the relative losses suffered by both sides, the Royal Navy's control of the North Sea remained inviolate. However, Fiennes went on to concede an unthinkable and previously unutterable anxiety: 'It is that the British Navy possesses the gates of its enemy, and has banged, bolted and barred those gates upon him. He *may* yet defeat that Navy. Nothing is impossible in war'.[51] In countenancing thoughts of possible defeat, Fiennes's article appeared to embrace the criticism of the navy underlying public concern since the war's outbreak. The criticism which had been piqued by the Scarborough raid and focused by the 'failure' of Jutland became intensified by the manifestation of a genuine threat of defeat by Germany's unrestricted U-boat warfare at the start of 1917. This campaign, and British shipping losses, were at their height when Fiennes's article was published.

The U-boat threat eventually diminished with the institution of a convoy system: concerns about Jutland, however, resurfaced in *War Illustrated* before the end of the year. An article by Lovat Fraser, appearing in November 1917, returned obsessively to the absence of detail and the aura of disappointment and indecisiveness which continued to cling to the action: 'The Battle was waged in mist and haze and darkness, and that atmosphere still envelops its story … The truth about Jutland is that it was not a victory for anybody'.[52] In this evaluation, the battle was deprived of the consolation of even strategic victory. Fraser's final, downbeat sentence was redolent of the sentiments of June 1916, and the persistent, unanswered desire for a confirmed and convincing victory: 'Jutland was manifestly no Trafalgar, nor is any British naval action which leaves room for doubt'.[53] Albeit interpretable as a victory, Jutland remained 'no Trafalgar', a condemnation by cultural association and traditional yardstick that even final victory in the war could not expunge.

Recorded in pictures by *War Illustrated*, the surrender of the High Seas Fleet in 1918 (an outcome predicated on the direct consequences if not the desired conclusiveness of Jutland), was anointed (without irony, and in further disparagement of Jutland) as 'Britain's Most Glorious Hour Since Trafalgar'.[54] In an accompanying article entitled 'Last Sailing of the Hun Armada', Edward Wright also described the capitulation of the German navy as an episode that both exemplified and outstripped an unbroken tradition: 'To the men of the island race, November 21st, 1918, was a day of victory such as Drake, Blake and Nelson had not known'.[55] Jutland was not mentioned by name in this report, but euphemistically, 'the only fleet engagement of the war' was conceded to have been part of the navy's contribution to Germany's ultimate defeat. This curious but valid recognition of the altered notion of victory at sea, achieved by sea control rather than fleet action, somehow still managed not to fully rehabilitate the navy nor the nationally dissatisfying but strategically conclusive battle, which had nonetheless facilitated it.

An obvious conclusion to reach from reviewing *War Illustrated*'s reporting and representation would be that the navy's image problem was inseparable from the problem of Jutland itself, as the battle was anticipated and interpreted as a fundamental measure against which success and failure, and therefore praise and criticism, pride and contempt, could be defined. When, where and how the navy was depicted appears predicated primarily upon the public perceptions of the service's role, and only tempered secondarily by admission of the war's realities. Strikingly, the absence or impotence of the Grand Fleet within the news is compensated or corrected by alternative, affirmative depictions. While the battle fleet was unseen and under-reported, there were unexpected, uncharacteristic yet positive images of the navy in circulation. These representations were sought and propagated perhaps in desperation, arguably as distraction from and obfuscation of the underlying problem of the navy's public image, or perhaps in recognition of a war being fought in unseen and unanticipated ways. In negotiating perceptions and propaganda, public expectations and strategic truths, *War Illustrated*'s naval coverage both admitted the criticism and strove to answer the questions of what the navy was and was not doing.

Notes

1 Anon., 'The Press: War Weeklies', *Time Magazine*, 25 September 1939, www.time.com/time/magazine/article/0,9171,761998,00.html (accessed 9 March 2013).

2 Thomas Hoerber, 'Prevail or Perish: Anglo-German Naval Competition at the Beginning of the Twentieth Century', *European Security*, 20:1 (2011), 65–79. See also Jan Rüger, 'The Symbolic Relevance of the Navy and the Sea in Britain and Germany, c.1880–1918' in Katharina Hoffmann, Herbert Mertens and Silke Wenk (eds), *Myth, Gender and the Military Conquest of Air and Sea* (Oldenburg: BIS-Verlag der Carl von Ossietzky Universität, 2015), pp. 55–68.

3 *The War Illustrated*, 22 August 1914. During 1915, photographic portraits of Royal Navy warships (the first example being HMS *Iron Duke*) occupied the inner covers of the magazine's editions in a series entitled 'Britain's Watchdogs of the Deep'.

4 Jan S. Breemer, 'The Burden of Trafalgar: Decisive Battle and Naval Strategic Expectations on the Eve of the First World War', *Newport Papers*, 6 (1993), 33–5.

5 Nicholas Reeves, 'Film Propaganda and its Audience: The Example of Britain's Official Films during the First World War', *Journal of Contemporary History*, 18:3 (1983), 464–6.

6 Anon., 'The Great Episodes of the War III: The Battle of Heligoland Bight', *The War Illustrated*, 26 September 1914, 122–3.

7 Anon., 'The Great Episodes of the War XIV: The Decisive Cruiser Action in the North Sea', *The War Illustrated*, 6 February 1915, 594–7; anon., 'The Great Episodes of the War XXI: The Demoniacal Destruction of the *Lusitania*', *The War Illustrated*, 22 May 1915, 318–19.

8 Anon., 'First Encounter of Warship and Submarine', *The War Illustrated*, 22 August 1914, 18.

9 *Ibid.*

10 Anon., 'Some Losses and Additions to our Navy', *The War Illustrated*, 26 September 1914, 124.

11 Anon., 'Germans Wildly Rejoice at our Naval Losses', *The War Illustrated*, 31 October 1914, 253.

12 Anon., 'The Commerce Raiders of the Indian Ocean: Rounding up the *Emden* and the *Koenigsberg*', *The War Illustrated*, 21 November 1914, 322–3.

13 *Ibid.*, 322.

14 Anon., 'Bombardment of Scarborough: Germany in Desperation Attacks our Defenceless Coast Towns', *The War Illustrated*, 25 December 1914, 450–1 (subsequent references: anon., 'Bombardment of Scarborough').

15 Paul G. Halpern, *A Naval History of World War I* (London: UCL Press, 1994), p. 40.

16 Anon., 'Bombardment of Scarborough', 450–1.

17 Fred T. Jane, 'What is the British Navy Doing?', *The War Illustrated*, 2 January 1915, 466, 468.

18 *Ibid.*, 466.

19 *Ibid.*

20 Anon., 'How Two German Cruisers Met Their Fate', *The War Illustrated*, 21 November 1914, 325.

21 Jane, 'What is the British Navy Doing?', p. 468.

22 Jan Rüger, *The Great Naval Game: Britain and Germany in the Age of Empire* (Cambridge: Cambridge University Press, 2007).

23 Anon., 'Ships that Swept the Germans off the High Seas', *The War Illustrated*, 26 December 1914, 442.

24 *Ibid.*, this page identifies the armoured cruisers HMS *Achilles*, *Cochrane*, *Natal* and *Shannon* as forming the Second Cruiser Squadron with Admiral Sturdee in the South Atlantic, but in fact none of these ships participated in the Battle of the Falkland Islands.

25 *The War Illustrated*, 2 January 1915.

26 Halpern, *A Naval History of World War I*, p. 93.

27 Anon., 'The Great Episodes of the War XIII: The Glorious Sea

Fight off the Falklands', *The War Illustrated*, 9 January 1915, 490, 492, 494.

28 Andrew Lambert, '"The Glory of England": Nelson, Trafalgar, and the Meaning of Victory', *The Great Circle*, 28:1 (2006), 11.
29 *The War Illustrated*, 27 February 1915.
30 *Ibid.*
31 *The War Illustrated*, 31 October 1914.
32 Anon., *The War Illustrated*, 21 December 1914, 416.
33 Anon., 'The Amazing Story of Submarine E.4', *The War Illustrated*, 26 September 1914, 125.
34 Halpern, *A Naval History of World War I*, p. 43.
35 Michael Paris, *Warrior Nation: Images of War in British Popular Culture, 1850–2000* (London: Reaktion, 2000), pp. 56–66.
36 Anon., 'British Submarines Turn Tables on Von Tirpitz/Hero of the Underseas Wins Fame on Terra Firma', *The War Illustrated*, 13 November 1915, 306–7.
37 Halpern, *A Naval History of World War I*, p. 203.
38 Anon., 'British Submarines turn Tables on Von Tirpitz', 306.
39 Anon., 'Humanity and Heroism of British Submarine Sailors in the North Sea and Baltic', *The War Illustrated*, 12 February 1916, 612–13.
40 Anon., 'With the Destroyers in Search of the Pirates', *The War Illustrated*, 1 January 1916, 475.
41 *The War Illustrated*, 5 February 1915.
42 Anon., 'Jellicoe and his Fleet in Readiness for "Der Tag"', *The War Illustrated*, 9 January 1915, 491.
43 *The War Illustrated*, 22 January 1916.
44 *The War Illustrated*, 17 June 1916.
45 Arthur Marder, *From the Dreadnought to Scapa Flow: The Royal Navy in the Fisher Era, 1904–1919*, vol. III, *Jutland and After (May 1916–December 1916)* (Oxford: Oxford University Press, 1978), pp. 240–4. See also Robert K. Massie, *Castles of Steel: Britain, Germany and the Winning of the Great War at Sea* (London: Jonathan Cape, 2004), pp. 660–2.
46 Percival Hislam, 'The British Victory in the North Sea', *The War Illustrated*, 17 June 1916, 418–19.
47 *Ibid.*, 419.
48 *The War Illustrated*, 16 December 1916.
49 Gerard Fiennes, 'All's Well with the Navy', *The War Illustrated*, 28 April 1917, 248.
50 *Ibid.*
51 *Ibid.*
52 Lovat Fraser, 'The Truth About Jutland', *The War Illustrated*, 10 November 1917, 249.
53 *Ibid.*
54 Anon., 'Britain's Most Glorious Hour Since Trafalgar' in J. A. Hammerton

(ed.), *War Illustrated*, album de luxe vol. 10 (London: Amalgamated Press, 1919), p. 3453.

55 Edward Wright, 'Last Sailing of the Hun Armada' in J. A. Hammerton (ed.), *War Illustrated*, album de luxe vol. 10 (London: Amalgamated Press, 1919), p. 3450.

10

Patriotism and pageantry: representations of Britain's naval past at the Greenwich Night Pageant, 1933

Emma Hanna

Using the grounds of the Royal Naval College as its stage, in June 1933 the Greenwich Night Pageant presented a showcase of English history. Various tableaux, including the christening of Elizabeth I, Drake's arrival on the *Golden Hinde* and the funeral of Nelson, were re-enacted by a cast of approximately 2,000 people. Accompanied by sea shanties and Sir Henry Wood's *Fantasia on British Sea Songs*, ten two-hour performances were seen by over 80,000 people, including prominent politicians, members of the aristocracy and senior members of the royal family. In terms of both its form and content, and particularly the personalities who created it, the production and reception of the Greenwich Night Pageant is an interesting case study that enables us to consider how representations of Britain's naval past featured in debates about the nature of national identity in an era of imperial decline and international instability.[1]

The history of pageantry in early twentieth-century Britain reveals much about the national understanding of the past and its relation to the present.[2] Drawing on the civic shows of the nineteenth century, and the German Festspiele, it was Louis Napoleon Parker who is considered to have invented the Edwardian pageant at Sherborne, Dorset, in 1905. Parker was a respected composer who had taken an interest in the English folk-song revival associated with Cecil Sharp and Ralph Vaughan Williams. He was an early disciple of Wagner, 'whose grandiose notions of a total theatre embodying the consciousness of a people he clearly sought to emulate'.[3] Parker was also inspired by William Morris's Arts and Crafts movement, which had regenerated interest in village culture.[4] After the success at Sherborne, Parker produced a number of large-scale pageants, for example at Warwick in 1906 and Dover in 1908. A pageant movement was soon created. Lots of other smaller pageants were held in Liverpool, Oxford and St Albans in 1907, and Chelsea, Cheltenham, Winchester and Pevensey in 1908. By the end of 1909, pageants had been staged at Bury St Edmunds, Colchester and York. Performed in open spaces, very often near historic monuments, pageants featured large casts of amateur actors and involved the work of local craftsmen. Gilbert Hudson's sizeable pageant at Pickering Castle, North Yorkshire, was staged in 1910 with the aim of attracting tourists to the area.

Pageants resembled chronicle plays where series of historical episodes were connected by prologues and epilogues, narrative and dramatic choruses, musical interludes and long parades.[5] Parker exported the pageant form to America during the First World War, where it thrived as a public spectacle under his disciple Percy Mackaye.[6] Pageants were performed on the Western Front, and in England pageants continued until the outbreak of the Second World War.[7] E. M. Forster scripted two – *Abinger Pageant* (1934) and *England's Pleasant Land* (1938) – which provided the inspiration for the Poyntz Hall pageant at the centre of Virginia Woolf's novel *Between the Acts* (1941). Besides Parker, the most well-known pageant makers were Frank Lascelles, Arthur Bryant and Mary Kelly. Kelly's *How to Make a Pageant* was published in 1936, and the book described the usual form of a pageant – having a 'Spirit of the Ages' or 'Father Time' who narrates the episodes. This type of pageant 'was by its very nature euphoric. The community that is any given pageant's subject is self-evidently alive and well at the end of the story and proudly re-enacting iconic episodes from its own past'.[8] Kelly felt it was best 'to end on a note of joy or hope', since to her the pageant was a commitment to the inevitability of progress. Pageants were therefore adaptable to progressive causes, for example E. M. Forster's liberal environmentalism and Cicely Hamilton's suffragette play, *A Pageant of Great Women*, performed in 1910.[9]

However, the majority of pageants were saturated with references to the Tudor period. Most productions contained a Queen Elizabeth scene and Kelly's instructions are most detailed on the casting of the queen as the most important role. Connections between pageantry and imperialism are also very evident in the representation of Elizabeth I as Gloriana, the founder of the British Empire. The Greenwich Night Pageant was indeed dominated by Elizabeth and the hero Drake, and as recently as 1930 the Aldershot tattoo had incorporated a pageant of Elizabeth I addressing her troops at Tilbury. Dobson has observed that 'in lieu of having a formally recognised national costume in which to dress up on special occasions, the English simply resorted to farthingales and doublet and hose as an instinctive default setting'.[10] The image of Elizabeth I as Gloriana had been emphasised in Parker's play at the Haymarket Theatre – *Drake: A Pageant Play in Three Acts* (1912) – which was successfully revived after the outbreak of the First World War. During the 1930s, a time of tumultuous social, political and economic challenges both at home and abroad, it appeared that 'Elizabeth's victory in 1588 still marked a convenient happy ending, the point after which there were to be no defining wars for national survival'.[11]

By the early 1930s, Arthur Bryant was one of the most successful pageant producers of interwar Britain.[12] The son of a courtier to the royal family, Bryant was an established historian, broadcaster and journalist who venerated order, place, ritual and historic tradition.[13] From the mid-1920s, he was concerned that the 'atrophying of patriotism' after the First World War constituted a serious threat to Britain's national character, unity and independence, and he aimed through his work to maintain the patriotism of 'ordinary people'.[14] It was perhaps Bryant's pageant at Hyde Park in 1932 which brought his talents as a pageant maker to the attention of Barry Domvile and his wife Alexandrina. Domvile had been born at the Royal Naval College in 1878 while his father, Admiral Sir Compton Domvile, served as Captain of the College. After a series of appointments both at sea and on land, including as a naval aide-de-camp to Queen Victoria (1888), Compton Domvile was appointed Director of Naval Ordnance (1891–4). Barry Domvile equalled his father's illustrious career path. Until the outbreak of the First World War in 1914, he was Assistant Secretary to the Committee of Imperial Defence, then commanded destroyers, flotilla leaders and cruisers in the Harwich Force for the duration of the conflict. Between 1919 and 1922, Domvile was Assistant Director and Director of Plans (Policy Division) of the Admiralty Naval Staff, and then Director of Naval Intelligence (1927–30), going on to command the Third Cruiser Squadron, Mediterranean Fleet (1930–1).

Domvile was reaching the end of a distinguished naval career when he was appointed President of the Royal Naval College in 1932. On their arrival, Domvile and his German-born wife Alexandrina appear to have found the Royal Naval College, and the local area of Greenwich, lacking in atmosphere. His diaries allude to the college as an institution which was regarded as something of a backwater, where the staff had settled into factions resulting in spats and infighting. Domvile's appointment as president of the college was not met with universal approval, and the couple made every effort to liaise with local politicians to garner support for the pageant. Accompanied by the town clerk, the Lord and Lady Mayoress of Greenwich paid regular visits to the college from September 1932. Domvile recorded that 'they were terrible excited about the pageant [the Mayoress] said there would be great competition for [the role of] Q[ueen] E[lizabeth]'.[15] The Domviles appeared in one of many public meetings on 2 November 1932 in Borough Hall where they and Bryant addressed the audience about the event.[16] The excitement generated around the pageant opened up the Royal Naval College. Domvile commented that people 'were too touching about our influence here – the only time the college has been accessible'.[17]

Early plans laid out by Domvile in 1932 detailed that '[t]he Pageant will be largely Naval in character and is intended to show the interest displayed by the various Sovereigns in Naval affairs and the gradual development of the Navy under their auspices'.[18] Of the Royal Naval College, Domvile said that

> the setting provided for such a show is very nearly ideal, and the History of Greenwich is the history of England, because a Palace has stood on this site since the 15th century. Both King Henry VIII and Elizabeth I were born at Greenwich, and to Greenwich came Sir Francis Drake in his famous GOLDEN HIND [*sic*] to make his bow to his queen. From the Painted Chamber at Greenwich Nelson's coffin was borne down to the river to be carried to its final resting place in St Paul's … Apart from this, the National Maritime Museum with its valuable and intensely interesting treasures will be inaugurated shortly … in the Queen's House at Greenwich.[19]

Domvile's diary records that, after a walk around the local area at Greenwich in July 1932, he had come to the conclusion that 'B[ryant] would do for my pageant – he is tremendously enthusiastic'.[20] Bryant was appointed by the Domviles under the auspices of the Greenwich Night Pageant Company Limited, and was offered payment of £400 (including expenses) – around £15,000 in today's money – to be the pageant's producer.[21] Bryant was a regular guest of the Domviles at Greenwich, and pageant business would very often be discussed after a lunch in the president's house and on walks in the college grounds. The plans for the event appear to have developed organically. In August 1932, Domvile records that there were discussions about having the principal actors 'using [the] river as well and the central path in the square'.[22] The first press interview the Domviles gave about the pageant was given to the *Kentish Mercury* in October 1932.[23]

Domvile was heavily involved with the production of the pageant, a little too heavily at times for Bryant whose correspondence indicates that the two men came to blows on a number of occasions. It was Domvile who came up with the idea of using the pensioners and their dreams as narrators of the pageant, and he also advised Bryant that '[l]ocal opinion will be very disappointed if you do not manage to work in Wolfe'.[24] Domvile's relations with the college's leading historian, Professor Geoffrey Callender, appear to have been particularly strained. Domvile originally intended that Bryant would work on the pageant with Callender.[25] Bryant visited Callender at Greenwich for meetings in September 1932, and Domvile records that Bryant 'had had a successful interview [with Callender] – so he said'.[26] However, Domvile and Callender were not to be close colleagues. In November 1932, his diary records in relation to pageant business that 'I see that the Professor has been busy poisoning people's minds'.[27] Bryant corresponded with Callender but this working relationship appears to peter out as Callender withdrew from discussions about the pageant due to his 'dislike of the limelight'.[28]

However, it was Domvile's wife, Alexandrina Domvile (née von der Heydt) who did the majority of the pageant's organisation. Domvile's diary records that Alexandrina – to whom he refers to as 'Pudd' – was working very hard on many aspects of the event. Domvile's diary is a fascinating insight into the couple's domestic life, and it becomes clearer from his own private words that Alexandrina was in fact the driving force behind the pageant as she was in many other areas of their life together. In August 1932, he described Alexandrina's business visits to London, and that 'she has many irons in the fire'.[29] As secretary of the Greenwich Night Pageant Company, established in 1932, Alexandrina attended meetings to publicise the pageant and garner local support, as well as hosting the many conferences required at the naval college. Nevertheless, Mrs Domvile is rarely mentioned in the cuttings and documents which record the planning and delivery of the pageant. Domvile's diaries are more forthcoming. By October 1932, Domvile said of his office that his wife was 'setting up her Pageant Kingdom in there'.[30] He records that 'Pudd has her table set in the corner of my office and I can watch my darling at work – she had some odd visitors in the course of the day – a grocer – a lady who wishes to supply cushions to the pageant and a keen actor from a printer's shop'.[31] Alexandrina attended a number of society gatherings to spread the word about the pageant.[32] Domvile noted that she was always 'working – working – working. She is a marvel'.[33] The workload increased at the end of 1932, and Domvile describes that 'Pudd has many things to do – the work is getting too much for her'.[34] In February 1933, Alexandrina made a speech about the pageant at a Scout concert in St Alfege Hall, and was asked if she would consider being a borough councillor. Domvile recalled that she was 'terribly elated. I must say she has done marvels with the people here'.[35]

The Greenwich Night Pageant demonstrates that the 'cult of the navy' – the ways in which the navy and the sea were celebrated in the decades before 1914 – had retained its strength in the interwar period.[36] Like the fleet reviews and launches of warships, the Greenwich Night Pageant was a spectacle of past power and pride where tradition and claims to the sea were staged to domestic and foreign audiences. Ritual and theatre merged with power and politics, and the implications of such a public entertainment show how the navy and the sea remained important metaphors of Britishness in the interwar period, enabling us to examine contemporary attitudes to the concepts of nation and empire.[37] Historians such as George Mosse and Hans-Ulrich Wehler have examined German national festivals and military spectacles as manoeuvres in the manipulation of the masses preceding the rise of the Nazis. In Britain, similar studies have been done which have interpreted public rituals as instruments of propaganda to induce imperialist sentiment and domestic consensus.[38]

It is also important to understand the context of the time in which the Greenwich Night Pageant took place. The early 1930s was a time of liminality, an extended period of international crisis in the aftermath of the First World War heightened by events in Germany. Pageants as 'rituals' were political mass spectacles used to overcome such crises, and the pageant movement 'was searching for origins, going back into history to construct a utopian vision of the future'.[39] Pageants as mass spectacles 'originated in a deep yearning for communal experience widespread in European culture at the turn of the century which stimulated the exploration of different kinds of fusion between theatre and ritual'. The events 'were conceived and intended as a bulwark against what was felt to be the evil consequences of industrialisation such as loss of solidarity, disintegration of society and disorder'.[40] Indeed, Louis Parker believed the social aims of pageantry should be a 'festival of brotherhood in which all distinctions of whatever kind were sunk in common effort', and that it 're-awakened civic pride' and 'increased self-respect'.[41]

Pageantry dramatises the past as a form of representation and performance, of re-enactment that encourages a visceral experience of the past on physical and emotional levels.[42] There are two principal characteristic features of a pageant: it involves a 'communitarian ethos' where large numbers of people from the local community are actively involved, and it claims authenticity, meaning the importance of place, of being held where the original events occurred.[43] The cast of the Greenwich Night Pageant was vast. Approximately 2,500 local people acted, and many were drawn from various organisations including The Old Contemptibles Association and local youth and athletic groups.[44] Domvile was particularly proud that so many local people were involved:

> Greenwich has a splendid history and they want the rest of the world to remember it … The whole borough has caught the enthusiasm of it. There will be 1,200 performers, and the great majority of them are Greenwich men and women. The Elizabethan crowd, with all its variety of yeomen, apprentices, gentry, strolling players and jugglers, will be made up mainly of Blackheath people.[45]

Indeed, the naval theatre of the 1930s 'was designed to affirm the unity of empire at a time when this unity was being challenged more than ever before'.[46] When Hitler's National Socialists came to power in January 1933 they embarked on a rapid programme of rearmament. This resulted in a rise in ceremonies and celebrations such as naval reviews and launches which became the prime sites of Nazi ritual.[47] A form of pageantry called *Thingspiel* or Thingplay was very popular in Germany from 1933. The plays featured national themes, subjects and ideologies, underpinned by the death and rebirth of a nation. It was enormously appealing at the time and was understood as a 'people's liturgy'.[48] In the context of the rise of Nazi Germany and its public pageantry, naval theatre reached a new climax in Britain in the 1930s. Jan Rüger has noted that 'the dual challenges of a rising rival on the Continent and a chronically overstretched empire abroad motivated a wave of renewed rituals which were designed to project confidence and continuity'.[49] The rise of public pageantry in Nazi Germany was mirrored by an increase in naval public theatre in Britain, but it should be underlined that this was not simply a right-wing phenomenon as the Popular Front staged its own pageants in Britain during the late 1930s.[50]

There had been voices which spoke against holding the pageant at Greenwich but the plans for the event were widely supported in the national press. The Greenwich Night Pageant was understood as a naval alternative to the Royal Air Force's annual display at Hendon, and the Army's tattoo at Aldershot, which only served to highlight the pageant's celebration of Britain's naval heritage.[51] Greenwich certainly had the support of the Royal Navy, which was underlined when Earl Beatty paid a well-publicised visit to witness the last stages of dress rehearsals.[52] Beatty emphasised that Greenwich was 'almost the birth-place of the Navy', surrounded as it was by royal dockyards, and that he hoped the pageant would teach people about the navy's history. However, Domvile was dissatisfied with Beatty's comments, saying that it was 'not a good speech – he would have done better to take the one I had written'.[53] Domvile, however, was very happy with the news-paper coverage of Beatty's visit the following day.[54] He was, though, annoyed that some members of the college staff who were not working in support of the pageant came to Beatty's reception, alluding to the division of colleagues who did or did not approve of the pageant's production at the college.[55]

The Greenwich Night Pageant was heavily publicised and had the support of the king and many of the Domviles' aristocratic friends. When his majesty 'consented to become a patron', Domvile wrote in his diary 'He is a brick'.[56] The event appeared in 480 publications providing local, national and international coverage running to over 5000 column inches. The press were treated very well, and were transported to report on two dress rehearsals by riverboat. The revival of the Whitebait Ministerial Dinner, a nineteenth-century tradition where the cabinet travelled to Greenwich by boat, was scheduled for the opening night and this imbued the plans for the event with an added historical and ceremonial element.[57] In January 1933, it had been reported that the government would be treated to 'the most romantic and historic dinner its members can ever have eaten'.[58] The article outlined the plans for the dinner and the pageant which were saturated in historical detail. The dinner would take place in the Painted Hall, designed by Wren and decorated by Sir William Thornhill, father-in-law to Hogarth, and where Nelson lay in state. The hall 'will be floodlit, and the Cabinet will sit down to an old-time dinner such as Pepys himself, who, as Secretary for the Admiralty, lived in the Hospital, would have enjoyed'. The stage directions were a tantalising foretaste of the planned spectacle:

> Silver-clad torch-bearers will light the Ministers from the river steps of the Hospital to the dining hall … the Lord Mayor, Sir Percy Greenaway … has been invited to come down by river in a naval launch. It is suggested that for the last half-mile of the journey he should transfer to a State barge and be rowed to the Hospital in the old style by liveried watermen, with the way lighted by searchlight from the banks … The roads leading into the Hospital will be lined by pikemen in the uniform of Charles II, who built the Hospital in its present form. The organ, on which Dr Malcolm Sergeant will accom-pany the pageant, is the one which was played at Nelson's funeral.[59]

It was also mentioned that Sir Arthur Bryant was currently writing a biography of Pepys 'in the very house where the great diarist lived', and that during the pageant the part of Nelson would be played by Captain Archibald Graham 'who lost his right arm in the war'. Further details of a shopping week and carnival organised to coincide with the pageant were also given.[60] Work on the stand began with Haig and Dickinson on 13 January 1933.[61] By March, it was being reported that the pageant's grand-stand would be 'the largest that has ever been put up in this country'. Accommodating 12,000 people, the construction was said to involve '30 miles of steel tubing and 15 miles of fire-proofed planking'.[62]

The Greenwich Night Pageant was open to all. The whitebait dinners were advertised widely and it was underlined that the restaurants would be fully licensed so 'there will be no reason why the Elizabethan scenes of the pageant should not be accompanied by Elizabethan cheerfulness'.[63] The pageant ticket office was close to Greenwich station, and the prices of seats ranged from 1s 6d to 12s 6d. A fish dinner was advertised in the Painted Hall at 5s 6d, approximately £10 today. All forms of public trans-port used to offer extra services to supply the demands of the pageant, and Empire Shopping Week was also held at this time.[64] An exhibition of Greenwich industries was also held nearby, to which those who attended the pageant would enjoy free entry. Much was made of highlighting the work and the products of factories in the area, as well as publicising the neighbourhood to potential residents.

The sense of place was key. The buildings of the Royal Naval College were used as a set, the colonnades acting as wings and the steps between as additional stage space. The event reeked of history. Many references were made not only to Tudor monarchs and the Palace of Placentia which had previously stood on the site, but to objects such as 'the Nelson relics'. This referred to the drums that were played at his funeral, which were brought back to Greenwich and played as if to summon up Nelson's spirit to the site where his body lay in state for three days in January 1806. However, the most striking, unique and effective part of the Greenwich Night Pageant was the use of the shadowgraph. A screen, 33 foot high and 120 foot long was erected between the colonnades of the King William and Queen Mary buildings which allowed for the projection of large-scale lantern images. This system was invented by Dr B. P. Haigh, profes-sor of applied mechanics at the college, and was of particular interest to the press because it was the first of its kind.

Perhaps taking some inspiration from the naval modelling techniques employed by British Instructional Films in the 1920s, models of ships were run along a small railway track in front of the lantern, at an angle which represented the approach and withdrawal of the vessels. Stencil slides were also used to project dates, for example, and the sea was conveyed by wave effects. But it was these technical elements of the Greenwich Night Pageant which made it both unusual and extremely challenging for Bryant and his team. He wrote that it 'is quite unlike the ordinary Pageant in its stage technique, and its production is much more the kind of work to which a producer of films is accustomed than a Pageant Producer'.[65] *Punch* magazine described the shadowgraph as 'entirely novel in the way of silhouettes, the undistorted movement of which across the screen is amazingly realistic'.[66] Images of ships, particularly sixteenth-century vessels, were the mainstay of the Greenwich Night Pageant. The imagery of ships and the sea is rich with symbolic meaning. Michel Foucault described ships as 'the greatest reserve of the imagination'. Their symbolic power as what he called 'heterotopias' signify that the vessels symbolically unite spaces or sites that would otherwise be seen as incompatible.[67] The Greenwich Night Pageant therefore underlined that the people and events hosted by Greenwich were at the centre of Britain's history, and that their heritage was inextricably linked with the sea and the vessels which sailed to establish a great empire.

However, the Greenwich Night Pageant also ventured into representations of the more recent past. A particularly striking scene took place just before the end, where the coming of war in 1914 is portrayed in a particularly dramatic fashion by 'robot soldiers' which echo Fritz Lang's *Metropolis* (1927). The stage directions detail that:

> a beam of light reveals a company of armed men marching across the top of the steps. Their helmets are of steel and their faces are pointed and phosphorescent, while their uniforms gleam with slime. Their motions are not of humans, but of rigid automata … another beam reveals their leader, who is Death, with a skull head and a white floating robe and riding a horse … Amid the thunder of artillery and the rattle of machine guns, and the shrieking sound of flying steel … sirens add to the inferno of noise.

You would not have seen that at Sherborne, and once again it gives us a window into the political and diplomatic undertones of the Greenwich Night Pageant. However, this appears to have been Bryant's idea. Domvile wrote to him saying,

> I have just read your epilogue … I think it is magnificent: a splendid finale that will bring down the house and make your name as a Pageant Master, that is to say if the actors are prepared to perform. I have an unpleasant

feeling that anything martial is not popular in Greenwich. However, the sooner they learn to become a bit more martial again, the better.[68]

In the run-up to the pageant tensions ran high. Domvile had tolerated weekly visits from the local mayor who insisted on 'meddling' with arrangements. They argued about publicity and the grandstand, and Domvile recorded that '[he] had already stopped the mayor sending off foolish letters – he is a bloody nuisance'.[69] Domvile's relations with Bryant, once so friendly, also suffered under the strain of staging the pageant. He complained '[t]hat wretched Bryant is once more in a state of panic – this time over traffic and dressing. He is an amazing fellow, lives his life in a series of crises'.[70] As the dress rehearsals were taking place, Domvile and Bryant had a series of rows by letter and in person, and Domvile was resigned that this disharmony 'was one of the things I must put up with for a pageant'.[71]

At 10pm on 16 June 1933, the Greenwich Night Pageant opened. Domvile recalled that the first night's audience 'were wild about the pageant … Hailsham said he would not ask me to the Tattoo! … we were overwhelmed with compliments … There is no doubt it is a very great success'.[72] Approximately 80,000 people went to see the pageant over nine performances. Demand for tickets exceeded expectations and an additional performance was added, and 3,000 seats were left unreserved. The *Daily Mail*'s account of the final performance gives an atmospheric taste of how the excitement built throughout the evening:

> Two hours before 8pm, when the gates opened, long queues were formed. By 8.15pm every seat had been taken, and until 10 o'clock, when the pageant started, a continuous stream of people hurried up to the gates in a fruitless attempt at admission … Those who crowded the grandstand last night were enthralled by the living pages of history which were unrolled one by one on the wide lawn, framed by the pillars of the naval college.[73]

Domvile was particularly pleased that instead of going to the producer, Bryant, 'all come to me' to lavish praise on the event.[74] The queen attended a performance on 24 June and 'arrived amidst great applause', but the king was absent 'because they were afraid of the damp'.[75] The pageant proved to be so popular there were calls to extend the run. Domvile's diary records that Lord Rothermere saw the pageant and 'decreed that it was to go on, and sent down a representative – a nasty piece of work, to make me a most tempting offer: that if I would prolong the pageant he would pay all expenses and leave me only profits. I returned a "no" in view of all the difficulties and the fact that I did not want to be exploited by the *Daily Mail*'.[76]

The Greenwich Night Pageant was typical in the prominence it gave to the Tudor period. However, the pageant's version of British history ignited debate in the national press. In the House of Commons on 18 July 1933, Labour's Isaac Foot asked the First Lord of the Admiralty, Sir Bolton Eyres Monsell, whether his permission had been sought in advance of the pageant. Foot also asked if the content of the performance had been submitted to him in advance for his approval, and if any public money had been used to fund the event. Eyres Monsell responded by underlining that the event was staged in aid of naval charities. He confirmed that the pageant had been given with his permission, that it had not been necessary for him to see the content in advance, and that no public money had been used. Foot continued to ask:

> Can we have the assurance that the sanction of the Ministry will not be given in future to a pageant which, while purporting to show how the heritage of the sea had been built up, contemptuously dismissed all reference to the Protectorate or the Commonwealth, and to the supreme service to the British Navy rendered by the Great Protector, by Vane and by Colonel Robert Blake, who, in our own parish church, is described as the chief founder of England's naval supremacy?'

Eyres Monsell replied that:

> I hope the hon. Member will agree that the pageant as a whole was a beautiful representation of British history. If we hold it again, as I hope we may, I will make representations about what the hon. Member says. I consider that Blake was one of the greatest of our British Admirals.[77]

Bryant responded that it had purely been a matter of space, time and continuity.[78] He said 'the only dramatic episode in the great Admiral's life which we could have presented adequately was his funeral ... We chose Nelson's, and honoured Blake in the only way left to us by making him the central figure of our posters'.[79] Foot replied that while public duties had denied him the privilege of watching the pageant, he appreciated 'the beauty and the public spirit of the enterprise ... [but] regarded the presentation in one respect as a perversion of our national history'.[80]

The technological developments of the 1930s meant that owners of cine cameras could film pageants. While there is a rough sound recording of the pageant, only the Gaumont newsreel of Beatty's visit survives.[81] Film footage of the Greenwich Night Pageant has yet to be found. Domvile's diary records that several visits were made to Greenwich by various film companies, for example Gaumont Graphic in April 1933,[82] and there is also reference to Paramount filming the rope-pullers during a dress rehearsal,[83] and discussions with a film studio based at Shepperton.[84] The event was listed in the *Radio Times* for broadcast on radio on Saturday 17 June, from 11.35pm, as *The Epilogue of the Greenwich Night Pageant* finishing with 'God Save the King'.[85] At the end of the run, Domvile reflected on 'a wonderful show, which has had a reception in the country far greater than I had ever anticipated, and only marred by the difficult nature of the producer'.[86] The day after the pageant closed Domvile enjoyed a relaxing day in the Royal Box at Wimbledon.[87]

Domvile was president of the Royal Naval College until 1934, when he retired with the rank of admiral.[88] He was knighted in 1934, quite possibly as a result of the successful staging of the Greenwich Night Pageant which made over £3000 (£110,000)[89] for local and naval charities such as the Royal Naval Benevolent Trust and the Dreadnought Hospital.[90] As the accounts were being closed in October 1933, Domvile was still railing against the imposition of the £3000 entertainments tax. Nevertheless, he reported that '[i]n view of this high tax and the necessarily high cost of a Production suitable to the dignity and glorious history of Greenwich, the Board regard the results as very satisfactory'.[91] However, once he had retired from the navy, Domvile's political views and subsequent activities led to the event being quietly forgotten. He made the first of many visits to Germany in 1935, where he mixed with senior Nazi officials, and became very critical of British policy and the way British newspapers represented Germany. The Domviles founded a pro-German organisation called The Link in 1937, which had over 4,300 branches all over Britain.[92] Domvile, his wife and his two sons were all under MI5 surveillance from at least the mid-1930s, although no reference is made in their file to the Greenwich Night Pageant.[93] In July 1940, Domvile and his wife were arrested under 18B regulations; Alexandrina went to Holloway and her husband was imprisoned with Oswald Moseley in what he referred to as 'His Majesty's stone frigate on Brixton Hill' until November 1943.[94]

The Greenwich Night Pageant is now remembered as being 'as close as England came to fascist theatre'.[95] Nevertheless, it supports the notion that the largest expressions of historical performance 'belong not to Hollywood in the days of Cinemascope but to the ruined castles and village greens of England between 1905 and 1939'. As Dobson has argued, 'the blossoming and passing into obsolescence of the spectacular communal dramatic form that evolved there reveals much about the understanding of the national past and its relation to the present, which briefly sustained a sense of imperial destiny, civic pride and ethnic identity in early twentieth century Britain'.[96] Early sound cinema did not wipe out the pageant immediately but it did adopt elements of the pre-war pageant within its output. Alexander Korda's *The Private Life of Henry VIII* (1933) was a swaggering pageant. In 1937, Korda made *Fire Over England*, adapted from A. E. W. Mason's novel, which ends with Elizabeth's visit to Tilbury in 1588. Certainly Arthur B. Wood's *Drake of England* (1935) was a film adaptation of Parker's pageant-play *Drake*.[97]

In the summer of 1933, in the wake of the pageant, Domvile basked in 'a revived interest in Greenwich'.[98] Bryant's letter of thanks to the pageant's cast said they

> had shown a larger world what Greenwich can do ... It is my hope and belief ... something may still survive to lighten the dark days through which all too many are passing and to bring nearer those better ones for which we and all Englishmen pray return to our country.[99]

After 1945 a few pageants were staged in small villages, especially around the time of the Festival of Britain in 1951, but 'after the Blitz ... it seemed much harder for the English to go on thinking of history as a providential fancy dress procession that was all about them but which they could simply sit back and savour as it passed by'.[100] In the early summer of 1933, however, as events in Nazi Germany began to escalate, the Domviles, Bryant and all who had experienced the Greenwich Night Pageant had witnessed an eclectic celebration of Britain's past glories in the shadow of a second total war.

Notes

1 Kevin Littlewood and Beverley Butler, *Of Ships and Stars: Maritime Heritage and the Founding of the National Maritime Museum, Greenwich* (London: Athlone, 1998), p. 61.

2 Michael Dobson, 'The Pageant of History: Staging the Local Past, 1905–39' in Mark Thornton Burnett and Adrian Street (eds), *Filming and Performing Renaissance History* (Basingstoke: Palgrave Macmillan, 2011), p. 173.

3 *Ibid.*, p. 164.

4 Erika Fischer-Lichte, *Theatre, Sacrifice, Ritual: Exploring Forms of Political Theatre* (London: Routledge, 2005), p. 91.

5 Fischer-Lichte, *Theatre, Sacrifice, Ritual*, p. 91.

6 Dobson, 'Pageant of History', p. 165.

7 Meghan Lau, 'Performing History: The War-Time Pageants of Louis Napoleon Parker', *Modern Drama*, 54:3 (2011), 265–86.

8 Dobson, 'Pageant of History', p. 165.

9 *Ibid.*, p. 170.
10 *Ibid.*, p. 167.
11 *Ibid.*, p. 169.
12 For Bryant's career see Andrew Roberts, *Eminent Churchillians* (London: Weidenfeld and Nicolson, 1994) pp. 292–4.
13 Reba N. Soffer, 'Political Ideas and Audiences: The Case of Arthur Bryant and the *Illustrated London News*, 1936–45', *Parliamentary History*, 27:1 (2008), 155–67.
14 Julia Stapleton, *Sir Arthur Bryant and National History in Twentieth-Century Britain* (Lanham, MD: Lexington, 2005), p. 49.
15 National Maritime Museum, London (hereafter NMM), DOM 49, diary of Domvile, vol. XLIX, 1 September 1932.
16 *Ibid.*, 13 November 1932.
17 NMM, DOM 50, diary of Domvile, vol. L, 3 February 1933.
18 Liddell Hart Centre for Military *Archives* (hereafter LHMCA), C22, correspondence re. Greenwich Night Pageant, letter from Domvile to Bryant, date illegible but from around mid-1932.
19 *Ibid.*
20 NMM, DOM 49, vol. XLIX, 6 July 1932.
21 LHMCA, C22, agreement for services as producer between Greenwich Night Pageant Ltd and Bryant. According to The National Archives' (hereafter TNA) money convertor, £400 in 1935 would have today's equivalent value of £14,792.
22 NMM DOM 49, vol. XLIX, 18 August 1932.
23 *Ibid.*, 4 October 1932.
24 LHMCA, C22, letter from Domvile to Bryant, 12 September 1932.
25 *Ibid.*, letter from Domvile to Bryant, date illegible but will be around mid-1932.
26 NMM DOM 49, vol. XLIX, 15 September 1932.
27 *Ibid.*, 2 November 1932.
28 LHMCA, C22, letter from Callender to Bryant, 6 February 1933.
29 NMM, DOM 49, vol. XLIX, 24 August 1932.
30 *Ibid.*, 3 October 1932.
31 *Ibid.*, 5 October 1932.
32 *Ibid.*, 24 October 1932.
33 *Ibid.*
34 *Ibid.*, 12 January 1933, emphasis in original.
35 NMM, DOM 50, vol. L, 25 February 1933.
36 Jan Rüger, *The Great Naval Game: Britain and Germany in the Age of Empire* (Cambridge: Cambridge University Press, 2007).
37 *Ibid.*, pp. 1–3.
38 *Ibid.*, p. 7.
39 Fischer-Lichte, *Theatre, Sacrifice, Ritual*, p. 90.

40 *Ibid.*
41 *Ibid.*, p. 91.
42 Lau, 'Performing History', pp. 265–86.
43 Fischer-Lichte, *Theatre, Sacrifice, Ritual*, p. 91.
44 LHMCA, C22, letter from The Old Contemptibles Association to Arthur Bryant, 24 June 1933.
45 *Daily Mail*, 19 June 1933, p. 21.
46 Rüger, *The Great Naval Game*, p. 269.
47 *Ibid.*, p. 262.
48 Fischer-Lichte, *Theatre, Sacrifice, Ritual*, p. 91.
49 Rüger, *The Great Naval Game*, p. 267.
50 Mick Wallis, 'Pageantry and the Popular Front: Ideological Production in the Thirties', *New Theatre* Quarterly, 10:38 (1994), 132–56.
51 Rüger, *The Great Naval Game*, p. 267.
52 *Kentish Mercury*, 19 May 1933, p. 3.
53 NMM, DOM 50, vol. L, 12 May 1933.
54 *Ibid.*, 13 May 1933.
55 *Ibid.*, 12 May 1933.
56 *Ibid.*, 25 February 1933.
57 LHMCA, C22, 'Report on results of publicity', Holmes Waghorn Editorial Publicist Services, report number 19733.
58 *Daily Mail*, 3 January 1933, p. 7.
59 *Ibid.*
60 *Ibid.*
61 NMM, DOM 49, vol. XLIX, 13 January 1933.
62 *Hull Daily Mail*, 14 March 1933, p. 14.
63 *Daily Mail*, 19 June 1933, p. 21.
64 *Kentish Mercury*, 19 May 1933, p. 3.
65 LHCMA, C22, letter from Bryant to Newington, 9 March 1933.
66 *Lloyd's List and Shipping Gazette*, 16 June 1933.
67 Rüger, *The Great Naval Game*, p. 140. See also Michel Foucault, 'Of Other Spaces', *Diacritics*, 16 (1986), 25–7.
68 LHCMA, C22, letter from Domvile to Bryant, 8 February 1933.
69 NMM, DOM 50, vol. L, 12 March 1933.
70 *Ibid.*, 14 May 1933.
71 *Ibid.*
72 *Ibid.*, 16 June 1933.
73 *Daily Mail*, 27 June 1933, p. 9.
74 NMM, DOM 50, vol. L, 19 June 1933.
75 *Ibid.*, 24 June 1933.
76 *Ibid.*, 26 June 1933.
77 *Hansard*, House of Commons Debate, 18 July 1933, vol. 280, columns 1681–2, 'Greenwich Pageant'.

78 LHCMA, C22, letter from Bryant to the editor of *The Times*, 19 July 1933.
79 *Ibid.*
80 LHCM, J6, letter from Isaac Foot MP to editor of *The Times*, 21 July 1933.
81 'Beatty visits Greenwich to see preparations for pageant', *Gaumont Sound News* 367, 19 June 1933.
82 LHCMA, C22, letter from Holmes Waghorn Editorial Publicist Services (the official Greenwich Night Pageant promoter) to Arthur Bryant, 7 April 1933. On 11 April, Alexandrina hosted a representative of the Gaumont film company to discuss filming the pageant, see NMM, DOM 50, vol. L, 11 April 1933.
83 LHCMA, C22, letter from Domvile to Bryant, 10 June 1933.
84 *Ibid.*, letter from Sound City Ltd to Bryant, 18 May 1933.
85 *Radio Times*, 9 June 1933, p. 664.
86 NMM, DOM 50, vol. L, 26 June 1933
87 *Ibid.*, vol. L 27 June 1933.
88 Admiral Sir Barry Domvile, *From Admiral to Cabin Boy* (London: Boswell, 1947), foreword.
89 According to TNA's money convertor, £3000 in 1935 would have the same value as £110,940 at the time of writing.
90 LHCMA, C22, letter from Domvile to an un-named newspaper editor.
91 *Ibid.*
92 Richard Griffiths, *Patriotism Perverted: Captain Ramsay, The Right Club and British Anti-Semitism, 1939–40* (London: Constable, 1998), pp. 39–40.
93 TNA, KV 2/834: PF 50327/V1, Surveillance reports, Sir Barry Domvile.
94 Domvile, *From Admiral to Cabin Boy*, dedication.
95 Littlewood and Butler, *Of Ships and Stars*, p. 61.
96 Dobson, 'Pageant of History', p. 163.
97 *Ibid.*, p. 173.
98 NMM, DOM 50, vol. L, 29 June 1933.
99 LHCMA, C22, letter from Bryant to Cast, July 1933.
100 Dobson, 'Pageant of History', p. 175.

Afterword

Britain and the sea: new histories

Jan Rüger

A century ago it was universally accepted by the educated world that naval history belonged at the heart of British history, but for much of the intervening period it has been relegated to the margins of serious history, regarded as a subject interesting, if at all, only to specialists and enthusiasts. It is still widely assumed that sea power mattered only in the context of empire; making it irrelevant and faintly embarrassing for the historian anxious to explore areas of relevance to modern debates.[1]

The defensive tone was striking when the British Academy used these words to announce a panel discussion on 'Does Naval History Matter?' in 2006. One could debate if 'irrelevant and faintly embarrassing' was an entirely accurate description at the time – arguably, the position of naval history was never quite as marginal as that. But even if some of the pessimism seemed exaggerated, it did reflect a broad consensus about the state of naval history as isolated from much of the mainstream of historical writing. As a review essay put it more recently, the history of the navy used to be an 'unfashionable sub-genre', seen as 'largely technical' and 'thoroughly unimaginative'.[2]

Much has changed since, as the chapters in this volume comprehensively demonstrate. The history of the navy and the history of Britain's relationship with the sea more generally have turned into a vibrant field in which different historiographies and disciplines interact. More than ever before, the naval past is being situated in broad political, economic, social and cultural contexts. Three distinct historiographical developments explain this renaissance. First, traditional naval history – with its focus on strategy, technology and war – has been reinvigorated from within. Second, the history of the navy and the sea has been discovered by scholars working on a vast range of topics that seem to lend the navy a new relevance beyond this traditional context. Third, the rapid rise of world history has redirected our attention to the sea as a historical space that matters more than before for historical narratives.

The best naval historians have, first, always been interested in much more than combat, strategy and technology – they were never only naval historians. It is hard to see how anyone reading Nicholas Rodger's or Paul Kennedy's work could come to the conclusion that naval history was 'faintly embarrassing'. Rodger's trilogy – *A Naval History of Britain* – is designed not primarily, certainly not only, as a history of the Royal Navy, but as a history of Britain told through the prism of the navy. Rather than a marginal object, to be explained by specialists as a specialism, the navy was a central actor in British politics, expressing the tensions in society as much as it had a bearing on them.[3] Paul Kennedy interpreted the navy similarly not only as an instrument for battle, but as a function of a broader set of issues concerning politics and conflict, both in international and national contexts.[4] His approach was influenced by continental historians who had integrated naval history with social, political and economic history earlier.[5] But while they explained the navy mostly as an instrument of domestic politics, Kennedy sought to bring this perspective together with foreign politics and socio-economic developments – 'the rise and fall of great powers'.[6]

There has been much revisionism and debate since Kennedy's work on Britain's navy and the Anglo-German antagonism came out more than thirty years ago, but his underlying approach, namely to relate seemingly narrow questions about technological change and naval strategy to broader historiographical issues remains acutely relevant. The recent debate about the Royal Navy before the First World War underlines this.[7] Its main protagonists are all naval specialists, but their work has a broader relevance for debates about Britain's relationship with Europe and the world. How much of a concern was the German fleet, rapidly built up from the end of the nineteenth century, for British policy makers? Was the Kaiser's fleet subsidiary to their worries about Russia and France? Or did the German naval programme prompt a British foreign policy realignment which ought to be seen as one of the underlying factors that explain why Europe went to war in 1914? The debate about these questions, which has occasionally been heated, demonstrates that naval history, in its traditional vein, continues to matter for broader historiographical questions that concern foreign policy and international relations.

As much as naval history has thus been reinvigorated from within, there would be little of a 'new history' had it not, secondly, been for the active interest shown by other historiographies. Since the 1990s, social and cultural historians working on a wide range of subjects have discovered and enriched naval history – in a process that resembles, but lags behind the integration of military history into the mainstream.[8] Most of the chapters in this volume are stimulated by this interdisciplinary opening. As diverse as they are, they share an explicit or implicit leaning towards 'culture' as a conceptual frame. This approach is obviously influenced by the success cultural history has enjoyed in other fields, but it has led to new insights that are specific to naval history. The fleet was never only an instrument of battle and deterrence, but also a cultural symbol which stood at the intersection of international and national, political and social, technological and economic contexts. There are two larger factors that explain this cultural role which expanded in the late nineteenth century. On the one hand, culture had an eminently political dimension in the 'age of the masses'. The new popular press, advertising and the rising cinema catered to an audience that had a new political function since the extension of manhood suffrage. Popularising the fleet in a broader cultural arena became a political necessity. On the other hand, the navy played a symbolic role not only for domestic, but also for foreign audiences. The Royal Navy was constructed to deter potential enemies from attack through its mere existence. Deterrence and the representation of power became just as, if not more important than the actual fighting of sea battles in this period: sea power was as much about performance and representation as it was about technology and operational capabilities.

It is worth dwelling on this point since it indicates why the cultural angle has particular potential for naval historians. Rather than regarding 'culture' as something peripheral or ornamental, as a quaint accessory, the new naval history understands it as intrinsically linked to questions of power and the function of the fleet. When Julian Corbett watched the assembled fleet at Spithead in 1902, he thought that the display of power would do much to project the 'silent pressure of sea power'.[9] Displaying the nation's deterrent was all the more important since there were few other ways in which the command of the sea could be claimed in times of peace. In a similar way, Cyprian Bridge differentiated between an absolute and a relative form of the command of the sea in his seminal essay for the 1911 *Encyclopaedia Britannica*. The 'absolute command of the sea', he wrote, was a 'condition … existent only in time of war'.[10] In times of peace, the command of the sea was relative. It was merely 'an attribute'.[11]

The more one nation's 'relative command of the sea' was contested, the more it had to be asserted symbolically. The fleet was, as Bridge put it, the 'visible sign of sea-power'.[12] Its primary peacetime role was the performance of power.

The representation of the navy and the sea thus directly expressed political claims and social conflicts. These conflicts are only imperfectly captured by phrases such as 'manipulation', 'propaganda' and 'mobilisation'. The press and popular culture, consumption and advertising played roles that do not fit neatly into the 'above' and 'below' dichotomy. Yet they were just as influential as government protagonists and political parties. Projecting Britain beyond its boundaries and claiming the sea as a space of influence was an immensely popular activity precisely because it was not the prerogative of one agency: a range of actors (official and private, commercial and governmental, local and national) drove this process without having to agree on an aim. Popular culture was more than a colourful collage of pictures and products. It was an inherently political arena in which socio-economic changes and the resultant demands for representation and participation were negotiated. It is therefore misleading to regard questions concerning gender and imagery, language and discourse, display and performance as 'merely' cultural in character. They were never isolated from fundamental political questions about power and entitlement, questions which were embodied powerfully by the modern navy. Culture was not a distraction from politics – it was inseparably bound up with politics.[13]

The third development that has motivated the renaissance of naval history is the rise of world history. Migration, trade, communication and transport – the vectors of globalisation – were all decidedly maritime in character. The sea was, as Linda Colley puts it in *The Ordeal of Elizabeth Marsh*, 'the vital gateway to a more interconnected world'.[14] The navy was an important factor for the operation of this gateway, no doubt, but it was not the only one. Commercial shipping, communication, the 'wiring of the world', the history of ports, islands and the environment are equally important for scholars working on the maritime world. In contrast to most naval historians they work primarily with a transnational approach.[15]

What is more, the maritime past has offered the authors of global and imperial histories a metaphor that allows them to structure their narratives outside traditional national frameworks. This goes back, of course, to Fernand Braudel, who established the Mediterranean as the Ur-Model for this sort of maritime history. It is fair to say that the Atlantic has overtaken the Mediterranean in historiographical prominence since, certainly in Anglophone scholarship. As Bernard Bailyn has put it, the 'Atlantic world' serves as a shorthand for the study of 'common, comparative, and interactive aspects of the lives of the peoples in the lands that form the Atlantic basin'.[16] A similar approach informs much of the recent writing on the Pacific and the Indian Ocean.[17] Yet there remains a tension between the function that the sea has acquired in world history on the one hand, and the older tradition of maritime history associated with Fernand Braudel on the other.[18] How does the aim to analyse oceans as spaces of world history square with the Braudelian idea of the sea as conditioning a regionally specific historical context? Are the seascapes of the past to be appreciated in their peculiar characteristics or should maritime history be understood primarily as a function of world history, giving a convenient spatial definition to investigations which would otherwise lack narrative focus?

One answer may be found in the 'historicisation of the ocean', which has gathered steam in the past decade or so and can be seen as a central tenet of the new maritime history.[19] Literary scholars and geographers have been just as much involved in framing this inquiry as social and cultural historians. The sea as cruel, the sea as a gendered space, the sea as a natural boundary, the sea as the stage on which race and empire were acted out, the sea as a national destiny: these ideas have been comprehensively deconstructed both by scholars who are naval historians by training and those who are not.[20]

More than anything, re-reading the ways in which maritime spaces were conceptualised in the past should prompt us to question the national framework which continues to dominate the writing of naval history. There is very little of a linear, national narrative to be had about Britain's relationship with the sea. Decades of historiography have made it abundantly clear that there is no one 'island story', no singular national history with the navy as its embodiment.[21] But what should replace the 'the nation' as the principal narrative tool that naval historians used to rely on? Will they cultivate their subject as a field which gladly receives attention from other historiographies, but continues to insist on its status as *sui generis*? Or will they step outside their genre and appreciate the navy as one subject among others? These are some of the questions prompted by the histories assembled here. It would be no small achievement if they resulted not only in a renewed interest in the naval past, but also in a rethinking of the idea of naval history itself.

Afterword

Notes

1 British Academy, 'Does Naval History Matter?', http://www.britac.ac.uk/events/2006/naval-history, 25 May 2006 (accessed 11 July 2013).

2 Matthew Seligmann, 'The Renaissance of Pre-First World War Naval History', *Journal of Strategic Studies*, 36 (2013), 454–79.

3 N. A. M. Rodger, *The Wooden World: An Anatomy of the Georgian Navy* (London: Collins, 1986); N. A. M. Rodger, *The Command of the Ocean: A Naval History of Britain*, vol. 2: *1649–1815* (London: Allen Lane, 2004).

4 Paul M. Kennedy, *The Rise and Fall of British Naval Mastery* (London: Allen Lane, 1976; with a new introduction, London: Penguin, 2016).

5 Eckart Kehr, *Schlachtflottenbau und Parteipolitik 1894–1901. Versuch eines Querschnitts durch die innenpolitischen, sozialen und ideologischen Voraussetzungen des deutschen Imperialismus* (Berlin, 1930); Volker Berghahn, *Der Tirpitz-Plan: Genesis und Verfall einer innenpolitischen Krisenstrategie unter Wilhelm II* (Düsseldorf, 1971); Hans-Ulrich Wehler, *Das deutsche Kaiserreich, 1871–1918* (Göttingen, 1973).

6 Paul M. Kennedy, *The Rise and Fall of the Great Powers: Economic Change and Military Conflict from 1500 to 2000* (New York: Random House, 1987). See also Paul M. Kennedy, *The Rise of the Anglo-German Antagonism 1860–1914* (London: Allen and Unwin, 1980). For a historiographical appreciation see Jan Rüger, 'Revisiting the Anglo-German Antagonism', *Journal of Modern History*, 83 (2011), 579–617.

7 The main positions in the debate are represented by Jon Tetsuro Sumida, *In Defence of Naval Supremacy: Finance, Technology and British Naval Policy, 1889–1914* (Boston: Unwin Hyman, 1989); Nicholas A. Lambert, *Sir John Fisher's Naval Revolution* (Columbia, SC: University of South Carolina Press, 2002); Michael Epkenhans, 'The Naval Race before 1914: Was a Peaceful Outcome Thinkable?' in Holger Afflerbach and David Stevenson (eds), *An Improbable War? The Outbreak of World War I and European Political Culture before 1914* (Oxford and New York: Berghahn Books, 2007); Christopher M. Bell, 'Sir John Fisher's Naval Revolution Reconsidered: Winston Churchill at the Admiralty, 1911–14', *War in History*, 18 (2011), 333–56; Matthew S. Seligmann, *The Royal Navy and the German Threat 1901–1914: Admiralty Plans to Protect British Trade in a War Against Germany* (Oxford: Oxford University Press, 2012). For the occasionally heated tone in the debate see Nicholas A. Lambert, 'On Standards: A Reply to Christopher Bell', *War in History*, 19 (2012), 217–40; Christopher M. Bell, 'On Standards and Scholarship: A Response to Nicholas Lambert', *War in History*, 20 (2013), 381–409.

8 Joanna Bourke, 'New Military History' in Matthew Hughes and William J. Philpott (eds), *Palgrave Advances in Modern Military History* (London: Palgrave, 2006), pp. 258–80.

9 H. W. Wilson (ed.), *The Navy League Guide to the Coronation Review, June 28th, 1902* (London, 1902), p. 7.

10 *Encyclopaedia Britannica*, vol. 24 (Cambridge: Cambridge University Press, 1911), p. 530. See also Cyprian A. G. Bridge, 'The Command of the Sea' in Cyprian A. G. Bridge (ed.), *Sea-Power and Other Studies* (London: Smith, Elder & Co., 1910), pp. 73–84.

11 *Encyclopaedia Britannica*, vol. 24, p. 530.

12 *Ibid.*, p. 560.

13 Jan Rüger, *The Great Naval Game: Britain and Germany in the Age of Empire* (Cambridge: Cambridge University Press, 2007), esp. pp. 50–139.

14 Linda Colley, *The Ordeal of Elizabeth Marsh: How a Remarkable Woman Crossed Seas and Empires to Become Part of World History* (London: Harper Press, 2007), p. 28.

15 Philip de Souza, *Seafaring and Civilization: Maritime Perspectives on World History* (London: Profile, 2001); Michael B. Miller, *Europe and the Maritime World: A Twentieth-Century History* (Cambridge: Cambridge University Press, 2012); John Gillis, *Islands of the Mind: How the Human Imagination Created the Atlantic World* (New York: Palgrave Macmillan, 2004); Jerry Bentley, Renate Bridenthal and Kären Wigen (eds), *Seascapes, Littoral Cultures, and Trans-Oceanic Exchanges* (Honolulu, HI: University of Hawaii Press, 2008); Helen M. Rozwadowski and David K. van Keuren (eds), *The Machine in Neptune's Garden: Historical Perspectives on Technology and the Marine Environment* (Sagamore Beach, MA: Science History Publications/USA, 2004).

16 Bernard Bailyn, *Atlantic History: Concept and Contours* (Cambridge, MA: Harvard University Press, 2005). See also Alison Games, 'Atlantic History: Definitions, Challenges, and Opportunities', *American Historical Review*, 111 (2006), 741–57, and Matt K. Matsuda, *Pacific Worlds: A History of Seas, Peoples, and Cultures* (Cambridge: Cambridge University Press, 2012).

17 Sugata Bose, *A Hundred Horizons: The Indian Ocean in the Age of Global Empire* (Cambridge, MA: Harvard University Press, 2006); Richard Hall, *Empires of the Monsoon: A History of the Indian Ocean and Its Invaders* (London: HarperCollins, 1996); Sunil Amrith, *Crossing the Bay of Bengal: The Furies of Nature and the Fortunes of Migrants* (Cambridge, MA: Harvard University Press, 2013); Thomas Metcalf, *Imperial Connections: India in the Indian Ocean Arena, 1860–1920* (Berkeley, CA, and London: University of California Press, 2007); Nicholas Thomas, *Islanders: The Pacific in the Age of Empire* (New Haven, CT, and London: Yale University Press, 2010).

18 Fernand Braudel, *La Méditerranée et le Monde Méditerranéen a l'Epoque de Philippe II*, 3 vols. (Paris: Armand Colin, 1949); abridged (trans. Sîan Reynolds) as *The Mediterranean and the Mediterranean World in the Age of Philip II*, 2 vols. (Berkeley, CA: University of California Press, 1995). See Gabriel Piterberg, Teofilo F. Ruiz and Geoffrey Symcox (eds), *Braudel Revisited:*

the *Mediterranean World, 1600–1800* (Toronto: University of Toronto Press, 2010); Peregrine Horden and Nicholas Purcell, 'The Mediterranean and "The New Thalassology"', *American Historical Review*, 111 (2006), 722–40.

19 Bernhard Klein and Gesa Mackenthun (eds), *Sea Changes: Historicizing the Ocean* (New York: Routledge, 2004); Kären Wigen, 'Oceans of History', *American Historical Review*, 111 (2006), 717–21.

20 See only Philip E. Steinberg, *The Social Construction of the Ocean* (Cambridge: Cambridge University Press, 2001); Kathleen Wilson, *The Island Race: Englishness, Empire and Gender in the Eighteenth Century* (London: Routledge, 2003); Klein and Mackenthun (eds), *Sea Changes*; Wigen, 'Oceans of History', 717–21; Rüger, *Great Naval Game*; David Cannadine (ed.), *Empire, the Sea and Global History: Britain's Maritime World, c. 1763–c. 1840* (Basingstoke: Palgrave Macmillan, 2007); Linda Colley, *The Ordeal of Elizabeth Marsh*; Mary Conley, *From Jack Tar to Union Jack: Representing Naval Manhood in the British Empire, 1870–1918* (Manchester: Manchester University Press, 2009).

21 Raphael Samuel, *Island Stories: Unravelling Britain* (London: Verso, 1997); David Cannadine (ed.), *Admiral Lord Nelson: Context and Legacy* (London: Palgrave, 2005); Holger Hoock (ed.), *History, Commemoration, and National Preoccupation: Trafalgar, 1805–2005* (Oxford: Oxford University Press, 2007); Jan Rüger, 'Insularity and Empire in the Late Nineteenth Century' in Miles Taylor (ed.), *The Victorian Empire and Britain's Maritime World, 1837–1901: The Sea and World History* (London: Palgrave, 2013), pp. 149–66.

Index

Index

Index

Index

Index

Lightning Source UK Ltd.
Milton Keynes UK
UKHW021300120422
401461UK00022B/409